AVID

READER

PRESS

Billionaire, Nerd, Savior, King

Bill Gates and His Quest to Shape Our World

Anupreeta Das

AVID READER PRESS
New York   London   Toronto   Sydney   New Delhi

Avid Reader Press
An Imprint of Simon & Schuster, LLC
1230 Avenue of the Americas
New York, NY 10020

First Avid Reader Press hardcover edition August 2024

AVID READER PRESS and colophon are trademarks of Simon & Schuster, LLC

Simon & Schuster: Celebrating 100 Years of Publishing in 2024

For information about special discounts for bulk purchases, please contact Simon & Schuster Special Sales at 1-866-506-1949 or business@simonandschuster.com.

The Simon & Schuster Speakers Bureau can bring authors to your live event. For more information or to book an event contact the Simon & Schuster Speakers Bureau at 1-866-248-3049 or visit our website at www.simonspeakers.com.

Interior design by Carly Loman

Manufactured in the United States of America

10 9 8 7 6 5 4 3 2 1

Library of Congress Cataloging-in-Publication Data

Names: Das, Anupreeta (Journalist), author.
Title: Billionaire, nerd, savior, king : Bill Gates and his quest to shape our world / Anupreeta Das.
Description: First Avid Reader Press hardcover edition. | New York : Avid Reader Press, [2024] | Includes bibliographical references and index.
Identifiers: LCCN 2024014139 (print) | LCCN 2024014140 (ebook) | ISBN 9781668006726 (hardcover) | ISBN 9781668006733 (trade paperback) | ISBN 9781668006740 (ebook)
Subjects: LCSH: Gates, Bill, 1955– | Businesspeople—United States—Biography. | Computer scientists—United States—Biography. | Philanthropists—United States—Biography. | BISAC: BIOGRAPHY & AUTOBIOGRAPHY / Rich & Famous | SOCIAL SCIENCE / Philanthropy & Charity
Classification: LCC HD9696.63.U62 G37429 2024 (print) | LCC HD9696.63.U62 (ebook) | DDC 338.7/610053092 [B]—dc23/eng/20240419

LC record available at https://lccn.loc.gov/2024014139
LC ebook record available at https://lccn.loc.gov/2024014140

ISBN 978-1-6680-0672-6
ISBN 978-1-6680-0674-0 (ebook)

To my parents.

Contents

Introduction

There is a photograph of Bill Gates—easily searchable on the internet, unmissable as a billboard—in which the Microsoft cofounder and billionaire philanthropist is standing facing the camera, his lips pressed into the service of a smile. There are four other men in the picture, taken in May 2011. Gates is second from right, dressed in a blue collared shirt and one of his usual sweaters. To his left stands a man with a buzz cut. To his right, at the center of the photograph, is a man with a tousled mop of salt-and-pepper hair, his arms folded. He is dressed in blue jeans and a half-zip sweater, the left arm of which is emblazoned with the American flag. On his feet are velvet slippers.[1] This man is Jeffrey Epstein, the convicted sex offender, social parasite, poseur, and pariah who died by his own hand in a Manhattan jail cell in August 2019. A month earlier, federal authorities had charged Epstein with sex trafficking of girls as young as 14, and the world was learning of his lurid activities and the astonishing array of high-profile men in his network. Of all the stars that studded Epstein's dark universe, from academics and entertainers to bankers and billionaires, Gates was the brightest. He was also the most mystifying. Here was one of the most recognized names and faces in the world, a visionary technologist who helped kickstart the computing revolution, and a path-blazing philanthropist with the lofty ambition of sav-

ing lives. Why was a deity of capitalism consorting with one of its Mephis-
tophelian bottom feeders?

There was no convenient label to affix to the relationship between Gates
and Epstein, and no label would have hidden the smudges that began to blur
the clear, unsullied outlines of the technology billionaire's do-gooder image.
The photograph, which surfaced in 2019, accompanied a story by *The New
York Times* detailing multiple meetings between the two men. Two years
later, in the middle of the coronavirus pandemic, Melinda Gates, his wife
of 27 years, would divorce him. Theirs had sometimes been a difficult marriage; for years, talk of Gates's womanizing had whirred in the background
among those who worked with the former couple. But the public airing of
his relationship with Epstein contributed to their breakup. As if to symbol-
ically distance herself from the man who had betrayed her, even though she
was tied to him forever by their shared philanthropy, Melinda inserted her
maiden name in between her first and last names. She would now go by
Melinda French Gates. Not long after their divorce, the world learned about
the affairs he had conducted during his marriage. Once a model of rectitude,
Gates had fallen into a slurry of ignominy. The large tear in Gates's public
image has forced us to reassess the man we knew, or thought we knew, a man
so brilliant, so rich, and so munificent that he had for decades been feted
and festooned like a king wherever he went. But the tear is also a portal to a
broader discussion about our obsession with billionaires, the vise with which
they grip our collective imaginations, and the repercussions of that cultural
and social dependency on our society.

Few billionaires have been in the public eye for as long, and in as many
guises, as Gates. He was an early template for a kind of billionaire that has
captivated the world since the 1980s—the "boy genius" who drops out of
college to start a technology company with little more than an idea, turns it
into a world-changing business, and becomes fantastically rich in the process.
Gates's personal tics, social ineptitude, and occasional condescension helped
bring to life the nerd, creating room in the public imagination for a version
of masculinity wherein mind mattered more than muscle. Just twenty years
after he cofounded Microsoft in 1975 with his high school friend Paul Allen,

the software company rose so far above its rivals that Gates seemed to levitate atop corporate America. He was the richest man in the world and a business mogul in his prime. But his relentless push to dominate the business, even at the risk of trampling a nascent internet industry, rendered him a monopolist in the eyes of many. In 1998, the United States government slapped an antitrust case on Microsoft. A gleeful media anointed Gates a twentieth-century robber baron in the style of John D. Rockefeller Sr., the monopolist of the Gilded Age. The boy genius had become a corporate villain.

In 2000, Gates began to step away from his technology career. Piece by piece, in full public view, he shed his monopolist's skin and metamorphosed into a kind of global benefactor. Given his deeply held belief in capitalism, whose rules had worked so winningly in his favor, his philanthropy was guided by the principles of the market. There was a huge unmet demand for global health "goods" that governments were often too disorganized, apathetic, or corrupt to provide. Private companies had little incentive to meet that demand because there were few profits to be had. Gates's charitable dollars could thus be used to support what he called "relentless innovation" that would solve stubborn public health problems.[2] The success of his strategy would be measured by the numbers—lives saved; crop yields improved. Over the next 20 years, Gates conducted a global philanthropic orchestra of such scale and ambition that it shook up multilateral organizations, astounded academics and activists, and transformed him in the public eye into a tireless savior of the poor.

The primary vehicle for his philanthropy is the Gates Foundation, formerly known as the Bill and Melinda Gates Foundation, which was founded in 2000 with initial bequests of $22 billion in Microsoft stock. Six years earlier, on New Year's Day, Gates had married French Gates, whom he had met at Microsoft and who was eight years younger. The auburn-haired engineer, a native of Dallas and valedictorian of her all-girls Catholic school, was as even-tempered as Gates was combustible, and as restrained in her manner as he was explosive. She left Microsoft in 1996 after giving birth to Jennifer Katharine Gates, the first of the couple's three children. Two others, Rory John Gates and Phoebe Adele Gates, would follow. Focused on raising their children, she was an occasional presence at the foundation in the first few years of its existence, but would eventually put her own imprint on it, helping to steer it and becoming the ambassador for its work on family planning and gender equity.

In 2006, the billionaire investor Warren E. Buffett announced that he would transfer the bulk of his multibillion-dollar fortune to the Gates Foundation. Buffett, the chief executive of Berkshire Hathaway, had met Gates in 1991 and the two became fast friends. Twenty-five years older than Gates, Buffett introduced him to the philanthropic ideas of Andrew Carnegie, the nineteenth-century steel magnate and another of the era's robber barons. One of the most significant outcomes of their philanthropic partnership was the Giving Pledge, an unusual and highly publicized effort in 2010 by the two men, along with French Gates, to get other billionaires thinking about charitable giving. Billionaires who took the pledge committed to give at least half of their wealth to philanthropy, either during their lifetimes or at death. Coming as it did right after the 2008 financial crisis, the Giving Pledge was morally compelling—America's wealthiest wanted to give back to society. But it was also a nonbinding commitment, effectively impossible to enforce or track, and in the end, perhaps little more than a showcase for a billionaire's generous intentions.

Today, the Gates Foundation has enough global heft that it can shape development agendas through its grant-making, particularly in low-income countries. It donates as much money to international organizations as some individual countries do. Along the way, Gates became a so-called thought leader, courted by world leaders and cheered by the press. Almost avowedly apolitical, he warmed to the role, speaking about topics like diseases, public health, vaccines, sanitation, agriculture, climate change, and, of course, technology. Long a canny user of the media to promote his business and philanthropic interests, Gates has a phalanx of handlers who work constantly to smoothen and polish his image, like taking sandpaper to a jagged frame. The billionaire has received an embarrassment of prizes, but the biggest of them all—the Nobel Peace Prize—has eluded him. To boost his candidacy for the big prize, some of his handlers for years strategically launched publicity campaigns when the world was nearing a public health milestone that the Gates Foundation was involved in.

At the same time, criticisms of the foundation's bigfooting abound. Its activities have been described as antidemocratic, neocolonial, technocratic, and top down, but its influence, which derives from Gates's star power and the roughly $7 billion the foundation has given away annually in recent years, is untrammeled. Even as the deployment of his fortune took the spotlight, its source remained hidden. Gates has an estimated net worth of over $120 billion, but most of it is no longer in Microsoft shares. His trove of wealth contains stocks, bonds, hotels, farmland, real estate, and even a bowling alley, managed by an investment firm called Cascade Asset Management.

His divorce from French Gates landed like a grenade in the typically placid world of philanthropy. The two had been partners in life and largesse, and their marriage, embedded in the foundation's origin story, was essential to its functioning. Little got done without their approval. Hundreds of nonprofits that relied on Gates Foundation grants, and foundation employees themselves, fretted about their future until it was clear that the two, in an odd power-sharing agreement, would remain at the helm as before. French Gates has since sought to build a separate identity as a philanthropist focused on women's rights, and on May 13, 2024, three years after they announced their breakup, she said she would resign from the foundation to carry on her work independently. The story of her personal and professional journey, including the pain of being married to a philandering, brilliant, and imperious man, and her struggle to be seen on an equal footing with him, has informed the public's perception of Gates in recent years. Like rust ruining iron, news of his personal conduct too has corroded his image and upset some of his closest friends, including Buffett. He has also become the subject of conspiracy theories about vaccines and the intentions of powerful men, as social media draws untruths and twisted truths to the mainstream. The boy genius who had turned into a ruthless monopolist only to turn into a benevolent philanthropist had shape-shifted yet again. And this time, Gates's image had turned into something darker, blurrier, and more divisive, making him an unexpected receptacle for one of the biggest debates roiling society—the influence of billionaires in an increasingly unequal world. The evolving image of Gates is thus much more than a story about one man, or a tale about capitalism and philanthropy. It is a story about American society and the peculiar cultural and moral ecosystem within which we operate. It is a story about how we embrace images mediated by the press and popular culture, from nerds to narcissists, and turn caricatures into truths. It is about our worship of billionaires, in whose spectacular success we see so much of the promise of America, and the articulation of the ideas we hold dearest: the rugged, frontier-pushing, fortune-seeking, self-made individual; the rag-picker turned rajah; the even, fertile earth upon which we plant the seeds of our dreams, where the harder you toil and the greater your skill and luck, the higher your ascent and the bigger your harvest. Gates's story is also a story about the swift rise of technology billionaires and their reign over our lives. It is a story about America's long-standing tradition of generosity su-percharged by billionaire money. It is a story about how billionaires actively and constantly manipulate their money and power to hide in the shadows or shine on the stage to achieve their preferred outcomes in collective goods such as education and the environment, as well as in business, politics, pol-icy, and philanthropy. Plutocrats, whether we know it or not, are our shadow rulers—private actors shielded by their wealth—and we are unwitting ac-complices to the perpetuation of this system.

The 400 people on Forbes's list of America's richest individuals have an estimated collective net worth of about $4.5 trillion. That's roughly 3 percent of the total wealth held by Americans, and nearly a trillion dollars more than the combined wealth of the bottom 50 percent.[3] Nine of the top 10 U.S. billionaires each have estimated fortunes of more than $100 billion. (For con-text, there are around 100 publicly traded companies in the S&P 500 stock index with market values of $100 billion or more.) If the average American family saved every cent of its $68,000 annual income, it would take more than 14,000 years to build a fortune of just one billion dollars. During the coronavirus pandemic, the rising stock market lifted the collective net worth of billionaires by 40 percent, even as millions of small businesses and liveli-hoods were decimated, and others were saved only because of government help. An individual billionaire might represent the promise of capitalism, but their growing numbers and wealth represent its cruelty. Even billionaires who have committed to giving more of their fortunes away find that descending the ladder of wealth is not unlike trying to run down an up escalator.

Asked about their success, many billionaires speak in terms of the American dream, selling a curated and emotionally resonant story of their arduous path to the top while omitting the messier, more complicated, more collective, more humbling—and more truthful—details that fill out the narrative. Aside from their talent and determination, hundreds of billionaires benefited from any number of advantages they had, including their race, class, and gender; education and networks that gave them a leg up; a timely insight from a schoolteacher or professor; a plan birthed within the cocoon of a comfortable job; government research that spurred the development of an idea; tax breaks, subsidies, and other policies favorable to their industries; and the sustained fattening of profit margins at their companies, often achieved by cutting worker pay and benefits.

We could choose to challenge these accounts rather than relying on the billionaires themselves to explain the nearly inexplicable, or accepting the idea that every dollar in a billionaire's pile is deserved, or that extreme wealth is ordained and there is no fighting the Fates, but as a society we don't. This stasis begets several questions. Why do we equate wealth with nobility and virtue, and often view the intentions of billionaires with an uncritical eye? Why do we get so easily swayed by the public personas of powerful people, placing them on pedestals so high as to make their downfalls that much more shocking? Are we so comfortable in the prison of our imaginings, satisfied merely as voyeurs and dreamers, that we don't want to navigate our way to reality? Is the astounding accumulation of wealth in recent decades justified by the scattershot philanthropy of billionaires, which is sometimes driven by their personal interests? Is ever-widening inequality a natural outcome of the vaunted individualist tradition of America or a symbol of dysfunctional capitalism? At what point does the argument that the fortunes of billionaires are covalent to the societal value they have created break down? Are certain fortunes "morally worthy?"[4] Who gets to decide what, if anything, billionaires owe to society?

Gates is the perfect prism through which to refract these thorny, moral questions into a myriad of themes—billionaires, wealth, and inequality; technology and pop culture; media and image; philanthropy, power, and influence. Seemingly switching between an entitled hero and a hubristic villain, and every shade in between, he is a protean creature, a Zelig who, according to his critics, has leveraged his money and his fame to go from one guise to the next. Because of the way his distinct turns on the public stage map onto the wider preoccupations of our society, Gates allows us to hitch a ride into our collective self, an opportunity to investigate the cocoon within which we exist, which so confounds and conditions us that we don't often recognize how our cultural, social, and economic beliefs contribute to and sustain a lopsided society. Looked at from the other direction, the little narratives about Gates's hubris, attitude, and behavior coalesce into a "grand narrative" of our society, to borrow a term from the French postmodernist philosopher Jean-François Lyotard. In tracing the arc of his evolving image, we might find a reflection of who we are, and why we are the way we are. Policy is prescriptive and politics are divisive, but as a society of immigrants, dreamers, and builders, there is room for a collective rethink of how our shared values built this ecosystem, and where to go from here.

Chapter 1

Why We Love Billionaires

Seeking Billionaire Wisdom

Dushime Gashugi is a bit of a stuntman. Every July, for five of the past nine years, Gashugi has flown or driven more than 800 miles from the east of Los Angeles, where he lives, to the small resort town of Sun Valley in Idaho. There, he lolls about, hoping to grab the attention of a billionaire or two as they swoop in from all over the world in their private jets for an annual confab dubbed the "summer camp for billionaires."

In 2017, Gashugi stood by the side of a road with an enormous sign that read: MESSRS. BLOOMBERG & GATES: ENTREPRENEUR FROM CA SEEKS ADVICE. COFFEE'S ON ME. He added his number at the bottom of the sign, which he had printed at a shop near his home and stuffed into his car, pulling down its backseat to be able to do so. Four years later, in 2021, he paid $1,500 to rent a spacesuit from Wonder-Works, a California company that builds replicas of space shuttles and other gear for movie studios and theme parks. Gashugi, who was working as a real estate agent at the time, squeezed his six-foot four-inch frame into the 30-pound suit as he stood by the roadside once again, holding another giant sign. This time, he hoped to catch the attention of Jeff Bezos, the Amazon founder who is commercializing space travel through Blue Origin, his aerospace company. In 2019, Bezos had shown off a four-legged moon lander that Blue Origin was building, which he said could deliver cargo and humans to the moon's surface by 2024. JEFF BEZOS, SEEK-

ING MOON COLONY LISTINGS. CAN SPEAK KLINGON. LET'S HAVE DINNER, the sign read.

Sun Valley, at an elevation of nearly 6,000 feet, is nestled at the foot of Bald Mountain, whose slopes fill with wildflowers in the summer and skiers in the winter. For the past forty or so years, it has been the venue for one of the most high-profile gatherings of billionaires and luminaries from the worlds of media, entertainment, and technology, where some of America's richest and most powerful executives gather to plot takeovers or exchange views about the state of the world over rounds of golf or quiet walks. Held at the Sun Valley Lodge—which, when it was built in 1936 in the style of an Austrian ski resort, was intended as a destination for celebrities and wealthy families—the conference, hosted by the New York investment bank Allen & Co., has long attracted media attention. Although the guest list is a closely guarded secret, it's not hard to spot the business moguls as they stroll the walking paths that wind around the lodge, or hitch rides on golf carts to get around. The dress code is informal, the atmosphere relaxed. Reporters and photographers are not invited to the conference, but they are tolerated if they maintain a respectful distance from the guests. Many attendees, however, are at ease and like to be accessible, so they often pose for photographs or stop to answer questions. Gates and Buffett are regulars, as are the media barons Barry Diller, Rupert Murdoch, and Michael Bloomberg and top executives from the world of technology like Mark Zuckerberg of Meta; Sundar Pichai of Alphabet; and Elon Musk of Tesla, SpaceX, and Twitter, now known as X.

Gashugi first heard about the Sun Valley conference in 2010, not long after he graduated from the University of Chicago, where he majored in economics. The son of Rwandan immigrants, Gashugi was born in Stoneham, Massachusetts, a suburb of Boston, but grew up in Berrien Springs, Michigan, a village of about 1,800 people where the boxer Muhammad Ali once owned a home. Berrien Springs sits in a prairie, attracting local visitors for its nature park. With just two traffic lights, it might be a pitstop to elsewhere. His father came to the United States in 1965 as a Watutsi dancer for the New York World's Fair. He spoke no English and carried only his high school transcript, hoping to make a life for himself in America. He eventually enrolled in a PhD program at Boston University. The family moved to Berrien Springs after he secured a teaching job at Andrews University, a Seventh-day Adventist institution. Gashugi's mother came to the United States to study nursing, sponsored by missionaries, and found work as a nurse practitioner at a VA hospital. Outside the university's cocoon of diversity, the population of Berrien Springs is largely white; in 2020, more than half of the county voted for Donald Trump.

Gashugi and his sister grew up in a modest but comfortable home in what he described as a "Christian setting." After college, the idea of a conventional path, say an MBA degree or a career in finance or academia, sounded boring to Gashugi. Relentless and restless, he had long itched to do something entrepreneurial. Success stories entranced him. He wanted to know how successful and powerful people approached business, and what he could learn from them. Gashugi speaks in torrents. He jumps from point to point, idea to idea, as if dashing across an imaginary whiteboard, marker in hand, scribbling furiously. He studs his sentences with references to Bezos, to Musk. One fall afternoon in 2022, he sat at a coffee shop in midtown Manhattan dressed in a bright red polo shirt and blue jeans, insisting that he had a plan but was too coy to share it. A copy of *Shoe Dog*, a memoir written by Phil Knight, the billionaire cofounder of Nike, lay on the table.

At Chicago, Gashugi had been a research assistant to Gary Becker, the renowned economist who won the Nobel Prize in Economic Sciences in 1992 for his groundbreaking approach to economics as a study of everyday human behavior. Gashugi recalled that Becker, who died in 2014, had once compared the ability to take risks to fertility: Both can diminish with age. Risks become harder to take as you grow older, the professor said, because life gets more complicated as mortgages and children enter the picture, and so on. Gashugi took that lesson to heart. If he wanted to become an entrepreneur, he would have to start taking his chances immediately. And he needed to learn from the best, by approaching influential people directly to learn about their principles and the lessons they had learned on their way to the top, and how he too could get to a position of power, wealth, and influence. "You can't become like people if you don't hang around them," Gashugi insisted. "You can't become a millionaire if you're hanging around with broke people."

At 22, he gave himself a decade to pursue the dream. But where to start? Buffett seemed like a good bet. The billionaire investor had bought Berkshire Hathaway in 1965 when it was a small textile manufacturer and used it as a vehicle to build an enormous conglomerate that owned everything from insurance to ice cream. He would know something about building a business. In the first week of July 2010, Gashugi flew to Buffett's hometown of Omaha on a one-way ticket, with the aim of securing a meeting with the billionaire and convincing him to give him an internship. But he soon learned that Buffett was out of town, and a quick Google search revealed that the investor was at a conference in Sun Valley.

Once Gashugi learned that the Sun Valley conference was a meeting place for billionaires, he set about researching the event. As he learned more, marveling at slideshows of the celebrity attendees on various news sites, he hit upon a crazy idea: Why not go to Sun Valley during the conference? It would be the most efficient way to get in front of as many billionaires as possible, so that he could ask them about their rules for success and apply them to his own life. "I don't have the money to go all over God's creation, so what's the most systematic way to find people?"

Gashugi bet that people would stop to talk to him, knowing that anyone showing up uninvited at Sun Valley would have gone to great lengths to get there. The airport closest to the lodge is in Hailey, about a half-an-hour's drive away. "At that level you have to respect a certain level of audacity," Gashugi said to himself. "You're a Black kid crashing a conference in Idaho."

When he got to Sun Valley the first time, in 2015, his mouth fell agape. "It's an out of body experience. Everyone who you can imagine is there," he said. He has since been to Sun Valley at least five times. In 2022, when he couldn't attend, Gashugi hired an aerial banner pilot to fly a banner over the conference for two hours, targeting Bezos and Musk. In 2016, his enthusiasm got the better of him, as he chased after attendees indiscriminately, often pestering them with questions. The July week of the conference, two

Black men, Philando Castile and Alton Sterling, had been fatally shot by police in St. Paul, Minnesota, and Baton Rouge, Louisiana, respectively. Amid protests about race and criminal justice, a sniper had shot and killed five white police officers in downtown Dallas. When Gashugi, dressed in a colorful dashiki, showed up at the Sun Valley Lodge, security officers were on high alert and ordered him not to trespass. Only later did he learn that photos of the sniper wearing a dashiki were circulating online, and he wondered if the officers were especially worried because of the coincidence. "That spooked me good." The following year, he returned with a plan. He created lists and stationed himself at strategic points around the resort—far enough that the security guards wouldn't have to shoo him away, but visible to the attendees. He had read enough billionaire memoirs and company reports so that he could go up to someone with a specific question. Over the years, he approached dozens of billionaires and executives, with a version of the same question: "What are your habits for success?" Most of the people he approached were nice and unassuming when he struck up a conversation with them. "If I didn't know they were billionaires . . . it's counterintuitive that the richer you are, the higher up you are, the nicer you are."

Alphabet's Sundar Pichai seemed like a "very nice guy." Bill Gates was "not very nice," because he didn't stop to entertain Gashugi's entreaties. Gashugi took a selfie with Jorge Paulo Lemann, the billionaire cofounder of 3G Capital, a private equity firm that owned a piece of the branded food giant Kraft Heinz. In 2017, just days after he held out a sign asking Bloomberg to call him, he woke up to a voicemail message from the former mayor of New York himself. A conference attendee had taken a photo of Gashugi's sign, on which he had scrawled his number, and sent it to Bloomberg. "I thought I'd give you the courtesy of a call," Bloomberg said in the voicemail message, which Gashugi saved. He said he would call again the following Monday, which he did. "How can I help?" As the two got to talking, it seemed to Gashugi that the billionaire, who made his money selling financial information to Wall Street firms, was genuinely interested in hearing about his background and offering his advice. Unnerved and trembling with excitement, Gashugi asked Bloomberg for tips for entrepreneurial success: how to build a team, how to raise money, and how to develop as a leader. Over time, Gashugi would ask for the same advice from the other billionaires who stopped to talk to him. The Sun Valley visits turned out to be what Gashugi called his continuing education. He became a bit of a local celebrity after he got written up by the *Idaho Mountain Express* for his stunts.[1] He even appeared on CNBC. That's when he realized that he could build a following by marketing himself: Stunts would bring him publicity, which he hoped to then leverage into building his business, no matter what the venture. As of 2024, Gashugi had no plans to give up his annual sojourn to Sun Valley, and neither did he plan to pull back on unusual public displays meant to draw attention. (He once crashed the sets of the *Today* show in another rented spacesuit to pitch himself as the first Realtor for Musk's planned colony on Mars.) He was also focused on getting a celebrity or a billionaire to endorse him, even willing to be a nuisance. "Money follows attention," he said. Sometimes, Gashugi wonders if he could be a "Black Rockefeller." Success in sports and entertainment was expected of Black people, he said, but there weren't many in the corporate world. "No one can tell me I can't be a billionaire, or that I can't do something."

The Billionaire Fever Dream

The wealthy have always been among us. We are entranced by the stories of how they came about their wealth. Like Gashugi, we want to learn about their paths to success, and how to emulate them. In a capitalist society built on the idea that material success is the inevitable outcome of individual merit and boundless opportunity, those at the top of the economic ladder would appear to hold all the secrets. We tend to uphold the wealthy as ideals, attributing to them valor, virtue, integrity, and brilliance. "Money ennobles rich people, and corrupts poor people," the essayist and editor Lewis Lapham, himself born into a wealthy family, once observed, although he dismissed the idea as "humbug."[2]

It's therefore no surprise that books, articles, and blogs abound that purport to distill the life experiences and stories of the rich into pithy, plug-and-play principles. University courses on business and entrepreneurship—pitched as a proxy for, and a route to, wealth—entice students by promising to equip them with the tools for success. The desire to get rich is partly what draws thousands of starry-eyed, ambitious youngsters to Wall Street and Silicon Valley every year. It's what prompts a schoolteacher to plunk her life savings into the cryptocurrency market and an immigrant to leave his family behind for a chance in America. But if wealth has always existed, whether through the accumulation of land, property, or currency, or simply in relation to the impoverishment of others, the term "billionaire" is a later construct. Merriam-Webster's dictionary traces its origins to 1844 in American English, and it became more common at the beginning of the twentieth century—a direct consequence of the explosion in wealth during the Gilded Age, when the term "millionaire" no longer sufficed. John D. Rockefeller Sr. is often considered the country's first billionaire, amassing an enormous fortune of $1.2 billion in 1918 dollars—about $24 billion today—from his oil empire.

The term came into its own in the 1980s, when the current cycle of wealth creation began, aided by the unusual confluence of technological innovation, financial engineering, and supportive government policies.[3] In that sense, the popularization of the word "billionaire" itself has become a metonym of sorts for the growing wealth disparity we have witnessed in recent decades. As billionaires become more numerous, more prominent, and more influential, they have become objects of fascination and wonder. We are united by a cultural voyeurism of billionaires, wondering what it would be like to live in their mansions with their armies of attendants; laze on their superyachts that float on international waters beyond the reach of nation-states; buy an entire company or an island on a whim; have a net worth larger than the GDP of some countries. Seen as the rock stars of capitalism and some of our biggest celebrities, billionaires make news not only for their fortunes—often numbers that are so enormous as to be unfathomable—but for their personal affairs, their physical transformations, their romances and dalliances, their purchases of sports teams and art at auction, their investments, their political contributions and their philanthropy, and even the number of children they have. They are both Emerson's singular figures and

Byron's romantic heroes. It is hardly surprising that billionaires are revered in a country that worships wealth. If monarchs throughout history, including in England before the Enlightenment, claimed a divine right to kingship as a way of retaining their grip on power, we have willingly conferred near divinity on our billionaires.

In 1892, Ward McAllister, a lawyer who sometimes served as a social director for Caroline Schermerhorn Astor, the high priestess of New York society during the Gilded Age, published a list of the 400 most influential people in the city in *The New York Times*.[4] That was the inspiration for Malcolm Forbes, the editor-in-chief of *Forbes* magazine, when he asked his reporters in 1981 to find the 400 richest people in America. Forbes, who had inherited the small family publication from his father, was intent on transforming it into a global brand synonymous with wealth, capitalism, and entrepreneurship. In 1982, the magazine published its first Forbes 400 list, kickstarting an annual tradition. That year, Forbes had 13 billionaires on its list of the richest Americans. Fifteen years later, the number of billionaires had shot up to 170, and a person needed to have assets of at least $475 million to make the cut. In 2021, all 400 were billionaires, and the twelve people at the bottom of the list were tied, each with a net worth of $2.9 billion. Every year, the list of billionaires whose fortunes don't make the cut gets longer. Since 1987, *Forbes* has also published an annual list of the world's billionaires; at last count, there were more than 2,600 people around the globe with estimated fortunes of at least one billion dollars.[5]

Rising wealth has given birth to an entire cottage industry of wealth tracking in America, where, in addition to *Forbes*, companies like Wealth-X and Bloomberg, through its Billionaires Index, calculate, quantify, rank, and track in real time the changing fortunes of billionaires, how they were sourced, whether they are "self-made," and how generous they are in terms of giving that fortune away. These lists are inexact but directionally accurate. Wealth managers subscribe to them so that they can target their services. Journalists, academics, and policymakers regularly cite them, especially the Forbes list. A search for "how to become a billionaire" on Google produces an infinite scroll of results, not all of them facetious. Investopedia, a site dedicated to financial information and advice, lists the do's and don'ts of becoming a billionaire. Amazon sells books offering strategies for making billions—essentially get-rich-quick lists upgraded to meet the moment. It also offers a broad selection of popular books about billionaires, from hagiographies to critical portrayals.

Even fictional billionaires, from Bruce Wayne, a.k.a. Batman (Forbes pegged his wealth at about $7 billion, although some fans put it at $100 billion, based on a DC Comics story plot) to Christian Grey (estimated net worth of $2.2 billion), the protagonist in *Fifty Shades of Grey*, are cult figures—one heroic and virtuous, the other kinky and chivalrous. The latter, an erotic love story between Grey, a young Harvard dropout turned billionaire, and a literature student, has sold tens of millions of copies since its 2011 publication, making author E. L. James a millionaire. It turns out that romance novels involving billionaires are a thing. Writing in *The New York Times Magazine*, the journalist Lydia Kiesling discovers that a search for "billionaire romance" on Amazon Books yields more than 50,000 results. It would appear, Kiesling writes, that "the only kind of book for which 'billionaire' is an explicit category is the romance novel, where it has developed into its own distinct subgenre."[6] Kiesling's essay was part of an entire issue that the magazine ran in April 2022 devoted to money, where writers examined the good, the bad, and the ugly of our fixation with billionaires.

And then there are the books that real-life billionaires have penned about themselves, where they share the insights gleaned on their way to the top. Dozens of superrich men and—a few—women, from Ray Dalio to Oprah Winfrey, have written memoirs detailing their life stories. It is a popular category with readers: Dalio's book *Principles* has sold more than 5 million copies worldwide since its 2017 release. Sam Walton's memoir *Made in America*, in which he charts his business journey from a single five-and-dime store to the Wal-Mart empire, remains an international bestseller some 30 years after it was first published in 1992. Some are better written than others, and many employ ghost writers, but the themes are common to many of them. The constant messaging is that their fortunes are the byproduct of what they loved to do, and that they got fantastically wealthy because they worked hard and added value to society. Asked about their reaction to billionaires in a June 2022 survey of American voters conducted by RealClear Opinion Research, 63 percent said they admired them or wanted to be them.[7] (Another 28 percent said they didn't think anyone should amass that kind of wealth, or that they outright hated billionaires.)

When talking about their stories, billionaires often underscore that their success is proof of the American dream. In July 2020, a House judiciary panel summoned the chief executives of Amazon, Apple, Alphabet, and Meta to answer questions about the business tactics that led to their dominance. Just years earlier, the same companies were heralded for their innovation. But the mood was darkening amid reports of their overwhelming dominance and alleged anticompetitive behavior, and their potential misuse and lack of oversight of consumer data. Lawmakers from both parties grilled the executives for more than five hours. Each executive—in addition to Bezos, Zuckerberg, Pichai, and Tim Cook of Apple were present, and all testified over video conference because of the pandemic—expressed humility. In his introductory remarks, Bezos sketched out his life story, speaking of the hard circumstances of his upbringing and how his parents instilled in him and his siblings that anything was possible with hard work and determination. From his grandfather, he took a lesson: If you have a setback, you keep trying until you invent your way to a better place. Those early lessons in entrepreneurial risk-taking came in handy when he left a cushy Wall Street job to start Amazon in a garage in the mid-1990s, Bezos said.[8] He also spoke at length about Amazon's contributions to the economy, how it had revolutionized online retail, helped equip small businesses for success using its technology, and the programs it created to serve underrepresented and underprivileged communities. He ended on a patriotic note, casting America as a country where rags-to-riches stories are possible, where risk-taking and entrepreneurship are welcome, and where immigrants like his adoptive father, who escaped Fidel Castro's Cuba, can make a home. "It's not a coincidence that Amazon was born in this country," Bezos told the lawmakers. "More than any other place on Earth, new companies can start, grow, and thrive here in the U.S. . . . . We nurture entrepreneurs and start-ups with stable rule of law, the finest university system in the world, the freedom of democracy, and a deeply accepted culture of risk-taking." Zuckerberg claimed for himself a similar narrative at the hearing, highlighting the uniquely American trajectory of Meta, Facebook's parent company. "Facebook is a successful company now, but we got there the American way: [W]e started with nothing and provided better products that people find valuable."[9]

By weaving their personal stories into the stories of their companies, Bezos and Zuckerberg were simply doing what many others of their ilk had done before them: They were selling the American dream. Foundational to the country, the American dream loosely holds that in a land of liberty, boundless opportunity, and free enterprise, individual merit, hard work, and a sprinkling of luck are the keys that unlock fortune. Your dream might be a car and a suburban home, or it might be a palace and a private plane, but it is a vision of upward mobility, of betterment, of easier and fuller lives for your progeny. In a society organized around the individual, the American dream is often cast as aspirational but achievable—and entirely self-made. The dream is at the heart of how Americans embrace our history and how we tell our stories. It is also America's pitch to the world, drawing immigrants from all over. The idea is constantly sold in popular culture and invoked in defense of the free market that has made the United States the richest country in the world. In signing the Giving Pledge, the initiative launched in 2010 by Buffett, Gates, and French Gates to encourage their fellow billionaires to commit to giving at least half of their fortunes away during their lifetimes or at death, dozens of the country's wealthiest men and women cite their success stories as the American dream come true. Many describe humble beginnings and fairy-tale endings. In speeches and memoirs, they talk of doing part-time jobs to pay for college, of growing up in immigrant households where the parents scraped and saved to send their children to school, of failure and perseverance. It is a message of empowerment, intended to tell listeners and readers that it is within a person's power to change their circumstances and achieve the outcomes they desire.

That American success stories would be self-made is a no-brainer given the very basis of the country's founding. Still, it would take roughly a century after the Declaration of Independence for the "self-made" pitch to become a distinct component of the American dream. The Gilded Age, a term coined by Mark Twain to describe the shine without and the rot within, was a period of roughly three decades beginning in 1870 when some enormous fortunes were made. Andrew Carnegie arrived in America from Scotland as a poor boy, educated himself at night school, and went from a factory worker in a mill to building a steel empire. Cornelius Vanderbilt, the son of a humble family from Staten Island, New York, got his start as a sailboat ferryman and used his entrepreneurial skills to build a steamship business, before turning to railroads and building a giant company. John D. Rockefeller Sr. built an oil monopoly before it was broken up by the federal government. Jay Gould, also born into poverty, did battle with Vanderbilt for control of railroads. John Pierpont Morgan was financier to many of them.

Their riches symbolized the opportunities of a world where the self-made man, and not an inheritor of wealth or an aristocrat, was at the top. The newly wealthy might not have the social status of old money, but they had the ambition and the money to muscle their way into polite society—a tension that is at the heart of *The Gilded Age,* a highly rated show on HBO. Although they were sometimes unscrupulous, crushing the competition, buying off willing politicians, and breaking up labor unions, the extreme success of the "robber barons"—a term that first appeared in *The Atlantic* in 1870—only underscored the American values of individualism and hard work, reinforcing the promise and possibility of the new world. A self-made success story was compelling, but it became profoundly emotional when it involved characters who survived the odds and hit paydirt with little more than luck and mettle—a storyline popularized by Horatio Alger, a minister who became a prolific author of books for young boys. By placing the individual at the center of his or her own destiny, the Alger stories provided succor and hope during a period of great wealth disparity. By one estimate alone, the 4,000 richest families in 1897, or about one percent of the population, had as much wealth as the collective monetary worth of 11.6 million families.[10]

More than two centuries after the robber barons held us in their thrall, there is perhaps no group with more power over our imaginations than today's technology billionaires. People often rationalize fortunes with value creation: A billionaire deserves his or her wealth because the individual created something of value for the wider world, and the wealth is proportional to the value created. But because technological innovations and inventions have prompted so many major cultural shifts and altered our daily lives, we see the people who built tech companies as even more deserving than the wealth that accrues to billionaires in, say, finance. If anything, the immense wealth of tech billionaires, the thinking goes, is dwarfed by the social, economic, and scientific progress they have created. Moreover, wealth creation in technology is seen as not a zero-sum game but an uplift for all members of society.

Lauding Billionaire Largesse

If the acquisition of money is an American fixation, so is giving it away. Americans give away more money than any other country in the world. They give to religious organizations, hospitals, schools and universities, arts and culture, nonprofits working for animal rights, and activists defending the right to abortion, among other causes. Some give because of their family values or religious beliefs. Others give as an expression of gratitude or a sense of civic duty. Deeply held beliefs about right and wrong spur people to send money to causes dear to them. Those who cannot part with their dollars give of their time. Individuals collectively give more money to charitable causes than foundations, corporations, and bequests combined, according to research by Indiana University's Lilly Family School of Philanthropy, which publishes an annual report called *Giving USA*, even though the numbers change from year to year. High inflation, an underperforming stock market, and a lethargic economy hurt giving, while global turmoil, political strife, and environmental catastrophes spur giving. Contributions flowed into nonprofits when the superstorm Sandy flooded lower Manhattan in 2012 and again when the coronavirus pandemic hit in 2020. Abortion clinics received an influx of dollars in 2022 after the Supreme Court struck down the constitutional right to an abortion. Nonprofits working on gender equality and sexual abuse saw a jump in donations after Donald Trump was elected president in 2016. Jeannie Infante Sager, the former director of the Women's Philanthropy Institute at Indiana University, said such "rage giving" was mostly made up of small-dollar donations from women. At the height of the coronavirus pandemic, when the stock market soared and the healthcare system was overwhelmed, philanthropic gifts broke new records. In 2022, as the pandemic receded and inflation became a greater worry, fewer people gave money away—although in dollar terms, the $319 billion amount was still higher than in 2019.[11]

The word "philanthropy" has its roots in Greek, and simply translates to "a love of humanity." The way we understand it today means using private resources for public good. The freedom to give voluntarily to whatever causes you want to, for whatever reason you pick, can be seen as a pure, uncoerced expression of individual liberty, and even an exercise of democracy. The tradition of philanthropy thus plays into the myth of American individualism, said Elizabeth Dale, who teaches nonprofit leadership at Seattle University. Through the ages, philanthropy has been "part of the American tradition of wanting to make it separate from government—that people could make their own decisions about how to use their own resources," Dale said.

Philanthropy, or at least a version of it, has a long tradition in American public life. Amanda B. Moniz, a historian and curator of philanthropy at the Smithsonian's National Museum of American History, divides the history of voluntary giving in America into five distinct phases that align roughly with the country's evolution, starting with the missionary organizations of the sixteenth and seventeenth centuries and tax-funded, local mechanisms for providing relief to the poor.[12] After the American Revolution, she notes in her article "Giving in America: A History of Philanthropy," residents of the newly formed nation took a more universal approach to charitable giving, moving away from religion, ethnicity, and other groupings to distribute aid to anyone in need. In the 1800s, Americans embraced charity with a nationalistic fervor, forming associations like the American Bible Society and other entities dedicated to social reform. It was this fervor that caught the eye of Alexis de Tocqueville, the French historian, on his nine-month journey through America. Writing in *Democracy in America*, Tocqueville observed that nineteenth-century Americans formed not just political associations, "but associations of a thousand other kinds, religious, moral, serious, futile, general or restricted, enormous or diminutive. The Americans make associations to give entertainments, to found seminaries, to build inns, to construct churches, to diffuse books, to send missionaries to the antipodes; in this manner they found hospitals, prisons, and schools."[13] By the late nineteenth century, the industrialists of the Gilded Age, their pockets bulging with new fortunes, introduced a more ambitious philanthropy, funding the country's cultural and educational institutions. With America's global clout growing, international charitable giving also grew. "World War I marked the first time Americans gave on a mass scale for foreign humanitarian relief," Moniz writes in "Giving in America." In the past five or so decades, as philanthropy has become a vast professional enterprise, the causes people pick have turned personal rather than national or universal, according to her.

Ever since he began to make money about four decades ago, Joel L. Fleishman has put away a portion of his paycheck for philanthropy. Initially, Fleishman set aside about 10 percent when his paycheck as an academic was relatively paltry, but over time he increased it to 30 percent. "It has made it so much easier to give away money because I overcame the reluctance early on about whether I should spend the money on myself rather than give it away," said Fleishman, a professor of law and public policy at Duke University, who also leads its center for strategic philanthropy and civil society. He said charity was an important part of his life, partly because of his religious beliefs. He gives to a variety of causes—to end child hunger, in support of relief to poor countries, to organizations serving the Black community. In addition, Fleishman set up a foundation in his parents' memory. But he admitted that giving money away is an acquired habit, like a late riser adjusting to a 5 A.M. wake up, or a meat lover adopting a vegan diet. To Fleishman, the nonprofit sector in America is dynamic because individuals and groups are free to give money to whatever they want to give to if they comply with the requirements of the law. Unlike in France, Germany, or Japan, where individuals require government approval to contribute money to things that the state deems within its purview, such as education, philanthropy is a free activity in America. "The great strength of the nonprofit sector has been that individuals can start foundations and give money to what they consider good ideas," Fleishman often tells his students.

Sometimes, an individual's impetus for giving is awakened by "mass philanthropy" campaigns; an early twentieth-century example is the March of Dimes in 1938, which raised collections from millions of Americans to fund polio research. The March relied on radio advertising, Hollywood celebrities, and President Franklin D. Roosevelt, who founded the organization, to get the word out. Even the pedestal of the Statue of Liberty was crowd-funded.[14] The publisher of *The New York World*, Joseph Pulitzer, put out an advertisement in his paper after funds for the construction of the base ran out. The ad brought in more than $100,000 in donations within six months, allowing the pedestal to be completed. Most of the contributions were a dollar or less. The same impetus that brought together Americans of earlier eras to form groups and start or fund institutions is echoed in the modern-day campaigns of online mass giving. Take the Ice Bucket Challenge of 2014. Initially dreamed up as a way to create awareness for amyotrophic lateral sclerosis, more commonly known as Lou Gehrig's disease, it became both a social media stunt and a viral campaign that succeeded in raising small-dollar donations from millions of people, who recorded themselves pouring a bucket of ice water over their heads, posting it on social media, and challenging another person to do the same, or donate $100 to the ALS Association (or do both). Celebrities and big philanthropists got involved in the challenge. The campaign eventually raised $115 million for the association, far outstripping the amounts it had raised in previous years, allowing it to direct much larger amounts to ALS research. Another online charity movement, GivingTuesday, started in 2012 to encourage people to make charitable donations one day a year, traditionally on the Tuesday after Thanksgiving. GivingTuesday now calls itself a "global generosity movement."

Individual philanthropy is also directed through corporations, which encourage generosity by offering company matches. At Microsoft, which applies its competitive culture even to donations, groups pit themselves against each other to see who raises more money. Managers offer prizes such as a dinner with the boss as incentives for employees to donate more. Once, a manager had to shave his head because he said he would do so if his team raised a certain amount. Buffett tipped his hat to this kind of philanthropy when he wrote in 2021: "Those who give their love and time in order to directly help others . . . receive no recognition whether they mentor the young, assist the elderly or devote precious hours to community betterment. They do not have buildings named after them, but they silently make those establishments—schools, hospitals, churches, libraries, whatever—work smoothly to benefit those who have received the short straws in life."[15] He made similar observations in his Giving Pledge letter in 2010: "First, my pledge: More than 99% of my wealth will go to philanthropy during my lifetime or at death. Measured by dollars, this commitment is large. In a comparative sense, though, many individuals give more to others every day. Millions of people who regularly contribute to churches, schools, and other organizations thereby relinquish the use of funds that would otherwise benefit their own families. The dollars these people drop into a collection plate or give to United Way mean forgone movies, dinners out, or other personal pleasures. In contrast, my family and I will give up nothing we need or want by fulfilling this 99% pledge."[16]

Small-dollar donations are mostly a reflection of pure generosity by individuals. It's therefore not surprising that philanthropy by the billionaire class is also seen as unadulterated generosity, except that it is supercharged. In 2022, very large gifts by individuals represented 5 percent of the nearly $500 billion that Americans gave to charity, according to the annual *Giving USA* report, and "mega-giving" by six individuals and couples alone totaled $14 billion.[17] Another study found that donations of more than $1 million accounted for 11 percent of the total number of donations, but measured by the number of dollars, they constituted 40 percent. As of the end of 2021, the top 25 U.S. billionaires had given away $169 billion as a group over their lifetimes.[18]

Hundreds of cultural centers, hospitals, museums, libraries, university departments, nonprofits, media organizations, and other entities have benefited from billionaire dollars, and that munificence is often recorded via news releases, articles, and renamed departments and institutions. In return for his $100 million gift to the New York Public Library, the private equity billionaire Stephen A. Schwarzman had his name inscribed on several of the library's iconic buildings. The Schwarzman naming spree irked at least one critic, who called it "crass."[19] Of his decision to buy a copy of the Magna Carta at auction, his fellow private equity billionaire David M. Rubenstein wrote in 2010 that he had bought it to keep the document in American hands.[20] He had the option to do so anonymously, but "I decided, though, that I wanted the public to know right then that I intended to place the document on long-term loan to the National Archives as a gift to the country and as modest repayment of my debt to this country for my good fortune in being an American."

To question billionaire philanthropy as anything other than noble, especially given its imprint on the social and cultural firmament, is akin to doubting the intentions of a soldier who goes into battle to save his country. Yet, the reasons for giving billions of dollars away are more complicated and can range from the moral to the merely expedient.[21] For those at the very top, philanthropic giving is often determined by a complicated calculus that, in addition to generosity, involves death, taxes, markets, egoism, and reputation. Decades of policy changes around death taxes (also known as estate or inheritance taxes), income taxes, and charitable deductions from those taxes have often controlled the philanthropy spigot. When estate taxes are high, people generally give more to philanthropic causes during their lifetimes and make larger charitable bequests as a means of reducing the taxes their estate will owe. A similar tussle happens between philanthropists and the government when income tax rates rise. The stock market's performance can also influence how much money is earmarked for giving.

The wealthy typically set up foundations to house their philanthropic dollars and direct those funds, or they put their money into donor-advised funds overseen by big money managers such as Fidelity. Money allocated to charity cannot be reclaimed by the donor, but it can be deducted from the total income on which an individual must pay taxes—an incentive meant to spur giving. Lawmakers, worried that the wealthy were directing big sums of money to their private foundations for the tax breaks without any accountability, passed the Tax Reform Act of 1969, which requires foundations to give away a minimum of 5 percent of their assets annually to maintain their tax-exempt status. Rising wealth has led to an explosion in the number of private foundations and the amount of investment assets they hold. In 2020, the most recent year for which data is available, there were more than 100,000 private foundations in the United States. More than $1 trillion sits in their coffers, a greater than fivefold increase from three decades ago.[22] Except for dips during the downturns following the 2000 dotcom bubble burst and the 2008 financial crisis, the amount of assets has grown steadily. Between 2010 and 2020, the number of foundations with assets of at least $1 billion doubled, from 65 to 136, according to calculations based on publicly available data by John Seitz, who runs a data organization called FoundationMark. Foundations with assets of between $100 million and $1 billion in assets also doubled over the same period.

Donor-advised funds, which have existed since the 1930s, too have exploded in popularity as wealth has risen. Like foundations, wealthy individuals get the tax benefit of the donation upfront, but unlike foundations, there is no annual disbursement requirement nor a time frame during which the money must make its way to a nonprofit entity. Such funds have become hugely popular in recent years; as of 2021, about $234 billion sat in donor-advised funds, according to the National Philanthropic Trust, which advises foundations, donors, and others.[23] That is more than double the $112 billion in assets, including donor contributions and market gains, such funds had in 2017. The number of donor-advised fund accounts has also risen from 471,000 to 1.3 million over the same time frame, introducing some cynicism into whether the noble intentions of philanthropy, as outlined by the government, are being abused.[24] Outflows from these funds are usually lower than the contributions people make, meaning that tax calculations are likely a bigger motivator than philanthropy. In 2020, more than $35 billion made its way from donor-advised funds to philanthropic causes—a record, as people were driven to directing the funds to charitable organizations during the pandemic. Still, the inflow of money into donor-advised funds for the year, at about $50 billion, was far higher than the out-flow.[25] In 2021, when the S&P 500 stock market index hit record highs, the inflows doubled to $72 billion. Payouts also increased, but by a much lower amount, according to the Trust.

Tax incentives aside, many billionaires also give to manage and burnish their reputations. Grand philanthropic gestures acted at least partly as a shield for the Sackler family even as they knowingly fed an opioid addiction crisis around the country, and made billions off selling Oxycontin through their company, Purdue Pharma.[26] For years, the Sackler name graced museum wings and art institutes, endowed university chairs, supported medical research and more, and family scions were often seen talking about their family's philanthropic traditions. (In 2021, following the growing outrage at Purdue's role in the opioid crisis, the Metropolitan Museum of Art scrubbed the Sackler name from some of its exhibition halls.)[27] Many billionaires also give money away because of the diminishing marginal utility of wealth. The media often casts big donations within the framework of selfishness and generosity; a billionaire who chooses to give money when he could have been buying yachts and mansions is seen as having taken the morally correct path. But generosity can be a forced choice. At some point, the relentless march of wealth accumulation—after the appetite for homes, luxury cars, custom-made private planes, yachts, expensive art, sports teams, and islands has been sated, and future generations provided for—brings no new joy. Rather, there is greater joy in giving the money back to society, picking and choosing the ways in which to do so, and building a legacy.

The growth of mega donors, and the overall rise of philanthropic donations by those on the wealthier end of the spectrum, could have potentially deleterious effects on America's giving culture. First, it skews the sources of funds for nonprofits. If ordinary Americans donate less money to, say, the nonprofit working on getting abortion care to women, it makes that nonprofit more dependent on the few givers at the top. If those mega donors go elsewhere, a nonprofit can suddenly become strapped for cash. The tilt of the field of philanthropy toward big donors also means certain already well-funded areas get more funding, such as top-tier universities and hospitals. Americans' attitudes toward donations by small donors and mega donors remain mixed. In a 2023 study titled "What Americans Think About Philanthropy and Nonprofits" published by the Lilly Family School of Philanthropy, respondents "somewhat preferred" a wider base of small donors to a narrower base of mega donors. At the same time, they also agreed that big gifts were more impactful and should be part of the giving landscape.[28]

Philanthropy experts are becoming concerned about another trend that is being masked by big, splashy billionaire donations: Fewer and fewer everyday Americans and households have been giving money away in recent decades. Even as the overall giving numbers are growing, the number of small donations is falling as a percentage of that total amount.[29] "The percentage of Americans giving to charitable organizations has been declining over the past 20 years," according to the authors of the 2023 report. "This is a key concern inside the sector and regularly garners media attention, as well. Yet only one in three Americans is aware of this key challenge to the future of philanthropy."

Chapter 2

The Ur Nerd of Capitalism

The Value Proposition

In the wee hours of the night, two young men are writing code, their faces pale in the blue light of the room. They haven't taken a break in hours. One of them—his sandy brown hair disheveled, his oversized glasses flecked with grease—pours Tang from the jar directly into his palm and licks the orange powder. The sugar hits his bloodstream. He can keep going. There is a deadline looming and not a moment to be lost. Earlier, he had told a company that he had exactly the software they needed. The reality was a little different, but the duo eventually delivered. Out of that first piece of code they wrote in 1975 was born Microsoft.[1]

We love origin stories of tech wunderkinds like Bill Gates and Paul Allen, the founders of Microsoft. Tales of sleep-starved young men (almost always men) building the companies of their dreams in dorm rooms and rented garages—fueled by little other than caffeine, drugs, sugar, and an unwavering determination to change the world, and becoming fantastically rich in the process—feed the narrative of American innovation and individual success. In recent decades, with successful entrepreneurs in Silicon Valley and elsewhere producing unicorns and decacorns by the dozen, the "nerd founder" has reached folkloric status. Nerds, with their unruly hair, social ineptitude, and uncanny brilliance, are objects of wonder, parody, and envy, and even worthy of emulation. They inspire both popular culture and academic study. Nerd brains and the fruits they bear have become American capitalism's greatest asset, creating immense value for society and cementing the country's top spot in technology.

"The lonely-nerd-turned-accidental-billionaire narrative has assumed the mantle of the Great American Success Story," the historian Nathan Ensmenger writes in "Beards, Sandals, and Other Signs of Rugged Individualism," his 2015 paper about how computer professionals of the 1960s and 1970s built a masculine identity around programming. The computer nerd, Ensmenger writes, thus became a "stock character in the repertoire of American popular culture, his defining characteristics (white, male, middle-class, uncomfortable in his body and awkward around women) well established."[2]

There is perhaps no nerd more representative of the early coalescence of technology, popular culture, and capitalism than Gates, the one with the greasy glasses. Of all the early tech savants, the Microsoft cofounder had serious programming credentials and a deep understanding of technology. But arguably, his biggest victory lay in his business vision. Gates saw a commercial market for software where none existed and built one of the world's biggest companies based on that vision. A year after Microsoft went public in 1986, Gates became America's youngest billionaire and the first to make his fortune from technology. He was 31 years old.

He was also an awkward young man who could be imperious and intolerant of others. He chewed so often and so furiously on the stems of his glasses that the plastic ends frayed. The rhythm with which he rocked back and forth in his chair was a barometer of his engagement with a topic. He displayed bouts of frightening intensity and passion, but he was physically unassertive. Software was his primary language. In story after news story and book after book, writers made a point of mentioning his appearance and behavior in the same breath as Microsoft's latest software. Even the occasional frosting of dandruff on his shoulders became a subject of private discussion among tech reporters. Gates still exhibits some of those tics. He slouches when he stands, slumps when he sits, often gesticulates wildly with his hands when he is animated or tucks them under his armpits when in listening mode. Sometimes, when making a point, his arms stretch as wide as the wings of an osprey in midflight. His feet tap in time to the pace of his speech.

He studs his sentences with words like "neat" and "cool." Gates once called his rocking and swaying body movements a "metronome" for his brain.[3] Social niceties and small talk meant to lubricate the start of a conversation are lost on him. Repartee isn't his forte, although people close to him say he has an offbeat charm that comes through in small settings; Buffett told this reporter that Gates has a "keen sense of humor." Still, it can be excruciating to watch him work the room at a cocktail party, say, in Davos, or at dinner after a conference. As Ken Auletta wrote memorably in *World War 3.0*, his detailed book about Microsoft's battle with the government over its monopolistic practices in the late 1990s, a conversation with Gates was "business sex, without the foreplay."[4]

In the 1980s, as Microsoft became more dominant, and Gates more visible, he bestowed mystique and prestige on nerdiness in equal measure, legitimizing both a personality type and the popular image of one. Gates was hardly the only technological genius of his era who shared his physical attributes and his ambitions. But he occupied a unique perch in the nerd pantheon because his nerdiness and his business instincts were so in balance that they appeared to be the core formula for Microsoft's success. His persona was as essential, it seemed, as Microsoft was unavoidable. He—the tech nerd and the businessman—was capitalism's darling, a blueprint not only for investors hoping to unearth the next badly dressed boy billionaire, but also for endless popular culture portrayals.

Bob Muglia, a longtime technology executive who joined Microsoft in 1988 and worked there for 23 years, said that Gates set the tone for a lot of what we classify as nerd behavior, from the glasses to the arrogance. "He was the perfect persona." In his long career in Seattle, and later in Silicon Valley as a top executive at Juniper Networks and chief executive of Snowflake Computing, Muglia, also a billionaire, observed that nerds are defined as much by their unpredictable behavior as by their physical appearance. "You hear things from them that you don't expect. It's not an uncommon characteristic, because they're always thinking about random things," he said. "They're all on the spectrum," he added, calling them "unique individuals" who have specific characteristics, including a taste for risk-taking, "which can get them into trouble in a number of ways, and the brilliance and the confidence that comes from that brilliance. They have a certain bravado that others don't."

When Gates entered Harvard University in 1973, the first cheap desktop computers were coming to market, made possible by advances in chip technology. But they needed software to become functional. As the Microsoft legend goes, Allen happened to read in *Popular Electronics* that the makers of a microcomputer called the MITS-Altair were looking for a programming language that could run on their hardware. The Altair was a foot and a half tall, and nearly as wide.

After Allen told Gates excitedly about the opportunity, they decided to make a pitch—without having written a single line of code. Gates then called Ed Roberts at Altair from his dorm at Currier House at Harvard, pretending to be Allen. They had decided that Gates would do the talking, but Allen, the older of the two, would be the one to go for the in-person meeting in case their ploy worked. "We've got a BASIC for the Altair that's just about finished, and we'd like to come out and show it to you," Gates said to Roberts.[5] Allen would later recount that episode in his memoir: "I admired Bill's bravado but worried that he'd gone too far, since we'd yet to write the first line of code."

But Altair executives bought their pitch, and Gates and Allen coded, as day turned into night, hurriedly adapting an existing software program to deliver the product they had promised. Micro-Soft was born in the fall of 1975 (they dropped the hyphen some years later). Originally based in Albuquerque, New Mexico, the company relocated to the Seattle area in 1979. From the start, their vision was that there would be a desktop in every home, and the software that ran them should be paid for. That software is worth paying for might seem like a no-brainer today. But Gates and Allen were trying to build a business around the invisible stuff that makes computers work when all the excitement was around the design and development of hardware. Software was largely something that math and engineering students and hobbyists tinkered with on the side and shared freely, despite growing demand for operating systems from computer manufacturers like

IBM. It was little surprise that the hobbyists, many of whom were reared in the 1960s counterculture movement that eschewed commercialism, irritated the young Gates. Their approach interfered with his business plan.

In the February 1976 issue of *Computer Notes* magazine, Gates wrote an open letter to computer hobbyists, lamenting the software piracy and lack of principles in their community. "As the majority of hobbyists must be aware, most of you steal your software," Gates wrote in the brief but well-worded missive. "Hardware must be paid for, but software is something to share. Who cares if the people who worked on it get paid?" Gates wrote with a rhetorical flourish, displaying his fundamental belief that software was intellectual property that must be protected.[6] By insisting that software was proprietary, Gates scrubbed off its countercultural ethos and imposed upon it the capitalist values that he had embraced from the start. A big helping of luck would soon supercharge his vision.

Once Microsoft gained some success with its programming language, it struck a deal with IBM to build an operating system for the hardware giant's personal computer, which had come to market in 1981. Gates was able to secure an introduction to IBM because his mother, Mary Maxwell Gates, served on a committee of the nonprofit United Way at the same time as IBM's then chairman John Opel, and happened to mention her son's young company. Opel then mentioned Microsoft to some other IBM executives, the story goes, and decided to invite Microsoft to build a software program for its computer.[7] Microsoft bought a disk operating system from Seattle Computer Products for around $50,000 and licensed it to IBM as MS-DOS. Microsoft also got IBM to agree to allow it to license MS-DOS to other hardware makers, thereby paving the way for it to sell software to as many computer manufacturers as there were in the market. The licensing model was Gates's real innovation; over the decades it brought Microsoft hundreds of billions of dollars in revenue. It was the equivalent of a person negotiating an open relationship just as the field blossoms with potential partners. Not only were there dozens of computer manufacturers when Microsoft secured its licensing agreement, but advances in chip technology were already bringing down the average cost of a PC, making it affordable to households. And Big Blue's PC was becoming the computer of choice in businesses and homes. Together, these events formed the bedrock upon which Microsoft built its empire.

Driven by a hard-nosed capitalism, Gates sought ways to build a business around Microsoft's core product, seeking competitive advantages where he could and defending his company's turf against potential threats. If that meant taking an existing program or application, tweaking it, and selling it as part of Microsoft's flagship Windows software, so be it. The public spats with rivals, the ugly accusations of plagiarism and theft, the labeling of Microsoft products as shoddy, and the dismissals about his programming credentials—even if they upset him—were simply the cost of doing business. His ruthlessness also extended to personal relationships; in his 2011 memoir *Idea Man*, Allen, who died in 2018, said that Gates had tried to dilute his stake in Microsoft and even tried to buy out his cofounder with a lowball offer in 1983. That year, Allen had been diagnosed with non-Hodgkin's lymphoma and begun working less, and Gates argued that Allen should therefore have a smaller stake.

At the same time, Steve Jobs—who, like Gates, could be mercurial and harsh, but who did not share the same nerdy traits—was building his reputation as an exacting design maven with a far more beguiling vision of what the personal computer could be. The Apple PC was an elegant, easy-to-use machine that Jobs had full control over, from the design specifics to the presentation. Gates and Jobs were early collaborators on software but also fierce rivals, each disdainful of the other. Jobs designed products that created desire—Larry Ellison, the cofounder of Oracle, once called Apple the only "lifestyle brand in the computer industry"—whereas Microsoft software, by comparison, was dull but dominant.[8]

In his biography of Jobs, Walter Isaacson compares the era of Jobs and Gates to the relationship between Albert Einstein and Niels Bohr in twentieth-century physics, or between Thomas Jefferson and Alexander Hamilton in early American governance. Those eras came to be "shaped by the relationship and rivalry of two orbiting superstars," Isaacson writes. "For the first thirty years of the personal computer age, beginning in the late

1970s, the defining binary star system was composed of two high-energy college dropouts both born in 1955. Jobs was more intuitive and romantic and had a greater instinct for making technology usable, design delightful, and interfaces friendly."[9] He made no secret of his utter disgust for what he viewed as Microsoft's shoddy products, with their lack of elegance and taste. "Bill is basically unimaginative and has never invented anything, which is why I think he's more comfortable now in philanthropy than technology," he told Isaacson. "He just shamelessly ripped off other people's ideas."

Who Is a Nerd?

The technology nerd did not emerge fully formed, like Aphrodite, out of a sea of computer cables. Rather, he is an artificial construct, Frankenstein's monster born of necessity, stereotype, and early mythmaking in the tech industry. The etymology of the term "nerd" is somewhat obscure. Some point to a poem by Dr. Seuss from the 1950s, while others say it is derived from the word "nut," meaning a crazy person. But the term itself didn't become part of the everyday lexicon until the early days of the computing revolution, when "nerd" came to stand for an eccentric male who preferred coding and hacking to human interaction, and often held antiauthoritarian beliefs popular with the 1960s counterculture movement.

Ensmenger, the computer historian, has thought a lot about nerds. Genial, thoughtful, and almost boyish in his appearance, Ensmenger studied civil engineering at Princeton before becoming interested in the sociocultural aspects of computing. An associate professor at Indiana University, his research focuses on how masculine culture works within the computing industry, and how early stereotypes were formed. In particular, he was struck by the fact that when mainframe computers were the norm in the 1950s, many early programmers were women. Yet, the foundations of the modern computer era were laid in a hypermasculine environment of hobbyists dominated by the perpetually adolescent "whiz kid."

In *The Computer Boys Take Over*, Ensmenger traces the rather arbitrary arc of that evolution. In the early 1960s, an IBM desktop computer cost millions of dollars, required roughly 10,000 square feet of air-conditioned space, and needed dozens of programmers to feed it operating instructions.[10] Ensmenger underscores that there were no preconceived notions of who could be a programmer, and there was even an initial conflict between casting programming as an art versus a science. A recruitment ad by IBM from 1969, for instance, was quite open to who could be a programmer—a music composer; a lover of geometry; anyone with an orderly mind who enjoys anagrams, chess, or bridge; or at least a person with a "lively imagination."

But as minicomputers moved from the worlds of science and academia to the broader market, their potential for use in business applications set off a mini manufacturing boom. And as computing technology evolved, the size of the computers too began to shrink, making them widely viable. The need for computer programmers increased, and with it, a more systematic way to recruit them. "It was clear that recruiting programmers a half dozen at a time with cute advertisements in *The New York Times* was not a sustainable strategy," Ensmenger writes.[11] From that desperate demand for people who could code emerged a set of qualities—often determined by aptitude tests, psychological profiles, and, generally, "deeply flawed scientific methodology"—that fed into the idea of the perfect programmer. "The primary selection mechanism used by the industry selected for antisocial, mathematically inclined males, and therefore antisocial, mathematically inclined males were overrepresented in the programmer population; this in turn reinforced the popular perception that programmers *ought* to be antisocial and mathematically inclined (and therefore male), and so on ad infinitum." This demand-driven, unplanned and almost whimsical way of finding computer programmers would ultimately feed into the definition of who is a nerd. Casting about for solitary males to fill programming seats was one way to spread the nerd gospel. Equally though, a few landmark pieces of cultural documentation helped flesh out both the characteristics of the nerd and the environment in which he thrived most.

In 1972, the writer Stewart Brand wrote a piece for *Rolling Stone* called "Spacewar: Fanatic Life and Symbolic Death Among the Computer Bums."[12] Brand, who by then had achieved some fame as the publisher of the *Whole Earth Catalog* magazine, immersed himself in the lives of early coders and programmers like an ethnologist, observing their habits and behaviors and capturing "hacker" culture, as they were known at the time. A rabbi for the Bay Area counterculture movement in the 1960s, Brand followed his subjects as they played a computer game called *Spacewar* that had been created at the Massachusetts Institute of Technology. In the article, one of Brand's subjects described the attributes of a standard computer bum: "A true hacker is not a group person. He's a person who loves to stay up all night, he and the machine in a love-hate relationship . . . They're kids who tended to be brilliant but not very interested in conventional goals. And computing is just a fabulous place for that, because it's a place where you don't have to be a PhD or anything else. It's a place where you can still be an artisan. People are willing to pay you if you're any good at all, and you have plenty of time for screwing around." The interviewee, Alan Kay of the Xerox Research Center, called the term "hacker" "a term of derision and . . . the ultimate compliment."

Who is Brand interviewing if not a self-described nerd? The term "hacker" has a very different connotation today than it did when Brand wrote his iconic piece, because it referred to a group of young men who braided their belief in the transcendent power of computing with aspects of the counterculture that rejected centralized authority—the very same people who so irritated Gates because they believed that software should be free, not proprietary.

Brand, in his robust and engaging prose, went further. Hackers were "a mobile new-found elite, with its own apparat, language, and character, its own legends and humor," he wrote. "Those magnificent men with their flying machines, scouting a leading edge of technology which has an odd softness to it; outlaw country, where rules are not decree or routine so much as the starker demands of what's possible."

Within a decade of Brand's piece, with the personal computing revolution at their doorstep, the anticommercial ethos of the hobbyists, the computer bums, and the hackers had been tamed by the staid ambitions of capitalism. The hacker was dragged from the frontier to the mainstream. At the same time, the conditions deemed essential to their success—the solitary environment free of traditional management rules, the competitiveness, the idea of work as its own reward—were kept intact.

In *The Soul of a New Machine*, published in 1981, the author Tracy Kidder described the race between two computer hardware companies, Data General and Digital Equipment Corporation, to build a new personal computer. Kidder, who won a Pulitzer Prize for the book, not only takes the reader into the deepest reaches of the computer itself, but also places us amid the dozens of young, sleep-deprived and sometimes self-taught engineers who work on their projects without a break, only the shadows on their chins marking the passing of time. We are invited into the drama of the competition, but equally, we are compelled by the creation of a new culture and mythology—of those who would come to be known as nerds.

Nerds 1.0 and 2.0

The 1980s were the go-go years for Wall Street. Hostile takeovers were new and thrilling, and celebrity dealmakers had cultural capital. It was a place driven by excessive greed, outsized bets, and financial scandal, and it was immortalized in books like *Den of Thieves*, *The Predators' Ball*, and *Barbarians at the Gate*. Ivan Boesky and Michael Milken, for a time, became synonymous with financial crime. The takeover of RJR Nabisco established the private equity business as an untamed, acquisitive new force with the potential for economic harm rather than good.

Literature and popular culture provided the harmony to the main tune of Wall Street in that decade. In *The Bonfire of the Vanities*, a bombastic tale of race, class, and politics, Tom Wolfe portrayed New York as a city seething with ambition, greed, and ego—the Masters of the Universe! But nothing established Wall Street as a cesspit of amoral, selfish, and scheming individuals who will stop at nothing to make their payday more than the 1987 movie *Wall Street*, which made Gordon Gekko a fixture in the public imagination—in particular, the line that "greed is good." Gekko, played by Michael Douglas, may have been making a more nuanced point about the nature of capitalism, but the line became a damning shorthand for Wall Street.

At the same time, a crop of young technology entrepreneurs was swiftly climbing up the ladder of influence and wealth. In addition to Gates and Jobs, there was Michael Dell, a college dropout who founded Dell Computer in 1984, rethinking the way that computers could be built and sold. Ellison, another dropout, cofounded Oracle in 1977, creating a commercially viable database software product to help businesses manage and store their data. Sun Microsystems, cofounded by Scott McNealy in 1982, changed the way computers talked to each other via networking software. The company remained independent until Oracle bought it in 2010.

Microsoft, Oracle, and Sun all went public in the same week in March 1986, but the "IPO of the year" title went to Microsoft, given the sheer excitement around the rapidly growing software company. In 1990, Microsoft became the first software company to cross $1 billion in sales. Five years later, in 1995, Gates became the richest man in America, a title he would hold for the better part of two decades. It had been twenty years since Gates cofounded Microsoft, and the company, now dominant and seemingly invincible, was long past its scrappy days. Gates, too, had lost some of his nerdy entrepreneurial sheen.

By the mid 1990s, America was in the throes of a hot and heavy love affair with the second iteration of the nerds: the drivers of the digital revolution. The sociologist Thomas Streeter has posited that part of the reason why the internet gained romantic status when it did was that Microsoft's dominance "represented the uninspiring end of the garage start-up days in microcomputing," motivating many technology-oriented students and young entrepreneurs to study the commercial potential of newer technologies. "Not only had the desktop computer become a commonplace of office life, but the companies that made microcomputers no longer seemed like the boisterous garage start-ups of popular capitalist mythology," Streeter writes. "By 1990, the least glamorous of the 1980s microcomputer companies, Microsoft, had achieved that much-prized and much-hated state common to technology industries: a practical monopoly. The gray, arrogant, predictable monopoly of IBM had been overthrown and replaced—by another gray, arrogant, predictable monopoly."13

At the same time, it was not lost on the new generation of would-be entrepreneurs or Wall Street investors that Microsoft's unfathomable success had generated massive wealth. An investor who bought one share of Microsoft when it went public on March 13, 1986, would get a return of more than 8,500 percent a decade later. Or if you bought $1,000 worth of Microsoft stock at its IPO price of $21 per share, you would be sitting on more than $4 million today—enough to pay off your student debt, buy a loft apartment in downtown Manhattan, or retire comfortably in a mid-priced city.

The combination of new technologies, investor enthusiasm, and media excitement—not to mention, the implicit search for the next Bill Gates—created the perfect conditions for the dotcom boom. Hundreds of graduates of business schools and other top universities who might have chosen to go to Wall Street instead made their way to Silicon Valley. Investment bankers rushed to cater to the financial needs of fledgling companies, and the number of venture capital investors swelled. The breathless rush for deals meant that companies with poorly formed ideas and no profits were suddenly tapping millions of dollars. In 1993, *Wired* magazine launched. Dedicated to chronicling emerging technologies and their impact on culture and society, it quickly became a media touchstone. According to one statistic, during the year 1996, a Valley company went public every five days, creating millionaires overnight.14

The biggest beneficiary of that excitement was Mosaic, a browser programmed by Marc Andreessen and Eric Bina, two students at the National Center for Supercomputing Applications at the University of Illinois. "Surfing the web using Mosaic in the early days shared certain features with the early stages of a romantic affair, or the first phases of a revolutionary movement: the dreamlike experience of pointing, clicking, and watching images slowly appear generated a sense of anticipation, of possibility. Mosaic was not a case of desire satisfied, but of desire provoked," Streeter writes. In April 1994, Jim Clark, a professor turned businessman who had found success with the hardware company Silicon Graphics, founded Netscape along with Andreessen. The two launched the Netscape Navigator browser six months later. Netscape's public offering in 1995 made front page news. *The New York Times* wrote: "A 15-month-old company that has never made a dime of profit had one of the most stunning debuts in Wall Street history yesterday as investors rushed to pour their money into cyberspace."[15] It had $100 million in revenue and no profit.[16]

Andreessen, at six foot four inches tall, loomed large both physically and metaphorically as tech's newest wunderkind, eliciting regular comparisons to Gates. Aspects of his persona became part of Netscape's storytelling, just as Gates's tics had once been studied and tied to his business maneuvers. People recount Andreessen showing up to meetings barefoot, in shorts, and proceeding to eat a messy Subway sandwich while discussing the intricacies of the browser.

Rosanne Siino, an experienced technology marketing executive who was one of the original team members of Netscape, saw the potential for a story centered around a 19-year-old founder who "doesn't know how to wear a clean T-shirt and eats sandwiches messily." Siino also pitched Andreessen as part of a new cadre of entrepreneurs different from Gates, who flew solo, and built the father–son dynamic between Clark and Andreessen into the company's creation myth. Once a perception, a brand, or a story is created, it no longer matters who the actual person is, Siino said. Details of Andreessen's "regular guy" life filtered through to the press. He appeared on the February 19, 1996, cover of *Time* magazine, barefooted, in jeans and sitting on a gilded throne. "The Golden Geeks," the magazine called Andreessen and a crop of other emerging tech founders. "Who are they? How do they live? And what do they mean for America's future?" At least one writer suggested that the "kid" could topple Gates.[17]

Andreessen, now a venture capitalist and arch defender of nerds, has dwelled on the type frequently, either to his 1.2 million followers on X, the company formerly known as Twitter, writing missives known as "tweetstorms," or in interviews. In a 2022 interview, he pointed out the staying power of nerds: A lot of people in finance with MBAs joined the tech industry in the 1990s only to leave as soon as the dotcom bubble burst, and then returned to the industry after realizing there was much more potential. "The Harvard MBAs left for a while, at least until after the new hills were discovered—smartphones, social networking, Web 2.0, cloud [computing]. Then those people came back into tech," he said. "That's why the nerds are predictive and the MBAs aren't."[18] In 2014, he wrote on X: "Silicon Valley is nerd culture, and we are the bro's natural enemy."

The bursting of the dotcom bubble was a mere blip in the long march of tech's domination, because the next generation of tech behemoths led by nerdy founders was already sprouting. In 1998, Larry Page and Sergey Brin started Google out of a basement. Jeff Bezos quit his hedge fund job to start Amazon. Also, that year, Peter Thiel and a few others cofounded PayPal, letting people make hassle-free money transfers online. In 2004, Mark Zuckerberg started Facebook out of his college dorm room. Apple introduced the iPhone in 2007, the same year Netflix, whose founders Reed Hastings and Marc Randolph had pioneered the concept of renting DVDs by mail a decade earlier, introduced its streaming service. Wireless, GPS, and Bluetooth technologies became widely available for commercial use.

When the global economy entered a recession following the 2008 financial crisis, which once again highlighted the greed and recklessness of Wall Street, young technology companies were the few specks of light amid the gloom. Since then, the technology sector has grown at warp speed, destroying old businesses and creating new ones, pushing the boundaries of what is possible, reaping billions of dollars of profits, making founders and investors obscenely rich, and consolidating America's position as the world's technology leader. Today, the tech sector accounts for more than a quarter of the S&P 500 stock index. Analysts even anointed Apple, Alphabet, Amazon, Meta, Microsoft, Nvidia, and Tesla the "Magnificent Seven"—a reference to the 1960 Western remake of Akira Kurosawa's *Seven Samurai*, in which seven gun-toting mercenaries team up to protect a village from bandits—because of their dominance and power. At $2.6 trillion, the digital economy, which typically includes software, services, and computing, made up just over 10 percent of the total gross domestic product of the United States in 2022, up from about 2 percent at the turn of the century, according to U.S. government data. For years, the sector has grown at a faster pace than U.S. GDP.[19]

The median annual wage for the computer and information technology industry was $100,532 as of May 2022, more than double the median annual wage for all other occupations.[20] In the next decade, computer and information technology jobs are expected to grow 15 percent, much faster than the average rate for other jobs. Although technology has killed jobs, it has also added new ones, and net employment in the sector has continued to grow. Venture capital firms have seen gushers of cash from traditional money managers hoping to get a piece of the next big thing. In 2011, as the economy found its footing following the recession, venture capitalists invested $262 billion in roughly 8,000 companies. By 2022, they invested four times as much money into more than 27,000 companies.[21] The first billion-dollar start-up was christened a "unicorn" because it was so rare. Unicorns then became so commonplace—there were more than 700 at the end of 2023— that the term "decacorn" had to be invented. At last count, 74 of the 400 richest Americans had made their billions from industries that can loosely be categorized as technology. Eight of the top 10 billionaires in the Forbes 2023 list of the world's 400 richest people were tech billionaires—Musk, Bezos, Ellison, Page, Gates, Brin, Zuckerberg, and Steve Ballmer. Each had an estimated net worth of more than $100 billion. Their collective net worth of about $1.2 trillion exceeded the 2021 GDP of the Netherlands. If Bezos were a country, his net worth of $201 billion would rank him at fifty-fourth on the list of countries based on their gross domestic product, coming in just below Iraq but ahead of Ukraine. The divorces of tech billionaires too have created new and enormous fortunes, including those of MacKenzie Scott from Bezos and of Melinda French Gates. Tech fortunes have eclipsed many of the biggest on Wall Street, including the founders of hedge funds and private equity firms. Also, tech billionaires have accumulated their wealth far more swiftly than billionaires in other industries.

The financial dominance and overwhelming importance of the technology sector has conferred upon entrepreneurs and innovators nearly unrestrained power over society, culture, and the public imagination, not to mention our daily lives, feeding into preexisting biases about who is best positioned to lead us into the future. There has been no other historical period than the past decade and a half when the pace and breadth of technological change has been this uncontained, even magical. We are able to shop for anything online and have it delivered in minutes, or connect with friends from anywhere in the world holding a six-inch device in the palms of our hands. We can type a query into a white search bar and find instantaneous results—so much so that "Google" is now a transitive verb. A chatbot employing artificial intelligence can hold a conversation with a human, or summarize billions of pages of data in seconds. Our data is stored virtually in the cloud, allowing us to access our email and our photographs from anywhere. Cars can now plug into electric sockets to recharge their batteries. Navigation, which once required paper maps, is now an application on a smartphone. Technology is so essential to the way we go about our lives that we no longer stop to think about it. Novelists might imagine futures, but technologists bring them to life.

Myths of the Nerd Ecosystem

"There are elements of truth in all mythology, along with a good dose of exaggeration that I have not contributed to," Gates once told *Playboy* magazine, speaking about himself at the height of Microsoft's reign in the 1990s.[22] Myths are sustained by our beliefs and our storytelling. They stretch reality to make the inexplicable explicable, and the irrational rational. Stereotypes, on the other hand, are sustained by our ignorance. They are lazy associations we make, signifiers with only a casual relation to the truth. In the twentieth and twenty-first centuries, perhaps no other industry has seen the cohabitation of sociocultural mythmaking and stereotyping as much as the technology industry, a combination of hype, hysteria, and hagiography. It is hard not to mythologize the individuals whose creations have transformed the ways in which we live and think at bewildering speed, and who even appear to predict the future. Since the Industrial Revolution, inventors of technology, from Thomas Alva Edison to Henry Ford, were seen as exceptional, according to Ensmenger, the historian. Early biographies of Edison portrayed the inventor of the light bulb in terms of the metaphysical—someone who brought "light to darkness," he said.

Gates may be known more for his philanthropy in the past couple of decades than his life as a technology executive, but the Microsoft cofounder helped build some of the stickiest myths about the environments in which technological greatness thrives. Take the myth that tech founders are young; often they are also college dropouts. Because so many successful technology companies have been started by wet-behind-the-ears twentysomethings, the young are seen as intuitively understanding that which is about to happen and that which is yet to come, while the skill of their venture capital backers (many of whom were once young founders) lies in betting on the right youngsters. That kind of you-don't-get-it attitude, as Streeter, the sociologist, describes it, creates an environment in which outsiders and even older entrepreneurs might be wary of criticizing or questioning what's in front of them. "Express doubts, and you risk being worse than wrong, you risk revealing yourself to be a dinosaur and thus no longer part of the privileged club; you just don't get it."[23]

The truth can be more nuanced. In a 2018 academic study, researchers found that successful tech entrepreneurs, on average, are in their forties. Their findings, based on tax filings, census data, and other federal data, help to show how certain images—the young white male, in this case—capture the popular imagination even when a closer inspection of the subject might indicate otherwise.[24] The researchers also found that only one-fifth of all billionaires are dropouts.

A second myth—so persistent as to be tired—is that of the garage, the dorm room, the basement, and increasingly, start-up accelerators like Y Combinator, as the starting point for world-changing innovation, mainly because some of the world's most successful companies, including Microsoft, Facebook, Apple, Google, and Amazon, got their start in one of those locations. The garage where Hewlett-Packard was founded is such a point of interest that it was christened the birthplace of Silicon Valley in 1989 and added to the National Register of Historic Places in 2007. It doesn't matter that these locations were favored because they were mostly rent-free or convenient, or that there are millions of technology start-ups that were founded in more welcoming spots. As entry points for someone's unimaginable success, garages, basements, and dorm rooms have also become entry points for our collective storytelling. The garage-to-billionaire stories of tech founders also map nicely onto the rags-to-riches storyline of the American dream.

Another of our most abiding myths, which feeds into the broader American narrative of the self-made individual, is that the founders of tech companies willed their creations into being simply with their brains and sweat. That is true to an extent, but several factors have propped up technology development over the decades. Silicon Valley's early success was largely subsidized by federal research funds that went to Stanford University that nurtured technologies, including the Defense Advanced Research Projects Agency (DARPA). The internet was built within the world of research with government funds. Global positioning system, or GPS, technology, was developed by the U.S. military during the Cold War and became commercially available in the 1980s. (The government still owns and operates the technology.) Until rising inflation forced the Federal Reserve to change monetary policy in 2022, a long stretch of low interest rates left big investors such as pension funds searching for better yields and returns on their investments, leading them to pour money into riskier assets—along with the fear of missing out on the next big tech hit. That ended up driving so much money into venture capital funds that they were able to support loss-making start-ups for longer, allowing fledgling companies a bigger shot at success. What's more, many of the start-up hits of two decades or so have come by repurposing traditional businesses for mobile platforms, which has been made far easier by falling costs of computing technologies—by now an almost formulaic rather than inventive approach.

A fourth myth is that start-up founders are out to change the world, reshaping and reimagining our lives to benefit all of humanity. And they largely have. In a poor country like Bangladesh, a mobile phone in every hand has meant its citizens can get direct deposits from the government without relying on an inadequate banking system. Communications technology allows seamless video calling between continents, via apps like Face-Time and WhatsApp, and enabled world-shaping meetings to be conducted entirely online during the pandemic. Cloud computing lets small businesses rent space without having to invest in their own data centers.

Elizabeth Spiers, a media entrepreneur and opinion columnist who founded the gossip blog *Gawker*, decried the myth, though, calling out founders and venture capitalists on their hypocrisy when they say they are out to change the world. "They're out to change the world, but they're not out to make money," Spiers said, rolling her eyes during a video interview. Wall Street speculators are hardly saints, but as Spiers pointed out, at least "hedge fund founders don't have that narrative about themselves, that we're out to change the world." But the myth, which we indulge, allows tech founders to claim credit for all the innovation and none of the downsides, Spiers said. We thus ignore the monopolistic practices of many of today's biggest tech companies and accept the giant toxic spew and total control of the ways in which we interact and inform—even if they have directly contributed to some of the worst tendencies today—as the price we pay for ease, convenience, and connection. As misinformation, disinformation, social polarization, and conspiracy theories threaten the very foundations of democracy, personal data and secrets about our lives and search habits get ever more monetized.

A fifth myth is that creativity and genius can manifest only through non-conformist behavior, outside of the drudgery of a job and unconstrained by the burden of formal clothing—and without government interference and regulation. At the same time, while entrepreneurs and venture capitalists want to be left alone in the name of innovation, they also want to be bailed out in the name of innovation. When Silicon Valley Bank failed in March 2023, a contingent of venture capitalists and other big investors who typically want the government to stay away, called on the very same government to help save the start-up industry, because the fledgling companies are the heart and soul of the so-called innovation economy.

The myths around how start-up founders are created and how they should behave are so pervasive that they have created an opportunity for

signaling and subterfuge, matched only by the greed of investors who sub-
stituted so-called pattern matching for due diligence. Elizabeth Holmes,
the founder of Theranos, the blood-testing start-up that collapsed in 2018,
contorted herself to fit the stereotype. Dozens of commentators have remarked that Holmes, a Stanford dropout who was sentenced to eleven years
in prison in late 2022 for defrauding investors in her blood-testing start-up,
adopted Steve Jobs's uniform of black turtlenecks and spoke in a deep voice
to establish her authority. When Channing Robertson, a professor at Stanford University, met Holmes, he realized that he "could have just as well
been looking into the eyes of a Steve Jobs or a Bill Gates."[25]

Once the nerd-philosopher-genius-king of the cryptocurrency industry before his nosedive into disgrace, Sam Bankman-Fried, the founder of
crypto exchange FTX, grew his empire rapidly on the back of $2 billion
raised from investors; at its peak, the start-up was valued at $32 billion.
He was as notable for the breathless rise of his crypto exchange as for his
shock of unkempt hair and cargo shorts, prompting *The New York Times* to
call him a "studiously disheveled billionaire." In fact, when a colleague told
Bankman-Fried to clean up his appearance, he demurred, saying that it was
all part of the image and would be helpful rather than harmful.[26]

Popular Culture Stereotypes the Nerd

In the 1980s, as the idea of using computer programming for commercial
benefit gained steam, personal computers infiltrated people's homes and offices. In 1982, *Time* put the PC on its annual "person of the year" cover—
calling it "Machine of the Year." University computer departments began
filling up; in 1965, there were 64 bachelor's degrees awarded in the field. By
1985, there were nearly 42,000 degrees.[27] Although far more students graduated with business and engineering degrees during the same time frame,
the enthusiasm around technology was partly a result of its newness and the
swift rise to fame and fortune of such a young group of people with similar
characteristics.

That's when Hollywood's interest in the nerd began. Nerds were portrayed as misfits who used their skills to outwit the jocks and the jerks, winning in the process social and financial capital—and, of course, the girl. A host of cult teen movies from that decade, including *Sixteen Candles*, *War Games*, *Weird Science*, *Revenge of the Nerds*, and *Can't Buy Me Love* (reprised in the 2003 film *Love Don't Cost a Thing*) are riffs on that core arc. Hammed up, popular culture's nerd is a composite character, picking up qualities much as a sedimentary rock picks up layers. The nerd is most often a heterosexual white male; a maladroit of formidable intellect who would rather look at the floor than make eye contact; uncomfortable in his own body; given to fits of rage and condescension; a dedicated fan of science fiction who plays video games to let off steam; and someone who can't be bothered to learn conventional modes of behavior or clothing. This character is also preoccupied with women, who were typically portrayed as objects of fascination and desire. Because dating women was an unattainable goal, the nerd sometimes used his tech skills to spy on them. (A few real-life examples that provide fodder: According to Gates himself, as a teenager he would rearrange class schedules at Lakeside, the Seattle private school he attended, using his computing skills to make sure he sat in classes that had the most girls. Before cofounding Facebook, Zuckerberg—allegedly in a fit of pique after being jilted by a girl—created a site on Harvard's campus called FaceMash, where students could rate their classmates on how hot they were, according to *Rolling Stone*.) Women could only gain entry to the male world of the nerd if they were "cool." In the hit show *Stranger Things*, the character Max is accepted by geeky middle-school boys after she outscores them in a video game.

There is also an emphasis on gaming, regularly mentioned in the biographies of tech company founders as though it were a rite of passage. Fantasy role playing games like *RuneQuest* and *Dungeons & Dragons*, creative video games like *Minecraft*, multiplayer games like *World of Warcraft*, and the abiding power of science fiction movies like *Star Trek* are part of the picture— an echo of Brand's university students and computer hobbyists who spent hours playing *Spacewar*. Just to take one example: Fred Ehrsam, a founder of the cryptocurrency exchange Coinbase, spent thousands of hours growing up playing *World of Warcraft*, which is how he learned about digital currency early on, according to *Forbes*.

In the 1996 PBS documentary *Triumph of the Nerds*, a software programmer named Doug Muise tells the anchor: "Eating, bathing, having a girlfriend, having an active social life is incidental, it gets in the way of code time. Writing code is the primary force that drives our lives so anything that interrupts that is wasteful."[28] That force also seems to drive the Red Bull–drinking, Adderall-popping Zuckerberg character played by Jesse Eisenberg in the 2010 movie *The Social Network*.

In *The Big Bang Theory*, which ran on CBS from 2007 to 2019 and is considered one of the all-time great sitcom hits, the protagonist Sheldon plays the archetypal nerd. He has no social skills or filter, no ability to recognize or engage in humor, and a brain that operates on multiple levels at once. He embodies a certain lack of empathy, and no real humility or tolerance of stupidity. As the ur nerd, Bill Gates appears in a cameo in Season 11 of the show. After one of the characters wells up at the sight of his childhood hero, Gates asks him if he needs a tissue. The other character unleashes a series of oh-my-gods in ascending pitches. In an interview about the show, Gates said: "It's fun to have a show where people are allowed to be a little nerdy, and a little bit smart, so I can relate to it, and I was thrilled when I got the chance."

In the HBO show *Silicon Valley*, a tech satire that ran from 2014 to 2019 and both parodied and idealized modern nerd culture, the protagonist, Richard Hendricks—portrayed as a skinny, neurotic, socially inept entrepreneur prone to vomiting when nervous—explains the historic opportunity for nerds: "For thousands of years, guys like us have gotten the shit kicked out of us," he says. "But for the first time we're living in an era where we can be in charge and build empires. We could be the Vikings of our day." In a later episode, Richard tells off a handsome entrepreneur seeking funding that tech is reserved for guys like him. "You listen to me, you handsome muscle-bound Adonis. Tech is reserved for people like me, okay? The freaks, the weirdos, the misfits, the geeks, the dweebs, the dorks." Gates also made a cameo appearance in *Silicon Valley*. He said of the show: "Personally, I identify most with Richard, the founder of Pied Piper, who is a great program-mer but has to learn some hard lessons about managing people."[29] (Jobs, by comparison, was so mythic as to be irreducible to stereotype.)

Sitcoms might embrace stereotypes for laughs, but there are real social consequences. Nerds are often described as being "mildly autistic," accord-ing to Jordynn Jack, a term that is casually tossed about as a shorthand for a certain type of male who prefers technology over social interaction, repre-senting a brain that is analytical and mathematical.[30] Autism became closely linked to the fields of technology, science, and computing in the 1980s, and in that decade was most closely associated with Gates, Jack writes. The media took the term and ran with it, citing statistics about how the rates of autism are highest in Silicon Valley. When Musk disclosed that he has Asperger's syndrome while hosting *Saturday Night Live* in 2021, it only embedded the storyline further. "For now, it seems that the persuasiveness of the Extreme Male Brain or Silicon Valley theories lies more in how those theories fit with our notions of gender, geekiness, and the late twentieth-century workplace than in actual statistical patterns," according to Jack. This gendered view of autism—and its cousin Asperger's—that is upheld in popular culture as well as scientific research does a disservice to the understanding of a complex disability that also affects women, she argues. But in an interview, Jack noted the flip side: Pop culture mentions of autism spectrum disorders can bring attention and resources to a poorly understood condition.

Many researchers have found that the stereotypical nerd image and the portrayal of nerds in hypermasculine environments can deter adolescent girls and women from entering science, technology, engineering, and math, or STEM, fields. Sapna Cheryan, a psychologist at the University of Wash-ington, and her colleagues have found that the bigger the sense of mismatch between a person and a cultural stereotype of what computer boys are sup-posed to look and behave like, the more it puts off people who don't see themselves that way, especially women.[31] In a 2013 paper, Cheryan, who has studied the role that cultural stereotyping plays in attracting women to or repelling them from certain careers, highlighted the same stereotypes: tech-nology oriented with strong interests in programming and little interest in people; solitary actors; singularly focused with no outside interests; without social skills; geniuses, brilliant; connection between nerdiness and computers, portrayed in the media; masculine interests like video games. "Taken together, the image of a computer scientist that emerges in the U.S. is one of a genius male computer hacker who spends a great deal of time alone on the computer, has an inadequate social life, and enjoys hobbies involving science fiction," Cheryan and her coauthors write.[32]

Nerds Turned Bros

Every July, as business moguls fly in from all over the world to Sun Valley for their annual conference, reporters and photographers jostle to identify the attendees. With little chance of covering the actual events or even peeking at the agenda since the media is not invited, reporting on billionaire fashion has become something of a tradition over the years. Reid Hoffman, the founder of LinkedIn, in a track jacket. Tim Cook, the chief executive of Apple, in a polo shirt. Facebook's Zuckerberg in one of his trademark gray tees. Barry Diller in a Dior aloha shirt. Michael Bloomberg in a lemon-yellow plaid button-up. Were those Allbirds on Sheryl Sandberg? Blue tinted lenses on Andreas Halvorsen, a hedge fund manager. Stacey Bendet of the fashion house Alice & Olivia in a floral dress. Buffett in a lime-green shirt patterned with the Geico mascot, a gecko.

Thus it was hardly surprising that in 2017, Sun Valley was where Bezos was noticed for his remarkable physical transformation. Gone was the nerdy, baby-faced founder of an online bookstore. In its place was a buff jock in aviator sunglasses, sporting a sleeveless puffer vest over a fitted T-shirt that showed off his bulging biceps, an appearance that gave rise to the meme "Swole Bezos." The media moment soon passed, but the image had staying power because the transformation from wimpy nerd to uber-masculine "bro" captured perfectly the potency of today's tech heroes. Others too have shed their nerd physicality. Zuckerberg took up jujitsu and competed in his first tournament in the spring of 2023, even winning some medals. He and Musk also challenged each other to an actual cage fight, which appeared to start as a joke on Twitter but quickly turned into a duel, revealing the bro, newly emerged from his nerd shell. (The two eventually called it off.)

Although Amazon and Microsoft are based in the Seattle area, Silicon Valley is the home base of tech exceptionalism. Considered to be the center of innovation and entrepreneurship globally, it's a place where chaos and failure are welcomed, and wild risk-taking is encouraged. People move there to get funding for what they hope are world-changing ideas, as well as to find talent and build networks. The Valley operates on a seemingly straightforward principle: a good idea will find money and money will find a good idea. For that simple exchange to happen, the thinking goes, the place must operate by its own rules, often beyond the bounds of convention and free of government interference. Seen this way, Silicon Valley is a hermetically sealed libertarian utopia that fuses the countercultural values inherited from the original nerds and computer bums of the 1970s with hard-nosed, no-holds-barred capitalism. "Silicon Valley is a mindset, not a location," LinkedIn's Hoffman once told the *Financial Times* newspaper.[33] Midsize cities around America have taken the message; there are dozens of mayors pushing to revamp disused downtown business districts into slick mini–Silicon Valleys, wooing young start-ups with lower rents and tech giants with tax breaks.

One reason why the Valley can be exclusionary is because it is so wedded to "disruption"—the idea that success comes to those who move fast and break things, and shake up business models, often without regard for consequences. "They have big ideas, but often they have very few ethics," said Rosanne Siino, the former Netscape executive who now advises start-ups and teaches a class at Stanford about organizational dynamics. She described the Valley as a place where there is no conversation about ethics or any consideration of it. "There were never enough safeguards in place, and an unregulated market allowed people to do whatever they wanted." Some forethought could have anticipated the downsides of social media, and Siino worried that the rush to build out products tied to artificial intelligence without thinking about the unintended consequences could have similar implications. "You'd think that with venture capitalists, there would be some sort of adult supervision in the room, but it's none of the adult supervision that we, societally, would benefit from the most. They too are concerned mainly with money, most of them don't care who they fund as long as they expect a certain return on investment," Siino said. But she pointed out that the online nature of our world and social media allows the misbehavior and misogyny of tech founders to come out. In the earlier days, none of the bad behavior could be tracked.

In November 2023, a tussle at OpenAI, the leading artificial intelligence start-up, illustrated the fundamental tension between building a "change-the-world" technology with caution and guardrails and rushing to commercialize it with reckless ambition. The board members of the nonprofit that governed OpenAI who fired the company's chief executive, Sam Altman, reportedly did so out of the concern that Silicon Valley's move-fast-and-break-things ethos, applied to AI, could have enormous implications for humanity. But Altman—like Gates did with software—had spotted the endless market for AI applications and had pushed hard to move quickly to build a business around it. Within days, those directors had been ousted and Altman was back at the company, even more determined to use artificial intelligence for profit.

A second reason why the Valley can be exclusionary is because it underplays the role of connections when it sells the idea that merit alone finds—and makes—money. Alliances are often created among people who went to the same schools, shared the same experiences, and have similar views of the world. Hoffman is among those who have weighed repeatedly on the power of networks. He introduced Thiel, one of the founders of PayPal, to Zuckerberg when the Facebook cofounder was looking for funding for his social media start-up. Hoffman and Thiel met as sophomores at Stanford, and famously are part of the "PayPal mafia" that includes Musk. Thiel made more than a billion dollars off his $500,000 investment in Facebook.

Underlying all this is a quality of "maleness," a nebulous concept but a helpful one because it captures the structural and institutional setup of the technology industry. As opposed to masculinity, which traditionally describes certain physical and social traits such as strength, vigor, muscularity, and assertiveness, maleness evokes an atmosphere—of comradery, of brothers-in-arms—where the scent of sweat and the fuel of testosterone propel people, and where bonding happens over coding, belching, and flatulence. Coders often sleep under their desks.

If the stereotypical portrayals of nerds that Cheryan writes about already deter many women from thinking about careers in technology, women entrepreneurs, venture capitalists, and technologists who do enter the Silicon Valley ecosystem often find themselves in an unwelcoming world. That makes it an exclusionary space for many women, men, and nonbinary people who don't see themselves thriving in this environment of maleness. It can also be intimidating for new immigrants, many of whom don't assert themselves for fear of being kicked out or not fitting in.

Cheryan became interested in the area when, as a first-year graduate school student at Stanford, she decided to apply for internships at technology companies. She remembers going to the office of one start-up where she walked past a conference room that was named after a Star Trek ship. "I remember thinking, I don't know if I'd fit in," she said. Instead, she took an internship at Adobe, purely based on what the offices of the software company looked like: airy space, a café and a gym. It provided her with a "sense of belonging."

There are statistics to prove it. More than 90 percent of venture capital funding goes to men. Women might be earning more than before now, and in more high-profile jobs, but they own less equity in companies, meaning that the wealth creation is lower when there is an exit like an initial public offering or sale of a company. Female representation in technology and related fields remains lower than in other sectors, including finance and healthcare, especially at the entry level, according to a 2021 report.[34]

In such an environment, even senior female tech employees have struggled to make it work in Silicon Valley. Ellen Pao, a former partner at Kleiner Perkins who sued the storied venture capital firm in 2012 for discrimination and bias, found herself a pariah amid venture capitalists after her lawsuit, which she lost. In it, she described a culture of all-male networking, including a ski trip to Vail that she was excluded from.[35] Susan Fowler, an engineer at Uber, wrote a detailed blog post in 2017 about a hostile work environment at the ride hailing company, describing a culture of sexism, sexual harassment, and retaliation. Recent efforts to promote more female founders and invest in companies excluded from the typical Valley networks hold promise, but largely, the tech world's underlying culture of maleness is just as rock steady as ever.

At the same time, stories of early women entrepreneurs like Ann Winblad, who built an accounting software company in 1976 with borrowed money, get lost in the bigger narrative. Winblad, who has long been a successful venture capitalist, came to the wider world's attention afresh in 2021, and that too for a tidbit about her past relationship with Gates, who had just gotten divorced. Many women who have succeeded in the Valley, mostly in the role of senior executives or venture capitalists, have learned to "play with the boys," in the words of one. Siino said she had risen through Silicon Valley's mostly male ranks by "not giving a fuck."

For all their talk of changing the world, having the world operate on their terms so far hasn't meant that tech founders have changed the terms for the better. Rather, they have simply extracted what they think they deserve. Some of the biggest tech entrepreneurs seem to be making up for a lost youth. Musk, who has said he was bullied in school, is not above behaving like a schoolyard bully, alternately taunting and picking fights, but also somehow desperate for approval. He has called his constant need to tweet a delayed adolescence.[36] But nerds are also displaying the high-handed behavior we often expect from those we label as moguls, kingpins, and celebrities. Their dominance and success have conferred upon nerds a certain cachet. Nerdcore is fashionable. Their newfound wealth is a magnet. They have access to Wall Street chief executives and top politicians and rub shoulders with Hollywood and sports superstars. Even their sexual exploits and unusual romantic engagements are news fodder. In *Brotopia*, the journalist and television host Emily Chang describes a Valley drug-and-sex scene that she suggests is a disruption of society.[37] "Their behavior at these high-end parties is an extension of the progressiveness and open-mindedness— the audacity, if you will—that make founders think they can change the world." These parties might not have the psychological verve of Stanley Kubrick's 1999 erotic thriller *Eyes Wide Shut*, but they do evoke a place where wealth can buy the most extreme sexual fantasies—although unlike in the movie, the masks are apparently off in Silicon Valley. In 2014, Andreessen mapped the evolution of computer technology from the 1950s to the 2010s onto the changing image of nerds in a series of Twitter posts titled "As the Nerds Turn." The 1950s, '60s, '70s, '80s, and early '90s were decades when all of computer technology was equated with "nerds," he wrote. By 2014, however, the sentiment shifted to: "Those nerds are completely out of ideas again, and now they're having sex too!"[38]

One longtime observer of the Silicon Valley scene and a partner at a venture capital firm observed that nerds have become more confident, even arrogant, because they have been proved right. "The hard part is that when you suddenly have all this wealth and all this attention and are at the center of things, you enjoy the trappings of it, you get invited to the Vanity Fair Oscar party, you get the girl," the person said. "Nobody even looked at you sideways, and now you're the center of attention, you do get in." The partner pointed out that society marvels at the genius that produces game-changing products and services, but like artists and musicians, that genius often comes at a price. "The fallacy is in expecting [nerds] to behave normally in every other way except their genius."

Chapter 3

Rockstar to Robber Baron

A Twentieth-Century Rockefeller

It was a sunny and pleasant San Diego morning in May 1998 when Tom Fragala arrived at the University of San Diego, a private Catholic institution not far from the Mexican border. Fragala, an entrepreneur and former soccer player, was there to attend his then girlfriend's graduation. It was to be an outdoor event, and chairs were arranged in three orderly sections. Fragala made his way to the section on stage right and picked a seat in the second row. He took casual note of the VIP sign blocking off the first row.

As he soaked up the sunshine, waiting for the festivities to start, a man and a woman walked up to the VIP row. The man, who looked to be in his forties, was in a business suit. The woman wore a floral dress and sun hat that made Fragala think of Julia Roberts in *Pretty Woman*. The couple sat down, with the man taking the chair directly in front of Fragala. It took him a moment to realize that he was sitting behind Bill Gates and Melinda French Gates. That month, the Department of Justice, the top U.S. antitrust regulator, and 20 states had filed suit against Microsoft, accusing the technology giant of using its dominance in one market to prop up its budding business in another, which it alleged was an abuse of monopoly power. By then, Gates was regularly pilloried in the press as a twentieth-century John D. Rockefeller Sr., the oil monopolist of the Gilded Age. It was not a good time for the Microsoft cofounder.

The moment Gates sat down, he cracked open a thick, hardcover book he appeared to be in the middle of reading. Fragala estimated it might weigh a few pounds. For the next two hours or so, as the graduation ceremony started, amid the pomp and applause, as diplomas were handed out, Gates never once looked up, barely moving except to cross and uncross his legs. About 15 minutes in, Fragala began to wonder: What could Gates be reading that so engrossed him? He tried to peek over his shoulder but only caught sight of the splintered plastic ends of his glasses. He noticed a little dandruff, but no luck with the book title. Fragala deliberately dropped his program on the floor, hoping to catch a view of the book's spine. No dice: Gates had removed the dust jacket.

About 90 minutes into the festivities, a young man, diploma in hand, came up to the couple. Clearly, they were there for his graduation. Gates remained absorbed in his book. French Gates, who had been following the program closely, her posture erect, stood up to greet and congratulate the young man. As she did, she elbowed her husband in a practiced move. Startled, Gates too stood up, hastily resting the book on the ground against the leg of his chair. Fragala saw his chance. He bent down quickly to peek and finally saw the title. Gates was reading *Titan: The Life of John D. Rockefeller, Sr.*, by Ron Chernow. It took Fragala a moment to recognize the irony.

Chernow's exhaustive and exquisitely detailed biography of Rockefeller, running at more than 800 pages, had arrived in bookstores in May 1998, just as the furor about Microsoft's monopolistic behavior had reached its crescendo. The book was notable not only for its heft but for its "eerie time-liness," as one reviewer put it.[1] Roughly a century earlier, the U.S. government had attacked Standard Oil, the company built by Rockefeller that at one point controlled 90 percent of the oil refining market, for engaging in monopolistic practices. The high-stakes trial, one of the most riveting of that era, had led in 1911 to the breakup of Standard Oil into 34 smaller entities. The trial had demonized Rockefeller, one of a handful of the Gilded Age's robber barons—so called because of their ruthless business practices and their willingness to stop at nothing, including bribing and flouting the law, to promote the interests of the massive companies they had created.

Comparisons between Gates and Rockefeller had existed for at least a decade, but they never got much traction. Mitch Kapor, the founder of Lotus Development Corporation, was one of the earliest to compare the Microsoft cofounder to the nineteenth-century oil titan. Kapor had railed against Gates since the 1980s, after Gates muscled Lotus 1-2-3, along with WordPerfect and other applications, out of the market. In 1984, Microsoft had made a bid to buy Lotus, whose spreadsheet and software programs led the market at the time. Kapor turned it down. Four years later, he told *The New York Times* that Gates was "an empire builder, someone who wants to build the Standard Oil of computing."[2] In the same article, Gates shot back at Kapor, calling him a "completely nontechnical guy who knows enough to sound technical."

By the mid-1990s, reporters and columnists had begun writing more frequently about Microsoft's bullying tactics. In a 1995 essay for *The New York Times Magazine* entitled "Making Microsoft Safe for Capitalism," the author James Gleick essentially suggested that Microsoft be broken down.[3] Gleick quoted a number of Microsoft's enemies in the piece, prompting Gates to write a letter in response defending his company and its products, and arguing that the PC industry remained competitive. Gates didn't see himself as a "grasping monopolist," but as Microsoft got snagged in the slowly grinding maw of government scrutiny, the comparisons with Rockefeller helped create an easy but resonant narrative of the Microsoft chief executive as a villain.[4] The Silicon Valley lawyer Gary Reback, whose clients were among the companies worried about Microsoft's dominance, gleefully embraced that line of attack. "The only thing J. D. Rockefeller did that Bill Gates hasn't done," Reback would tell anyone who cared to listen, "is use dynamite against his competitors!"[5] With the trial looming, the idea that Gates was indeed a monopolist of what many had christened the second Gilded Age certainly didn't hurt the case that lawyers for the Justice Department were making.

The comparison is worth investigating. Rockefeller and Gates were the richest men of their eras. The circumstances of their ascents were similar: Standard Oil floated to the top in the 1880s, when industrial activity was buzzing and humming.[6] Microsoft helped set off the personal computing revolution in the 1980s, shaping an industry that was similarly vibrant. Rockefeller was born poor and Gates came from affluence, but both displayed an unerring instinct for business, leveraging developments in science and technology with business acumen in pursuit of profit and scale. Like Rockefeller, who created many of Standard Oil's corporate practices out of a sense of self-preservation, Gates too was terrified of Microsoft losing its edge.

Between 1870 and 1880, Standard Oil went from being a small company based in Cleveland, Ohio, to conquering more than 90 percent of the petroleum market. Its size not only brought economies of scale but allowed it to secure price concessions from railroads to move its barrels.

Gates, too, had become untamable, according to his critics. Microsoft's flagship Windows software operated roughly nine out of 10 personal computers, and the company had used its dominance in personal computing software to offer discounts to computer hardware manufacturers. Now, it was parlaying that dominance to control the emerging market for applications and bundling Microsoft's Internet Explorer browser into every copy of Windows 95 and later versions of the software and displaying it prominently. That allowed its browser to become the preferred way to surf the internet, while strangling Netscape, its fledgling competitor in the browser market. Netscape's Navigator may have been more popular, but it didn't have Microsoft's dominant software platform. At the same time, Gates portrayed the decision as an efficient one that customers could use easily. The strong-arm tactics used by Rockefeller, America's first billionaire, caught the attention of the public, particularly after a 19-part magazine exposé about the corrupt and unethical practices of Standard Oil by the investigative journalist—called a "muckraker"—Ida Tarbell. Microsoft too was accused of strong-arming competitors and rapacious conduct and called the "Standard Oil of the Information Age."

Microsoft pushed back on the comparisons. Its practices were not monopolistic, Microsoft argued, because it was defending intellectual property. Unlike petroleum, which was a scarce resource because there was a finite amount of it in the world, there were no limits to IP. How could Gates be controlling a sector where the barriers to entry were so low that anyone with a new idea could patent it and reshape the industry? But the barrage of negative news, spurred by a systematic campaign by Silicon Valley to taint Microsoft's reputation, found some receptive ears in Washington.

The Behemoth that Behaved Like a Start-up

On August 24, 1995, Gates stood onstage with fellow Microsoft executives as "Start Me Up" played in the background. The occasion was the launch of Windows 95, the latest iteration of Microsoft's software. Gates, dressed in a beige polo shirt, didn't dance to the guitar riffs of Keith Richards so much as shuffle to them. Steve Ballmer, the president of Microsoft, was less restrained. The company had shelled out several million dollars to the Rolling Stones to use their 1981 hit as part of an extravagant $300 million campaign to drum up enthusiasm for Windows 95. The Empire State Building was lit up in Microsoft's colors of blue, green, yellow, and red. Jay Leno, the era's top television host, was recruited to create buzz and cohost the launch with Gates. Jennifer Aniston and Matthew Perry, two of the stars of the 1990s era sitcom *Friends*, gave the world a tutorial on Windows 95 in a faux episode arranged by Microsoft. The arrival of the software, marketed as consumer friendly and easy to use, created the kind of fervor that has come to symbolize the launch of a new iPhone. Around the world, people lined up to get hold of a copy. It was inescapable. As *The New York Times* asked, "Haven't heard of Windows 95? Where have you been hiding?"[7] Gates was a rockstar in the business world, inviting the kind of adoration reserved for Hollywood celebrities and sports stars. He may not have looked the part, with his tousled brown hair and suits that never quite fit right, but he was striding down the corridors of corporate America in full mogul mode. Five years earlier, Microsoft had become the first software company in history to cross more than one billion dollars in annual sales. By 1994, Microsoft would make nearly five times as much, dominating the desktop market. Microsoft's soaring stock had made it the most valuable company in the world, making Gates the youngest billionaire in history to have made his own fortune. He would end 1995 atop the Forbes billionaires list.

Microsoft's success also transformed Seattle, Gates's hometown, creating new wealth for thousands of employees and changing the region's economics. The Seattle that Gates, who was born on October 28, 1955, grew up in was a small city with a tightly knit community that portrayed itself as innovative and forward-thinking. It had a big aerospace industry anchored by Boeing. The Space Needle, a famous landmark, opened in 1962 for Seattle's World's Fair. Its futuristic design—the top resembles a UFO—complemented Seattle's ambitions to become a hub of technology and science. The second of three children, Gates, along with his sisters Kristianne and Libby, grew up with all the accoutrements of an upper-middle-class existence. There were games of tennis, carefree summers spent at vacation homes. His parents were well-known in the local community. His mother, Mary Gates, served on the board of United Way, the charity. His lawyer father, William Gates Sr., was closely involved in civic affairs. As a child, Gates was highly intelligent, and highly argumentative. His older sister, Kristi, once said of him: Bill "didn't see that he was not normal. He didn't perceive himself as different because he was so introverted."[8] Gates's parents thought he was underachieving in school, and when he got into trouble as an 11-year-old, they sent him to see a psychiatrist.[9]

Gates attended Lakeside, one of Seattle's most prestigious private schools, where he was introduced to computers at an early age, befriended Allen, and took to programming with an obsession. In Allen's telling, Gates liked to show people that he was smart.[10] He also identified in his friend and business partner an early competitive streak. Whether it was chess, games, or math, Gates hated to lose.

In 1979, he relocated Microsoft's headquarters from Albuquerque to Seattle. Before moving to the Emerald City, Gates had considered Silicon Valley, but decided against it because he felt that it would be harder to protect business secrets in a small and gossipy community, and hard to retain talent because there would be greater poaching.[11] That decision benefited Seattle handsomely, especially after Microsoft's initial public offering, which created hundreds of millionaires in the city. Unlike Seattle's old-school wealthy— the Nordstroms, the Weyerhaeusers—the so-called Microsofties stood out for their nonconformity. Many dressed modestly and expressed the view that they embraced technical careers not for the money but for the potential to change the world. "The Microsoft class may well make up the first large group of American millionaires from technical backgrounds," wrote Timothy Egan in *The New York Times* in 1992.[12] Thousands of newly minted Microsoft millionaires drove such a frenzy of consumption, from houses to horses, that it temporarily threw the Seattle economy off kilter.[13] The city has long had a "nerdy DNA," said Leonard Garfield, director of Seattle's Museum of History and Industry. Its transition to a largely knowledge-based economy started in the 1980s with Microsoft, but Gates's influence was generational, because the first wave of Microsoft millionaires went on to create a whole set of subsidiary businesses, attracting more talent to Seattle, according to Garfield. That in turn attracted other technology companies, including Amazon and Expedia, making Seattle one of the fastest growing cities in the United States, with a population of more than 708,000 and median income of $85,654 as of 2021, far above the national median income of $59,611.[14]

When Robbie Cape joined Microsoft in 1993 as a 23-year-old engineer on the Visual Basic team that was developing a programming language, he quickly picked up on two things. One, Microsoft was centered on individual achievement rather than collaborative work. And two, people at the company, especially young engineers like him, worshiped Gates. Between his junior and senior years at Princeton University, Cape had interned at Microsoft, so the company's culture wasn't entirely a surprise when he joined full time. A Canadian who grew up in Montreal, he came to the United States for college and never went back. "I fell head over heels for Microsoft, for the Pacific Northwest, and for Bill and Steve," he said, referring to Ballmer, a top executive and friend of Gates's who would later become the company's chief executive. "Like a lot of young people who joined the company in the 1980s and 1990s, I'd say we deified them," Cape recalled. "The leaders all wanted to lead just like him. Young people like me wanted to grow up to be just like him. He was a technologist, a visionary, a businessman, and a leader." Hundreds of starstruck young programmers joined Microsoft because of Gates, known inside the company as "BillG." Even if they were too far down the ranks to meet him, they hoped to learn at his feet.

Although Microsoft was nearly a 20-year-old company when Cape joined, with about 15,000 employees, its internal culture was very much a reflection of Gates's relentless, hard-charging attitude. Long known for his competitive streak and his maniacal devotion to work, Gates was notorious for not taking vacations. In Microsoft's early days, he memorized the license plates of his employees' cars so that he could keep tabs on when people were coming and going—now a piece of lore woven into the company's informal history. Many Microsoft meetings would go on for hours without a break, as he drilled down into the minutiae of a product, peppering his engineers with questions. He was prone to expletive-laden fits of rage, often berating colleagues if he didn't think their work met his exacting standards. There was "definitely a culture at Microsoft of being the smartest person in the room," Cape said. Now an entrepreneur who helps run two start-ups, one of which is investing in regenerative farming—"I like meat but consider it a vice, so [I'm] trying to find healthier ways to grow and manage livestock," he said—Cape retains idyllic memories of his time at the company. In his telling, Microsoft was a place with no limits on ambition.

The business culture at Microsoft was "intensely masculine," said Margaret O'Mara, a historian of Silicon Valley, in an interview. It was called a "frat house," she said, but was not too different from other tech companies. In its early decades, she said, Microsoft "behaved like an overgrown start-up. Gates was sharp-elbowed, very argumentative, it was all about 'show us what you've got,' intensely gendered, and the whole company took on the tone of the 20-something young man who was still behaving as though you had to be incredibly aggressive to get a toehold in the market."

Although that sort of corporate environment has since come to be frowned upon, many say that Gates and Ballmer embodied and normalized that internal culture. That led to Microsoft's push for what Cape called "excellence, even at a high cost." As an entry-level worker, Cape only saw Gates from afar, except for a few big meetings, but the company was awash in tales of interactions that more senior executives and team leaders had with Gates, and "the way individuals would end up being almost deposed." Cape interpreted these secondhand stories as examples of Gates's push for excellence. Cape ascribed a purity of intent and a nobility to Gates's mission, whereas many others crumpled under the intense—and sometimes terrifying—scrutiny applied by him. "Compassion was not part of the culture of Microsoft," he said.

The experience of senior executives who worked more closely with Gates was sometimes different. In one email exchange, a Microsoft executive wrote to another that Gates was being "amazingly, unnecessarily rude."[15] Gates once sent a long email to the developers of a Microsoft program called Movie Maker—a rant, dripping with sarcasm, about his frustration at not being able to download the software. Gates may not have acknowledged it publicly, or even thought about it privately, but stories about his ruthlessness and arrogance were feeding into his growing image as a business bully. To Gates, free markets rewarded competition and innovation, and if a company took its eyes off the ball and stopped improving its products and innovating, it would quickly lose the race. "We can't rest for a second," he told *Playboy* magazine.[16]

Michael Cusumano, the SMR Distinguished Professor of Management and deputy dean of the Sloan School of Management at the Massachusetts Institute of Technology, studied Microsoft's business strategy extensively in the 1990s. Cusumano observed that Gates was influenced by the ideas of Andy Grove, the founder of Intel with whom he worked closely. In his famous book *Only the Paranoid Survive*, Grove wrote about how swift change can turn a successful company into a has-been, but managed right, change can also present an opportunity for the leader of the business to redirect the company's course. That business philosophy makes sense because the technology industry often has low barriers to entry, which was Microsoft's main argument, and tech companies can sometimes die if they aren't flexible and innovative enough. However, Microsoft's problem was that it underestimated its own size and influence. "They were really not as vulnerable as they thought they were," Cusumano said in an interview. As a result, according to Cusumano, "they continually broke the law or came right up to the line— and they did it multiple times."

Beginning in the 1990s, Microsoft had begun to look for ways to leverage its dominance in personal computers to enter new areas of business. It wanted to control the electronic gateway from the home to the world and charge fees for just about every recurring revenue product imaginable that could fit onto a desktop computer. What it couldn't build, it tried to buy. Microsoft had already made a habit of acquiring the top company in fields it wanted to enter: Softimage, a maker of computer animation programs; Forethought, which brought it PowerPoint; and others. Between 1994 and 1999, Microsoft's prolific deal-making had resulted in its owning all or part of 130 companies.[17]

In 1995, Windows 95 launched to much fanfare. Windows 95 was the latest version of a software product that Microsoft had begun building in the 1980s, borrowing the idea of a graphical user interface from Apple, its closest competitor. Microsoft had also been building an operating system in partnership with IBM called OS/2, but in 1989, it launched its own updated software called Windows 3.0, leading to a feud with the hardware giant.

In its June 5, 1995, issue, *Time* magazine put Gates on its cover, with the title "Master of the Universe." Gates was courted by heads of state looking to bring Microsoft's business to their countries. President George H. W. Bush had awarded him the National Medal of Technology in 1992 in recognition of his contributions. He golfed with President Bill Clinton on Cape Cod.

The paranoia inside Microsoft predated the Windows 95 launch. Based on his conversations with Microsoft executives in the early 1990s, Cusumano found that the central tension was between whether the company was a "platforms and applications" company that focused on building versatile products for different operating systems, or whether the entire ecosystem would continue to grow around its core Windows product. When some executives made the argument that it was the former, Gates disagreed, and his key lieutenants had to abide by his decision. As it turned out, Microsoft's dominance was its failing, in the sense that Windows became such an enormous stream and source of power in the industry—with Office attached to it—that they had to protect it.

Microsoft's business tactics had not endeared it to rivals or regulators.

One of its practices involved "per processor" contracts with computer manufacturers. The company used its dominance in the software market to lure
hardware makers into restrictive, long-term contracts. Microsoft offered discounts on its operating system licenses to those manufacturers in exchange
for them giving Microsoft a royalty payment for every computer they shipped
that used a certain kind of microprocessor, even if that computer didn't use
Microsoft's operating system. That put computer manufacturers in a difficult spot, given that they wanted to offer customers the industry's dominant
software, and dissuaded them from carrying other operating systems. The
move effectively stifled competition in the market for operating systems at a
time when demand for personal computers was exploding. If you wanted to
use a PC, chances are you would have to use Microsoft software. As applications for the operating system developed—spreadsheets, word processors,
graphics—developers of applications began to complain that Microsoft gave
its own application developers an advantage by sharing with them what the
next version of the operating system would look like.

It wasn't long before regulators began sniffing around Microsoft's business
practices. The United States enacted antitrust laws to rein in future excesses
in the aftermath of the nineteenth-century robber barons like Rockefeller,
when a wave of industrialization after the Civil War led to the formation of
massive companies known as trusts. Now, the same law that broke up Standard Oil in 1911 would be used by the Department of Justice to build its
antitrust case against Microsoft.

In July 1994, Microsoft signed a consent decree with the Federal Trade
Commission, agreeing to limit certain business practices related to its licenses
for operating system software. U.S. Attorney General Janet Reno played up
the settlement, announcing it on national television. The decree was the result
of a nearly four-year investigation by the FTC, which had alleged that Microsoft used restrictive licensing practices to keep rival software makers out of
the market. Some critics of Microsoft were disappointed with the settlement
because it was narrowly focused on operating system licenses when the company was trying to leverage its dominance in the software market to control
the emerging market for applications that could be built atop that software.

Microsoft too saw the FTC settlement as a victory. So, it was little surprise that just three months later in October, Microsoft announced that it planned to buy Intuit, a maker of personal finance software, for $1.5 billion. Microsoft would use its stock to pay for what was going to be the software industry's biggest acquisition ever. Microsoft's interest in Intuit was understandable. Based in Menlo Park, at the heart of Silicon Valley, Intuit had been founded in 1983 after Scott Cook had the idea for a personal financial software program, following his wife's complaint about the tedious nature of paying bills and balancing checkbooks.[18] The company went public in 1993, one of the early Valley success stories when people were still figuring out what personal computers could be used for beyond basic documents and word processing. Intuit's software was essentially an "application" that could be integrated into Microsoft's Windows operating system.

Electronic commerce and online banking were nascent, but the financial and technology industries could see their potential, expecting that one day, people would use their computers to do everything from transferring money and paying others to shopping from home. Microsoft wanted not only to ascend to the top of the market with Intuit, but also beat banks and credit card companies that saw the opportunity. Seven million people—or roughly 70 percent of users—used Intuit's Quicken software to file taxes, track their spending, do personal banking, and make other financial transactions.[19] Microsoft had launched its own version of the product, called Money, in 1991, but Quicken was by far the most popular. Although Money was the second-largest player in the personal finance software market, it was woefully behind, with less than a quarter of the market and about one million users.

Dread in the Valley

In the mid-1990s, the Valley had yet to achieve the reputation it enjoys today as the center of technological innovation. Although companies like HP, Fairchild Semiconductor, and Intel had built headquarters there, followed by Apple, Oracle, and others in the 1970s, tech behemoths including Alphabet, the parent company of Google, and Meta, the parent company of

Facebook, hadn't yet been born. Instead, it was a hub of fledgling companies that for years had watched Microsoft copy or demolish their businesses or buy them outright. Many entrepreneurs also found Microsoft unpalatable and bellicose; the company's executives were known to call venture capitalists with lowball offers to buy their portfolio companies, and if they didn't want to sell, the Seattle giant's attitude was: "Fuck you, we're going to crush you," in the words of one former Microsoft executive. The arm-twisting left many young companies—which often had little more than some technology and the makings of a business plan—and their backers quaking. One sure-fire way for a start-up to not get funding was to put in its pitch deck that Microsoft was one of its main competitors.

There was good reason for companies to feel that way, according to O'Mara, who wrote in *The Code*, a book about the tech industry, that many start-ups came close to being annihilated by Microsoft's dominance in that decade. "Microsoft was the 800-pound gorilla, it was 'the software industry' for a while," O'Mara said in an interview. "If there had to be one bad guy, [Gates] was it. It was about nimble start-ups versus the bigness of Microsoft. It fell into a very familiar American narrative." When Microsoft announced its intention to buy Intuit in the fall of 1994, it was as though the shark was at the Valley's door, jaws open and ready to bite. Intuit was a homegrown Valley darling and many of the company's managers did not want to see it swallowed by Microsoft. Not long after Microsoft and Intuit agreed to merge, a group of Silicon Valley companies—they remain unnamed—hired Reback, the lawyer who had loudly compared Gates to Rockefeller, to explore how they could thwart Microsoft.[20] A graduate of Stanford and Yale Law School, Reback worked at the prestigious Valley law firm of Wilson Sonsini, which specialized in antitrust law. Then in his mid-forties, Reback retained a boyish, youthful look and had an appetite for a fight. His first move was to write a friend-of-the-court brief on behalf of his anonymous clients, complaining that Microsoft was violating the terms of its 1994 consent decree with the Federal Trade Commission. Under the Tunney Act of 1974, courts are required to periodically review such settlements to ensure that the companies are abiding by their terms.

In his brief, filed in early 1995, Reback argued that the consent decree was too narrow and wouldn't stop Microsoft from using its dominance in the market for operating systems software to control new and emerging applications. Microsoft's proposed acquisition of Intuit, Reback wrote, would allow it to enter a new market and create a monopoly in electronic commerce and online banking. In other words, Microsoft could easily stick the popular Intuit applications atop its Windows operating software and crowd out other personal finance app developers.

In April 1995, officials at the Justice Department said they would investigate the planned Intuit acquisition, citing antitrust concerns. The deal was valued at nearly $2 billion at the time, because of the appreciation in Microsoft's stock. Anne Bingaman, who led the department's antitrust division, said that the combination would stifle innovation and raise prices for consumers. But she also listed a greater worry, echoing Reback's argument: that Microsoft could use its dominant position in personal computing to seize markets of the future, including home-based banking. "To give you a sense of antipathy involved, on the day the news broke the government said they were gonna sue him to block the acquisition of Intuit—there was wild celebration on the Intuit campus, cheering literally from each of the buildings," Reback recalled. "They didn't want to work for [Gates]." Three weeks later, Microsoft abandoned the deal. Today, Intuit is a giant in personal financial and business financial software, with a market capitalization of more than $150 billion. Esther Dyson, a former tech analyst and a venture capitalist, told *The Washington Post* at the time that the deal's failure would likely make Microsoft look "a little less nasty, a little less invincible," and that it would humble the tech giant.[21]

The humbling would take a few more years. While Microsoft was focused on the software market, a different sort of excitement was spreading in the Valley. Young entrepreneurs were captivated by what they considered the future of computing and communication: the World Wide Web. They could see the commercial potential of the internet and were beginning to bet their futures on it. In addition to Netscape, Jerry Yang, a young Taiwanese American graduate of Stanford, cofounded an internet website called

Yahoo along with David Filo in 1994. Companies such as Infoseek and Lycos, hoping to grab the new opportunities offered by the internet, were springing up by the dozen, funded by eager venture capitalists. They wanted to protect this new thing they'd found from the beast in the Northwest, but the distance that Gates kept from Silicon Valley meant that he didn't see the internet coming.

Of course, the Microsoft cofounder had paid some attention to the internet. In April 1994, he published a memo called "Internet Strategy and Technical Goals" that he had written during his annual "think week," when he went to a secret hideaway cottage every February to read prodigiously and delve deeply into Microsoft papers.[22] He also sent a confidential memo to a group of Microsoft executives describing the rise of electronic communication as a "sea change" that the company was going to lose out to rivals on.[23] But he considered it a side project inside Microsoft. The internet was going to be a free service, and there was little money to be made, he told Microsoft executives and board members. He expected the PC and not the internet browser to be the gateway to future products and services that could be offered to consumers. Also, Microsoft executives were preoccupied with testing and perfecting Windows 95, which had already suffered from multiple delays.

Gates's first book, *The Road Ahead*, was an instant bestseller. Coauthored with Microsoft's chief technology officer Nathan Myhrvold and Peter Rinearson, a company vice president, and published in 1995, the book laid out Gates's vision for the future of the digital revolution, although it barely mentioned the internet. Published simultaneously in multiple countries, it had an initial print run of 850,000 copies. Gates donated the $2.5 million advance he got for the book. But many critics were scathing in their reviews. Writing in *The New York Times*, the journalist Joseph Nocera called the book little more than a "positioning document" for Microsoft, lacking any real vision of what a future based on the internet might look like and more about the software giant's short-term business plans. "If this book really represents the sum of his vision for the future, then his own road ahead is going to be a long, hard slog," Nocera wrote.[24]

Sometime between 1994 and 1995, Gates suddenly changed his mind about the internet. He had initially failed to foresee how quickly and profoundly the internet would change the future of computing. But the more closely he followed its swift rise, the more troubled he was by what he saw. The PC was not going to be the center of the next generation of computing. Rather, it was the internet, which ran on a network of connected computers that delivered information and emails to users. The gateway to the internet was a browser, and Microsoft was nowhere in that market. Just three months before the launch of Windows 95, Gates wrote a long memo to employees called "The Internet Tidal Wave" that laid out, in precise detail, how computing was evolving under their very eyes, and how Microsoft would have to pivot to incorporate web-based features into all its products and applications. Caught flat-footed and recognizing that Microsoft had to catch up to rivals, Gates pushed his employees—nearly 18,000 of them—to build their own product while also trying to find ways to defang the competition. The "tidal wave" memo would later come to be seen by the government as evidence of Gates's monopolistic intentions. However, the contents of the memo also catapulted him to oracular status for its clear-eyed ability to visualize how the digital revolution would unfold. When Gates realized that the world could move on without Windows because the internet was a neutral platform, he wouldn't stop.

In June 1995, Reback got a call from Jim Clark of Netscape, which was building its Navigator browser to run atop different kinds of operating systems, including Windows. Clark told Reback that Microsoft was withholding technical information that Netscape needed to write a version of its browser for Windows 95. Instead, Microsoft had offered to let Netscape put its browser on other operating systems and older versions of Windows while keeping its own browser, Internet Explorer, on Windows 95. If Netscape agreed to it, the deal would effectively divide the market and ensure that Netscape could never become the browser of choice for the biggest chunk of consumers. After Netscape had said no, Microsoft eventually provided it with the information it needed after Windows 95 launched.

The first version of Internet Explorer, Microsoft's browser, launched alongside Windows 95 as part of a special package. But within the next year, the browser was loaded into every copy of Windows 95 for free, offering customers a way to hook up to the internet. That hurt Netscape's Navigator because it suddenly had a tougher route to the user. In a 1996 memo to employees, Gates talked about how Microsoft had reorganized itself around building internet software while retaining a focus on Windows. That memo would also become part of the Justice Department's evidence as it built its antitrust case. Elsewhere, Microsoft used the word "jihad" to describe its attitude toward the browser wars. There was an urgency to Gates's memos and emails and a barely concealed sense of alarm that the world was changing faster than Microsoft could.

Clark would later compare Gates to the "Wagnerian dragon" Fafnir who, in Nordic mythology, is a symbol of greed, having slain his father for treasure. "For all his nerdy ways and offbeat charm for the press, I feel Bill Gates is happiest when he is crushing the life out of companies that dare establish territory on the borders of Microsoft's sprawling dominion," Clark wrote.[25]

By then, a chorus of Silicon Valley companies—which some took to dubbing the "noise coalition" and included companies ranging from Sun to Netscape to Oracle—had started becoming deeply uncomfortable about Microsoft's ambitions. Reback and his colleagues, who had written a brief explaining how Microsoft was extending its dominance in the operating system into the applications market, now wrote a white paper on behalf of Netscape saying that the company was repeating those behaviors to dominate the browser market and shut Netscape's browser out. Microsoft, the paper said, offered computer manufacturers discounted prices, cash payments, and other incentives that made it hard to feature Netscape's browser on Windows. The two documents would doom Microsoft and change Gates's path forever.

Reback, once unleashed, was virtually unstoppable. With a flair for narrative and hyperbole, and a willingness to engage with the press, he was for a time the face of Silicon Valley's brewing deathmatch with Microsoft. As

Microsoft continued to push into new markets and threatened some young companies with its ambitions, Reback became their attack dog. "I came to be kind of a symbol for that, but it really wasn't me," Reback said. He attributed his role as Microsoft's chief nemesis at least partly to the fact that Wilson Sonsini's client roster included some of the biggest names in the Valley. Reback wasted no time in knocking Microsoft at every opportunity—using the press, writing court briefs, and attacking Microsoft's practices. Reback in court briefs in the 1990s said Microsoft engaged in promoting "vaporware," or announcing products that didn't exist, particularly in hopes of stopping the competition.[26]

Even decades later, Reback relishes recounting the stories of working on his clients' behalf to discredit Microsoft. "If you didn't live in Silicon Valley, it's hard to understand the antipathy toward Gates and Microsoft at this time," he said. Once, his synagogue was interviewing rabbis for a position. When one candidate, who had flown in from New York, happened to mention Microsoft favorably, "people started to hiss," Reback said. They were joking, he said, but "it gave you an idea." Another time, Reback attended an event at which a government lawyer spoke and implied that Microsoft wasn't so bad. "You could see the ice crystals forming on the windows of the room," Reback said. "Here's this guy who wants to take away our future. When Gates at that point said he was going after Intuit, and the banks were dinosaurs and he was the ultimate disrupter, being bred on Valley culture I understood it."

Inside Microsoft, though, the view couldn't have been more different. The message to workers was that the company was under attack and had to defend itself. Bob Muglia, who was a senior executive during Microsoft's troubles with the government, said the company tripped up because "we just didn't know any better." Muglia, now retired, said the culture inside Microsoft was "go, go, go" all the time, with not a moment to stop and think. "The first time I was called a monopolist by a customer, I was shocked," he recalled. Microsoft took a long time to learn that the world was looking at the company and its practices very differently than the company did from the inside out, Muglia added. "You can't behave as a small company does when you've grown so large."

At the time, Gates dismissed the claim that Microsoft was trying to shut out the competition by saying that his vision of the personal computer had always included the idea that it would be a tool through which to communicate. It was just that the idea hadn't caught on until the internet came along and there were new standards set, driving PC sales because people had a lot of information at their fingertips. And although he identified the internet as an important piece of Microsoft's future in 1994, the internet grew so fast that he had no option but to call the troops to war. "You can't just keep doing the same thing you were doing. You have to take your skills and attack the new frontiers," he told Charlie Rose in 1995. "It was our biggest opportunity and biggest challenge."

Starting in 1997, as lawmakers and regulators slowly turned up the heat on Microsoft, bringing things to a boil with the antitrust suit in April 1998, Gates seemed personally wounded. Lawyers from the Justice Department had crafted a narrative around Gates as an evil monopolist who would stop at nothing to beat competitors. He could not understand it. Microsoft was a source of American pride. The Seattle computing giant had created tens of thousands of jobs. With a market capitalization of more than $200 billion, it was one of the biggest technology companies in the world. It was an innovator. The consternation that Gates felt was palpable to many of his close advisors. "This makes no sense to me at all," Gates would say, in the words of one former Microsoft employee who spoke with him often on the company's media strategy. "I don't understand how your government comes for you when you're one of the bright lights and contributing to the economy."

Gates, the son of a lawyer, and given to a black-and-white way of thinking, saw the government case purely as a legal one that would be won or lost on its merits, and he insisted that the government's case had no merit. If anything, the very things Justice was attacking Microsoft for—such as offering its internet browser as part of its Windows software—were essential to a better customer experience, his thinking went. Almost naively, he didn't quite grasp the power of politics and optics to overtake logic and erode image. The more others painted him a villain, the more he thought himself a victim.

"Bill was confused into thinking [by Microsoft's lawyers] it was a legal case, when it was always political. Bill didn't understand that," said Muglia, who was among the senior executives called on to testify at the trial. He reflected that Gates had a tough time processing the way things had turned out, and that in his view Microsoft's lawyers did a poor job of outlining the dynamics and politics that were driving Justice, especially the campaign by the "cabal" in Silicon Valley, including Netscape, Sun, and Oracle. "It really hurt Bill. It was a personal attack on him," he said.

The Microsoft trial captivated the entire country. Gates was, after all, the richest man in the world, starring in the biggest antitrust case of the era. He didn't help his case, and was by turns indignant and contemptuous of questions about Microsoft's business practices. But nothing could compare to the three-day deposition Gates gave as part of the trial. As David Boies, the primary lawyer for the government, interrogated Gates, the Microsoft cofounder wore a disdainful expression, his mouth shaped into a sulky, inverted U. On occasion, he shrugged as if to disagree with the premise of a question. He rocked back and forth in his chair, as he often did, but his combative approach only made him look like a petulant child. At one point, he debated the meaning of the word "if." Gates rejected the very notion that the government had a legitimate case and argued that by blocking his company's ability to design and incorporate new products, it was stifling innovation in a rapidly changing technology landscape, where it's hard to retain monopolies anyway. "He did look like he was going through a root canal," Cusumano said of Gates. "I suppose it would be hard to find a performance that is worse, unless someone just said they are pleading the fifth."

By 2000, Gates's image was badly tarnished. The trial also devastated the company, former employees said. "It completely changed everything inside the company, consumed the executive team for multiple years," Muglia said. By 2001, Microsoft had been sued more than 200 times in the United States because of the antitrust conduct highlighted by the Justice Department.[27] It settled in 2002 and agreed to restrictions, including living with a special master to oversee its conduct for the next 10 years. Every manager underwent antitrust training. Its cases with Europe took several more years to settle. But it was a very critical juncture for the world, given the rise of the internet and the shift to online computing.

Gates did turn out to have been right about two things. First, he was correct in predicting that Microsoft's "dominance was ephemeral in many ways," Cusumano said. He saw that the internet would become an alternative computing platform, providing a new way to launch apps and threatening the future of Windows. Gates also saw and understood the development of mobile platforms as a big threat. In the meantime, the browser wars had moved on.

Do No Evil

In April 2018, some 20 years after Bill Gates's disastrous run-in with the government, Mark Zuckerberg found himself thrust into the middle of a crisis. Two years earlier, during the 2016 presidential election, a researcher got hold of the personal information of millions of Facebook users and sold them to Cambridge Analytica, a firm hired by the Trump campaign that specializes in psychological targeting, which it then used to build psychological profiles of voters. Facebook, cofounded in 2004 by Zuckerberg out of a Harvard dorm room, had already morphed from a cheery social network where friends and family could connect, to a hive of misinformation. Its other platform, Instagram, had become a site where gun sellers were advertising their weapons, and where pedophiles could track child-sex content. Lawmakers had begun to look closely at the company. The Cambridge Analytica revelations pushed Facebook further into an image crisis, turning the Silicon Valley company's platforms into something far more sinister than anyone had anticipated. Amid calls to #deleteFacebook and lawmakers pushing for more information on the mishandling of customer data, Zuckerberg was called to testify in front of Congress.

As he dealt with the crisis, Zuckerberg sought advice from one person he knew had gone through a similar experience: Gates. Zuckerberg, who, like Gates, is a Harvard dropout and considers the Microsoft cofounder a mentor, sought his advice on how to manage the public relations disaster and build bridges with politicians, according to news reports and two people who worked at Facebook at the time. Gates suggested that Facebook hire someone like Brad Smith, the longtime Microsoft executive who has been at the company for close to three decades; Smith became Microsoft's general counsel in 2002 and has been its president and vice chairman since 2021. Affable and skilled at building relationships, he played a key role in expanding Microsoft's presence in Washington following its bruising antitrust trial.[28]

"Who's our Brad Smith?" was a question a former Facebook employee recalled being bandied about inside the company. Eventually, Facebook (now known as Meta) settled on Nick Clegg, hiring the former deputy prime minister of the United Kingdom in October 2018 as vice president for global affairs and communications. Clegg started in the thick of the Cambridge Analytica scandal and eventually became the company's voice on data privacy issues, and he is now its president of global affairs.

When Zuckerberg went to testify in Congress in April 2018, answering questions from lawmakers about misinformation and the use of personal data by outside firms that was not authorized by Facebook, the setup had echoes of the Gates antitrust hearing. But whereas Gates had taken a tone of condescension and refused to concede a single point, Zuckerberg was far more conciliatory and deferential, apologizing to lawmakers often and messaging that he would be open to making changes.

Many technology industry executives and analysts say that Gates's behavior in front of Congress became an example of what not to do for founders and chief executives of a later generation of tech giants. Along with Zuckerberg, top executives of Google and Google's parent Alphabet, Amazon, Apple, and others who have been hauled to Congress several times in recent years have remained civil and humble even when they have provided little information to lawmakers. In the summer of 2020, Zuckerberg, Jeff Bezos, Tim Cook, and Sundar Pichai testified in front of the House Judiciary Committee on whether technology companies have too much power. As lawmakers accused the executives of everything from abusing their dominance to right-wing bias, they each sat upright without slumping, their facial expressions showing no emotion. Bezos began many of his responses to lawmakers with the phrase "with all due respect." No matter how combative the hearing got, and how evasive the executives turned with their responses, it never got to the point of arguing about the meaning of the word "if" as it had with Gates.

Tech executives have been thoroughly advised by people with experience in politics—as well as former Microsoft executives who now work at companies like Meta and Alphabet—about what not to say and do, even when lawmakers have asked questions that are not technologically savvy, according to people who have studied or worked on these issues. In 2020, when the Justice Department filed a complaint against Google, employees were also advised not to leave a paper trail discussing business strategies that could be entered into evidence, and not to speak about matters of antitrust, especially by using language such as "crush" the competition, according to a *New York Times* report.[29] Emails that Gates had sent Microsoft employees about the nature of its fight against emerging internet companies were part of the evidence the Justice Department used in its case against the company.

Microsoft influenced the younger generation of tech companies in other ways. There was a palpable we're-not-Microsoft sentiment that drove the early approach to business of Sergey Brin and Larry Page, who founded Google in 1998 out of a Stanford dorm. The young company's "do no evil" motto was very self-consciously anti-Microsoft, according to O'Mara. They sought to build a product based on open-source software and a free flow of information, rather than license it for a fee, as Microsoft had done. In those early years, Google even hired communications professionals to privately badmouth Microsoft to reporters. The kinder, gentler appearance of tech giants, and the insistence by their executives that the primary motive of their companies is to make the world a better and more connected place, rather than maximize profits, is at least partly a direct reaction to Microsoft's behavior as a capitalist bully hell-bent on protecting its turf.

In the first decade of the twenty-first century, regulators looked at the emerging crop of technology companies, like Google, Facebook, and Amazon, as the next harbingers of innovation. New products and services, many of them convenient and free to use, were changing people's lives and habits. There were few worries that these companies would become big enough to merit government scrutiny. Rather, the approach from lawmakers was, "what can we do to help this new industry flourish?" O'Mara said.

But just as Microsoft had risen swiftly from a nonentity to a dominant tech company in a decade and half, many of the tech companies of the past two decades appear to have reached escape velocity before the mood against them shifted, and lawmakers started poking around. It took a while for people to realize that today's tech industry is almost full of near monopolies or duopolies, and along the way, many of these companies have destroyed jobs and entire industries. Alphabet's Google controls more than four-fifths of the search engine market. Meta has long dominated social media and messaging through its massive acquisitions of Instagram and WhatsApp.

Even older companies like Apple and Microsoft have conquered new markets. Apple, which controls more than half of the smartphone market in the United States and is the single biggest player in the global market, controls the iPhone's entire ecosystem, from hardware to software and applications, and takes a meaningful cut of the revenues of any app developer that wants to offer its product on the app store. Amazon redefined the consumer retailing business, becoming a trillion-dollar company with its razor-sharp focus on logistics and cutting costs—including using its power as a dominant buyer squeezing its suppliers and slashing worker pay—to fatten its profit margins. Its Amazon Web Services unit is one of two giants in the business of providing cloud computing services to business—the other being Microsoft Azure. Some of this dominance is the natural outgrowth of network effects—the idea that the more people use something, the more value is created because others want to be on the same platform. Om Malik, writing in *The New Yorker*, points out how in Silicon Valley, it's almost all "winner takes all" now.[30]

Mitch Kapor, the founder of Lotus whose feud with Gates in the 1980s is well documented, said in 2013 that he didn't see Zuckerberg and Page as all that different from Jobs and Gates. "I think that in all generations . . . leaders in the industry had a very complicated mix of motives that are partly idealistic, partly pragmatic, and partly Darth Vader."[31] The key difference is how powerful their companies have become. "What you do isn't just affecting 5 or 10 million nerds and geeks, it's everybody and everything," he said.

Sensitive to the criticisms and government scrutiny, some of the largest tech companies have increased their lobbying armies in Washington. In 1998, the year Microsoft faced its trial, it had 61 lobbyists and spent just under $4 million. Recognizing that its inconsequential presence in Washington, D.C., may have hurt its case, the company hired an additional 107 lobbyists in 2000, according to data from OpenSecrets. In the last two decades, it has employed, on average, 111 lobbyists every year; in 2023, Microsoft spent $10.5 million on lobbying.[32] Andy Jassy, who has been Amazon's chief executive since 2021, has made it a point to visit lawmakers and other government officials in Washington, D.C., often, and the company has increased its lobbying spend from about $2.5 million in 2012 to $21.4 million in 2022.[33] Similarly, Meta has steadily increased its lobbying expenditure from $8.7 million in 2016, the year the Cambridge Analytica scandal unfolded, to about $19.2 million in 2022. Broken down into markets that Alphabet plays in, its biggest lobbying spend as of the first quarter of 2023 was tied to Google's business and the internet.

During his first term in the White House, President Joe Biden signaled that regulating the technology industry was a priority by appointing Lina Khan, one of the harshest critics of "Big Tech," as his chief antitrust enforcer. Khan, the youngest-ever head of the Federal Trade Commission, shot to fame in academic and policy circles after her influential 2017 paper "Amazon's Antitrust Paradox," in which she argued the dominant framework through which antitrust law had been applied for decades—the notion of consumer harm—was inadequate and compared it to the trusts of the Gilded Age. Biden also appointed Tim Wu, a professor of law at Columbia University, as a special assistant to the president for competition and tech policy in 2021. Three years earlier, Wu had drawn a through line from the trusts of the Gilded Age built by Rockefeller and his cohort of robber barons to Microsoft's aggressive acquisition, or kill-the-competition, tactics, and on to the twenty-first century's tech giants. "The tech industry became essentially composed of just a few giant trusts: Google for search and related industries,

Facebook for social media, Amazon for online commerce. While competitors remained in the wings, their positions became marginalized with every passing day," Wu wrote in a 2018 article.[34] Wu spent nearly two years helping the White House figure out how to employ antitrust law more forcefully.

In the fall of 2023, the FTC and seventeen states accused Amazon of "illegally maintaining monopoly power" through strategies that squeezed rival merchants from offering lower prices on platforms other than Amazon's and of promoting its own products, thus harming consumers. Amazon has denied the accusations. Also in 2023, Google went to trial three years after the Justice Department accused it of cutting off competitors to maintain its dominance in search and advertising—the first big tech company trial since Microsoft. In March 2024, the Justice Department laid the groundwork for a Microsoft-style antitrust spectacle when it sued Apple, accusing it of maintaining an illegal monopoly in the smartphone market. In remarks accompanying the suit, Assistant Attorney General Jonathan Kanter said that the department's successful litigation against a "different platform monopolist," meaning Microsoft, had helped to foster the growth of mobile phones. But now, Apple—one of the biggest beneficiaries of the smartphone revolution—was, according to the DOJ, essentially engaging in the same kind of behavior to protect its iPhone ecosystem.

The companies have routinely said that their activities are not anticompetitive, borrowing the same argument that Gates had used during Microsoft's trial: Barriers to entry are low in the technology industry, and competitive edges can easily be lost. Microsoft, whose market capitalization briefly crossed $3 trillion in early 2024 as it jousted with Apple for the title of the world's most valuable company, itself is undergoing renewed scrutiny. In the aftermath of its antitrust trial, as Gates stepped away from his daily duties, the battered and bruised company lurched around unable to find its footing and falling behind in the race to capture the consumer internet. In 2014, the Indian-born Satya Nadella took the reins at Microsoft and pushed the company in a direction beyond Windows. He focused on becoming a lead provider of office productivity tools, and building Azure, its cloud-based software for enterprises. He also began turning around its internal culture. Where Microsoft had once been driven entirely by individual success, Nadella encouraged more collaboration, both internally and externally, becoming an ally to Valley companies rather than the tyrant from the Northwest that the company had been under Gates. For instance, Microsoft struck a partnership with VMware, once a fierce software rival. Its deepening ties to the Valley also meant that it landed the biggest coup of all: a big stake in OpenAI, the artificial intelligence company—although that too could face regulatory scrutiny after Khan said her office will focus closely on the emerging field of artificial intelligence, as the biggest tech companies rush to define and grab the market.[35]

The FTC and the European Union, which has always taken a tough antitrust stance, had also blocked Microsoft's acquisition of the video-game giant Activision Blizzard, but the $75 billion deal went through in May 2023 partly on the ground that the video-game market is a small one.

In a 2019 interview, Gates mused about the situation that tech founders and their companies found themselves in then—and still do today—drawing similarities with his own experience. "As soon as tech became important, with the personal computer and the internet, there was certainly a duality where people were saying, 'Oh my God, this is brilliant stuff,' but they were also looking at me, or other leaders in the industry, and saying, 'What motivates their work? Do they understand the potential negative side effects?' I'm sort of the poster boy of that original duality. By some measures I was extremely popular and by some measures I was extremely—you know, people worried what Microsoft was up to. What's happening now is more of a mainstream thing. The concerns are legitimate, and they're touching more areas of life now."[36]

Chapter 4

The Pivot

New Spin

On February 21, 2008, Gates stood in the main auditorium of Carnegie Mellon University in Pittsburgh, about to deliver a speech to more than 700 students. Two years earlier, he had announced his intention to transition from his day-to-day responsibilities at Microsoft, of which he was chairman, and turn full-time to philanthropy. Now, he was months away from doing just that. After the thundering applause and the flash of cellphone cameras faded, Gates began. He spoke at length about software, innovation, entrepreneurship, and philanthropy, topics that were dear to him, and his vision for all the ways in which technology would continue to transform lives and society. He dwelled on the potential of 3D technology. He talked about how far speech recognition software had to go.

And then, with a simple but attention-grabbing statistic, he explained why his latest pursuit, philanthropy, was necessary: Because malaria research gets only 10 percent of the funding that goes to research on cures for baldness. "The market directs itself to solve problems based on economic signals," Gates said to his rapt audience, moving about the stage, gesticulating, as he explained why. Because of their profit-seeking nature, he said, companies put money into pursuing products and solutions that have the most demand. Since there are about two billion people at the top of the economic ladder who don't like being bald and are willing to spend to find a cure, companies will channel resources to finding ways to reverse baldness. At the same time, the bottom two billion of the world's population suffers because it doesn't have the means to direct funds into malaria research. Large numbers of their children therefore die from an easily preventable disease caused by mosquito bites.[1]

This was an avatar of Gates that the world had increasingly become acquainted with: the billionaire philanthropist who explained why the same market that failed people could also be alchemized, by charitable dollars, to serve people. With facts, figures, and flashes of the geeky showmanship that had begun to define his philanthropic talks, Gates dazzled his young audience of mainly computer science and engineering students. One of the world's foremost research institutions, Carnegie Mellon was founded in 1900 as the Carnegie Technical Schools with a $1 million gift from Andrew Carnegie, the steel mogul and philanthropist of the Gilded Age. In 1967, the training institute merged with a scientific research center endowed by Pittsburgh's other wealthy family, the Mellons, to form Carnegie Mellon. But that day, Gates's audience was so taken by his speech that most of their questions at the end were about careers in philanthropy rather than technology.

It was a stark change from Gates's visit to the campus four years earlier, when he had stopped by to talk to students about computer science. By 2004, Gates had already begun to focus on philanthropy in a very public way. That year, the Gates Foundation donated $20 million for a new science center at Carnegie Mellon. Called the Gates Center, the futuristic looking building, with a zinc exterior, took five years to build and houses the school's undergraduate computer science programs. But Gates didn't have a halo quite yet. If anything, he was still linked closely to Microsoft. At the end of that talk, the Q&A with students got a little contentious, with many of them quizzing Gates about Microsoft and its business tactics, and why it sought to crush Silicon Valley companies.

"He gave the talk in the same room, but in that first talk it wasn't Bill Gates the philanthropist," recalled Jared Cohon, then the president of Carnegie Mellon, who introduced Gates to the audience. "He was viewed by much of the student body as the emperor of evil empires." By 2008, though, Gates's image transition to philanthropist was complete. And so to mark both his second career and the venue he was speaking at, Cohon brought onstage a unique thank-you gift: one of the original desk chairs that Carnegie—whose writings on philanthropy deeply influenced Gates's thinking—had used in his office at Carnegie Steel. The rather modest wooden chair was accompanied by a black-and-white photograph of Carnegie at his desk. "We thought it would be fitting to connect you, the greatest philanthropist of the twenty-first century, with the greatest philanthropist of the twentieth century," Cohon said to Gates as he presented him with the chair. It was one of the few occasions when Gates, who typically doesn't accept gifts, appeared delighted. "I got the impression that Bill was very pleased by that," said Cohon, who stepped down as president in 2013. "He is not very demonstrative."

Cause and Effect

In 1999, as Gates approached his twenty-fifth year running the company he had cofounded and tended to for the better part of his life, his energy was leaching away. He had been fighting the government for more than a year, and every arrow loosed upon him hurt his morale. Reporters, commentators, and Microsoft rivals employed an arsenal of increasingly harsh adjectives to describe Gates. They called him arrogant, disdainful, indignant, angry, snide, condescending, petulant, contemptuous, truculent, evasive, hyperaggressive, despotic, bullying, an enfant terrible of the tech industry, and a robber baron. His three-day deposition at Microsoft's antitrust trial the prior year had been disastrous. If Gates was exhausted, Microsoft was desperate. The company's top executives were distracted by the government's attack. It was fighting the worst public relations crisis in its history, and unsure how to fight back.

Microsoft was no novice when it came to dealing with the media. When Pam Edstrom joined Microsoft in 1984 as its first director of public relations, she took the raw material of Gates's personality and presented him as a nerdy genius out to change the world, putting him at the center of the company's origin story.[2] In some cases, spiffing up the Microsoft boss meant doing so literally—down to brushing his hair and polishing his glasses. But as Microsoft's heft in the computer industry grew, its public relations strategy was geared toward building buzz around new company offerings. It often involved parceling out "exclusives" and access to Gates, typically by inviting small groups of reporters for briefings where they could ask questions of him directly. Trips to the Microsoft campus, and even tours of the Gateses' home, kept the mainstream press engaged. Microsoft arranged overnight getaways called "pajama parties" for reporters to Gates's vacation compound in Washington's scenic Hood Canal area. Microsoft's media team also reached out to technology-focused publications, whose reporters—early "influencers"—built excitement around its software by testing new versions early.

Gates himself was an astute, if not enthusiastic, user of the press to promote Microsoft's products. He understood that public appearances and stories about the company served as important tools for recruiting top talent. He regularly monitored the media's coverage of Microsoft; as he pored through monthly reports on the state of the business, he would study press write-ups of the company's products, including individual applications like its Excel spreadsheet, down to the last word. If it looked like a reporter missed the point, the PR person in charge would get the critique. But because he placed communications strictly in the business toolkit, Gates rarely pitched himself as part of the story. Many reporters from the 1990s recalled his barely concealed irritation at having to talk to them. Sometimes, he could be condescending or sarcastic; one recalled a press conference where a fellow reporter asked Gates why flat-panel televisions were becoming all the rage. "Because they're cool," Gates responded. Another time, during the antitrust trial, a reporter asked Gates if his budding philanthropic activity was a public relations scheme. "If it was, I'd find a more cost-effective way to do it," Gates said dryly.

It's not that Gates was unaware of his shortcomings. In August 1997, as Steve Jobs strode around the stage at Apple's Macworld event in Boston, electrifying the audience with his forceful, clear, and magnetic delivery, Gates sat in one of Microsoft's television studios thousands of miles away in Seattle, watching his nemesis. Jobs had just returned to Apple as its interim chief executive through the company's acquisition of NeXT and was about to announce a partnership between Apple and Microsoft. Gates, who had refused to travel to Boston to join Jobs onstage, was to make a brief speech via satellite link. As he observed the loose-limbed ease with which Jobs spoke to the audience—the pauses at just the right moments, the speech dappled with humor, the sheer performative theater of it—Gates was filled with admiration and envy. He turned to a colleague and asked: "How does he do that?," recalled a person who heard the exchange.

Gates could never capture for Microsoft what Jobs did for Apple. But he was everywhere, keynoting big tech conferences like the Consumer Electronics Show. If he had to tolerate personal questions in the name of pushing the Microsoft brand, or if he thought his presence would help sell the "product," he would put up with it, said one former Microsoft executive who worked closely with Gates. Edstrom, who by then had cofounded her own public relations firm, was one of the few people whose feedback on his media performance Gates respected, partly because she was direct. One former Microsoft employee in the communications department recalled Edstrom sharing an email she had sent Gates about an interview he had fumbled. Edstrom's feedback to Gates was specific, and she had marked the interview transcript with comments like, "here's where you lost the reporter," the former employee said. "There was no coddling or sugarcoating."

However, even Edstrom—and Microsoft's vast in-house communications team—couldn't convince Gates that his thin-skinned but dismissive attitude toward media questions about the antitrust trial only fed into the case. In 1994, when the government began poking into Microsoft's practices with vigor, Gates appeared on television for an interview, but walked off the set in a huff when the CBS News anchor Connie Chung pushed him on the matter—although not before demonstrating that he could indeed jump over a chair, as he had been known to do. Microsoft didn't immediately go on the counteroffensive. Instead, people in Gates's inner circle, including direct reports, advisors, and communications officers, deferred to his wishes, embarking on a PR strategy to dismiss the government's stance and unleash a campaign designed to argue on the merits of the case, rather than counter the image that had been forming of the Microsoft leader in the media. Over the span of five years starting in 1995, Gates went from being seen as a brilliant entrepreneur and innovator to being portrayed primarily as a ruthless businessman. People may have fallen in love with the computer nerd on his way to stardom, but they hated the hard-nosed businessman with his unrelenting desire to obliterate the competition. A ravenous press couldn't get enough of the narrative. In 1998, the Microsoft cofounder achieved the heights of pop culture notoriety when he showed up in an episode of *The Simpsons*, telling Homer Simpson he intended to buy his online business rather than risk competing with it, even though he didn't know what it made. About three years later, the actor Tim Robbins played a Gates-like character in the action thriller *Antitrust*, about a young programmer and the menacing billionaire founder of the company he worked at. Although the movie was panned by critics and flopped at the box office, the very fact that his alleged villainy became Hollywood fodder showed how the theater of the trial had seeped into the wider world. The king of software had been dethroned—swiftly, embarrassingly, and rather gleefully—in the court of public opinion.

Eventually, Microsoft's despairing public relations team decided to launch a media blitz aimed at salvaging Gates's reputation. The company hired Mark Penn, a longtime political strategist who had been an aide to President Bill Clinton. Penn was skilled at polling and applying political strategies to determine public opinion. He specialized in negative ads, which were designed to sow doubt about the target. But initial polling showed that Gates had a better public reputation than Justice Department officials and the media did, according to a person with knowledge of the campaign. Gates was "the ultimate Horatio Alger story" in people's minds, according to this person, not unlike Henry Ford who was able to develop a product that became universal—and therefore deserved to be the world's richest person. "The robber-baron view was a little overstated in the public eye," this person added.

The polling also found that people knew little about the Microsoft cofounder or his family, his charitable giving, or his thoughts on American innovation. Rather than pursue negative advertising, Penn and his team focused instead on what they deemed Gates's positive attributes. They began to fashion an image of Gates centered on three things: family, philanthropy, and innovation. By then, Gates was a new father and had stepped up his philanthropic efforts. With his prognostications about the future of computing and the web, he had also come to be regarded as a tech visionary. Gates wasn't initially on board, but the pollster and spinmeister got through to him the only way anyone could: He appealed to his intellect and made a rational, data-based case. Penn would patiently explain to Gates that people were making judgments about him based not on the facts but on his behavior. It was only after he and his pollsters showed Gates data charting the changes in public mood that Gates realized that his behavior had contributed to the anti-Microsoft sentiment. Gates "didn't care about his image" until that moment, said a person involved in those conversations. "He was like a lot of people. Until Washington comes knocking, you're just doing your business, you're not focused on the external world at all." Once Gates understood that interacting with the media was essentially a game where you could score points based on performance, and the data reflected that thesis, his competitive nature kicked in. Gates would sit through hours of media training on how to respond to tough questions by journalists. Rather than responding to their questions literally, he practiced saying what he wanted them to take away. Concerned with being portrayed as "dehumanized," he once asked a member of his public relations coterie if they could make him "more human."

On February 5, 1998, Gates was in Brussels, on his way to meet European Union regulators about Microsoft, when he was pied in the face by two people. Photographers for U.S. newspapers paid thousands of dollars for the image of a surprised Gates wiping cream off his face and glasses. Just three days later, Gates made a day tour of Silicon Valley, where he said he was "humble and respectful."[3] He appeared on TV in an interview with Barbara Walters, crooning "Twinkle, Twinkle, Little Star" to his young daughter. He appeared in ads for golf clubs. He offered mea culpas on the *Charlie Rose* show. Microsoft ran essays in national newspapers, penned by several of its senior executives, defending the need for innovation. Gates himself appeared in a series of ads calling for the "freedom to innovate." In 2000, as the government pushed Microsoft to break up into two parts, Gates appeared in several television commercials for the company, including one that came to be known as the "blue sweater" ad. In the brief commercial, Gates, dressed in the kind of V-necked sweater that would become his signature, is talking about the software giant's products. *The New York Times* described it as a "visual antidote" to the way Microsoft and Gates were being portrayed in the press.[4]

To squeeze out some additional image points, Microsoft's media team also began highlighting the occasional philanthropic gifts that Gates and French Gates had begun to make. In 1994, Gates had bought a codex of Leonardo da Vinci's for a record $30.8 million, one of his first billionaire purchases. The 72-page manual, which Gates named Codex Leicester, contained the Italian Renaissance painter and scientist's elaborate drawings and musings on the science of water, including on tides and how they connected with the earth and moon. The codex had been on a museum tour since the Gates purchase. When it made its way to the Seattle art museum, Microsoft communications employees jumped at the chance to hold a Q&A with students where Gates could tell them about his interest in hydraulics.

The press, however, was buying none of it. The blue-sweater commercial elicited derisive comparisons to Mister Rogers, the kindly and beloved television show host famous for his colorful V-necked cardigans who reigned over children's public television for decades. Cynical writers called it a blatantly obvious attempt to launder the billionaire's image and reputation. Writing in *The New York Times*, the columnist Frank Rich didn't mince his words: "As a hard-knuckled tycoon he was at least true to his arrogant self," Rich wrote. "Now he is morphing into another phony full-time actor in the sentimental P.R. pageant that has become American public life. He must turn himself into a lovable character that the entire populace will adore, if that's what it takes to deflect the Feds."[5] In his book on the Microsoft antitrust trial, Ken Auletta notes that Gates's charitable activities became "significantly more visible" after the company settled with the Department of Justice.[6] By the following year, Auletta writes, "Bill Gates became America's most generous living philanthropist." When the Gates Foundation made a $100 million donation to establish a children's vaccine fund, Auletta wrote: "The Gates Foundation . . . had made many generous gifts in the past, but what was unusual about this gift was that it was made in such a public way."

Gates did receive some favorable coverage. In the August 1999 issue of

Newsweek magazine, the tech journalist Steven Levy portrayed Gates as a family man "who just wants to have fun."[7] As Gates told Levy, "When somebody's successful, people leap to simple explanations that might make sense. So you get these myths. People love to have any little story. Yes, I'm intense. I'm energetic. I like to understand what our market position is. But then it gets turned into this—the ultra-competitor. It's somewhat dehumanizing. I read that and say, 'I don't know that guy.'"

Selling a Philanthropist

In early 2000, Gates announced that he would step down as Microsoft's chief executive, but would stay on as chairman, a role he finally stepped down from in 2014. Microsoft created for him the role of "chief software architect," which allowed Gates to stay close to software development, but also yanked him out of overseeing the company's operations as it tried to remake its public image. Despite its dominance in the software industry, the antitrust trial and focus on Gates's public behavior had become enough of a challenge that Microsoft risked losing clients and employees and found it harder to attract new talent. Understanding that he needed to get out of the way, Gates told the press that he would focus "100 percent" of his time on software, which is what he liked best. He would also make time for his philanthropy. One former Microsoft employee recalled asking a confidante of the billionaire why Gates had decided to step down. "Bill feels like he's at the top of a very narrow peak, and the only way is down," the confidante replied. His switch to philanthropy once again elicited comparisons with Rockefeller, who had turned to prolific charitable acts partly to change his reputation as a hard-charging, extractive monopolist. Philanthropy was always something Gates was going to turn to; he had grown up in a family that encouraged charitable giving. On the eve of his marriage, his mother, Mary Gates, had written his then fiancée French Gates a letter about the couple's obligation to do something bigger with their vast fortune, which ended with the words: "From those to whom much is given, much is expected." However, the timing had always been undecided. Gates wouldn't acknowledge it at the time, but in recent years he has admitted that the bad publicity surrounding the Microsoft trial hastened his move to philanthropy.[8]

Gates started his philanthropic career with conventional donations in the early 1990s, some years after he became a billionaire. One of his earliest gifts was in 1991, when he gave $12 million to the University of Washington to start a new department of molecular biotechnology. It was, at the time, the single largest commitment by an individual to the Seattle-based institution. As part of the donation, the university created the William Gates III endowed chair in biomedical sciences. He also made donations to Stanford University and United Way, the nonprofit his mother had been closely involved with. In 1995, a year after he married French Gates, the couple gave $10 million to the University of Washington in honor of Gates's mother who had recently passed away, and who had been a major influence on his thinking about charitable giving. The prior year, he had started the William H. Gates foundation with a gift of $94 million, roping in his father, William Henry Gates Sr., to oversee it. The elder Gates, who died in 2020, was a longtime community leader and retired lawyer who ran the foundation's activities from the basement of his house. The foundation initially focused on community development in the Pacific Northwest and health-related causes. It also looked at funding curricula in U.S. schools. Three years later, Gates recruited a Microsoft executive, Patty Stonesifer, to start a second foundation with a primary focus on wiring the nation's libraries. At the time, many American libraries, especially those in smaller communities, were still without internet access. Stonesifer oversaw a program to provide hardware, software, and training to libraries around the country. Choosing to support libraries was partly a nod to Carnegie, whose money funded the creation of a network of more than 2,500 libraries around the country—and whose ideas on giving back had shaped Gates's thinking. But his philanthropic efforts remained ad hoc for a few more years. The former couple donated $20 million to Duke University, French Gates's alma mater. They gave money to the Seattle Public Library and the city's theater endowment fund. Gates made other gifts sporadically, including $2 million to aid refugee health and $50 million to PATH, a Seattle-based global health organization, to help with cancer research.

The Bill and Melinda Gates Foundation came to life at the turn of the century after Gates merged his two separate philanthropic efforts and added his then wife's name. Its initial bequest was about $22 billion through transfers of Microsoft stock, which meant that the foundation had to give away hundreds of millions of dollars annually in keeping with U.S. law governing nonprofits. As Gates often did when tackling a new subject or challenge, he dived into philanthropy with the same intensity that he had used to build Microsoft. He read endlessly, learning about the intricacies of diseases, poverty, and healthcare in developing countries. He met with leaders in the field and sought insights from experts. He fired off emails at all hours to the small group of staffers at the foundation. He flew to New York to meet with leaders at the United Nations. He sought partnerships and collaborations with other foundations and corporations, all the while learning from their operations. Doors opened easily for the world's richest man and business legend. People lined up to meet him, and they welcomed his interest and his dollars.

When Trevor Neilson joined the Gates Foundation in 2000 as its first spokesman, one of his tasks was to create a firewall between the foundation and Microsoft to ensure that the budding organization could build an identity separate from the company. At the same time, Microsoft had to reprogram its communications strategy following the antitrust trial, ensuring that announcements from the company didn't collide with foundation-related news. A former staffer in the Clinton White House who had returned to his hometown of Seattle to work with the city's public schools system, Neilson tried to shape the foundation's image around Gates, taking the essential elements of his approach to philanthropy—his reliance on metrics to establish why donations were needed, as well as his desire to be an engaged partner rather than a passive donor—and fashion it into a pitch. "I had to reverse engineer the themes that Bill Gates spoke about to create a message and story around the foundation's focus," Neilson said. Although he left the foundation after a few years and parlayed his Gates Foundation credentials into a philanthropy advisory business, Neilson said Gates never once specifically asked him to polish his public image. "All this was driven by this profound sense of what is right and what is wrong, in terms of equity and justice."

No sooner had he started his new career than the accolades began pouring in. In 2001, the Gates family was presented with the Carnegie Medal of Philanthropy in recognition of their commitment to giving. Four years later, Gates, French Gates, and Bono, the rockstar, were named *Time* magazine's Persons of the Year for their contributions to global poverty relief. Gates had first met Bono at the World Economic Forum in Davos in 2002. By then, the U2 front man was already a well-known activist working on improving the financial health of people in Africa through an alliance called Debt, AIDS, Trade, Africa (DATA), and his legendary band had won more than ten Grammy awards. But Gates, the newly minted philanthropist, was slowly discovering the world beyond Microsoft, and had never heard of the singer or the band before then. Later, DATA, and another campaign led by Bono, would merge into an organization called ONE, with funds from the Gates Foundation and led by one of its executives. Gates's joint philanthropy with Bono also sparked a friendship. In Seattle for a U2 concert in May 2005, Bono stayed with the billionaire, who attended the band's concert along with "20,000 screaming fans."[9] However, despite their yearslong friendship, Gates admitted in 2020 that he knew very little about Bono's life growing up until he read *Surrender*, the singer's memoir. In 2005, Gates also received an honorary knighthood from Buckingham Palace, joining other Americans such as Rudy Giuliani, the former mayor of New York; the movie director Steven Spielberg; and former President Ronald Reagan, who had received the dubbing before. The following summer, Gates was absent from Microsoft's annual meeting for the first time since the company's founding, on sabbatical in Africa.[10] His full-time role at Microsoft was shrinking by design. And his pivot to philanthropy was well on its way. By 2008, the man who had been labeled a rapacious capitalist a decade earlier was calling on the world's leaders at Davos to practice "benevolent capitalism."[11]

Today, the world has a completely refurbished image of Gates, the jagged edges of the monopolist softened by the halo of the philanthropist. His uniform of trousers and a sweater, worn over a collared shirt, signals an everyman look. Although he owns two Gulfstream jets, Gates does not appear to embody his wealth. His hair is grayer but still messy and slightly disheveled. His skin is now more tan than wan, but his glasses still appear more functional than fashionable. The image-making around his philanthropy is endless, an iconography building around a billionaire. There he is, learning about grain production from a farmer in Nigeria. Administering the polio vaccine to an infant in India. Rocking in his chair and chewing on his glasses onstage as he ponders a question about math education in American schools. Out in the field, dressed in khakis and a plaid shirt, listening intently to a community activist. Sitting on a colorful rug on the dusty earth with French Gates, knees folded, deep in conversation with a woman holding her baby. Shaking hands with a head of state. Getting "trained" by Roger Federer ahead of a charity tennis match to raise funds for Africa. Playing finger puppet soccer with David Beckham in an Instagram post as the two discuss the challenges of addressing malaria. Engaging in a fireside chat about growth—from bacteria to babies, from economies to empires—with one of his heroes, the Czech Canadian scientist Vaclav Smil. Pushing companies and governments to take climate change seriously. Gates's star power, wealth, and influence are so potent that he has become a sought-after voice on global health and development, vaccines, viruses, pandemics, sanitation, education reform, climate change, philanthropy, and, of course, technology, including the emerging field of artificial intelligence. His skill at digesting and explaining complicated topics—he once took an online MIT course on solid state physics, even doing the homework—and his ability to envision and map how the future might play out have made him a roving scientist-statesman of sorts.[12] Gates can come across as professorial in his public appearances, but people who have interacted with him offstage say that he is often in student mode, deferring to the expertise of academics, constantly learning and responding to new information. Occasionally, he steps into the role of Cassandra, as he did in 2015 when he appeared to predict the coronavirus pandemic by remarking on the likelihood of such an event, and its threat to humanity.

Gates is not above stunts to make a bigger point. At a TED conference in 2009, he unsealed a jar of mosquitoes onstage to make the point that the insects killed dozens of people in poor, tropical countries because they can carry the parasite that causes malaria. (The mosquitoes were shipped from a lab at the University of California, Berkeley, and spent a night in the hotel room of a foundation employee before making their way onstage.) Gates reassured the rather unsettled audience that those mosquitoes were not infected. In 2018, he took a sealed jar of human feces with him onstage in Beijing at an expo about reinventing the toilet. The stunt was meant to draw attention to the problem of open-air defecation; for years, the foundation had made grants to researchers to develop innovative toilet technology.

The evolution of his image might seem to be a natural byproduct of his activities. The reality is anything but. Rather, it is the outcome of a yearslong campaign by a small army of communications professionals, at both the Gates Foundation and Gates Ventures, the billionaire's personal investment and image management firm, who are paid to shape the public persona of Gates in a way that elevates his stature to benefit his foundation's goals and burnish his individual brand. The Microsoft cofounder's very public image switch from an all-knowing, imperious boss of a technology giant to an earnest student of the world and a thoughtful practitioner of philanthropy is largely a manufactured one, according to several people with insight into those efforts. Gates isn't someone who wakes up each morning thinking about how he comes across in public. If he has to speak to an audience, he's more focused on rehearsing his talking points. If the day involves travel, he might be preoccupied with what's in his book bag and the emails he needs to fire off. If there's a meeting at the Gates Foundation, he's lining up the questions he wants to ask and perhaps, the gaps of logic he wants to point out in a briefing document.

However, people in Gates's orbit, including current and former advisors, foundation employees, and communications professionals, say that as a philanthropist, the billionaire is far more receptive to the importance of creating and controlling his media personality, and projecting certain attributes to sustain his personal brand, than he ever was at Microsoft, having learned that image management lesson the hard way. It took plenty of coaching and training to get Gates in shape for his role as front man for the foundation, people who worked with him said. The task was to "transition Bill's profile from wealthy technologist to inspirational global leader," according to internal documents from the time. There were rehearsals and run-throughs, mock Q&A sessions. Foundation employees had to remind him not to condescend to someone asking a question he found dumb, and to respond in broad brush strokes rather than the technical style that was his instinct. It also helped that he saw real returns: The more he put himself out there, the more positive feedback he got about his foundation's work. "He liked the transformation of his image and the adulation for obvious reasons," one former senior foundation employee said. "Rubbing shoulders with celebrities and heads of state, the king's welcome all over the world, people desperate to hear his opinion. He liked the impact of putting himself out there." The foundation and its mission—which the former employee described as Gates's "we can save the world" thinking—also resonated in a world exhausted by America's protracted war in Iraq and the great financial crisis of 2008.

The media was largely receptive to the new Gates. News stories breathlessly charted his evolution as a public intellectual on global health, disease, education, and climate change. In 2005, the *Wall Street Journal* published a story about Gates's "think week."[13] Gates would take similar trips while at Microsoft, but the peek into this bit of his life helped to crystallize the brainiac image. The technology columnist David Pogue found himself confronting the "apparent contradiction between Bill Gates, the merciless businessman with ambitions for world domination, and Bill Gates, the compassionate scientist whose goal is to save millions of lives."[14] The 2019 documentary *Inside Bill's Brain: Decoding Bill Gates*, a three-part film on Netflix, treats Gates's brain like a national treasure, juxtaposing events from the billionaire's childhood with his philanthropic endeavors. Directed by Davis Guggenheim, who made *An Inconvenient Truth* and *Waiting for Superman*, the film received mixed reviews. Some found it inspiring. Others dismissed it as hagiography.

Build "Bill's Brand"

Some called it the gold prize. For years, some employees in the Gates orbit had made it an informal goal to push their boss's name for the Nobel Peace Prize. Gates and French Gates had won multiple public service laurels, including the highest honors from countries like India, so it wasn't a stretch to eye the top prize. It was a "front and center" goal among some employees at Gates Ventures and the Gates Foundation to push Gates's name periodically as a contender for the Nobel prize, according to several people who were aware of those conversations, although another person said he wasn't aware of any specific strategy conversations during his time at Gates Ventures. There would be an open and ongoing conversation about how to massage Gates's so-called brand to appeal to the Nobel Prize committee, and about how the team could opportunistically use global health milestone moments—the potential eradication of polio, or breakthroughs in malaria research—where the foundation played a big role to create a media campaign about his candidacy.

At the Gates Foundation, it was more chatter and aspiration than a "ten-step plan," according to one former senior employee of the foundation. Many saw such a prize as validation of the work they had signed up to do. It was especially buzzy as the foundation suddenly began playing an outsize role in global health and development, supercharged by Buffett's decision in 2006 to turn over billions of dollars to its endowment. The Giving Pledge, the campaign started by Gates and Buffett in 2010 to get more billionaires to engage with philanthropy, put him on an even higher pedestal, coming as it did right after the financial crisis, which spotlighted the country's widening economic inequality. "Everything was done with an eye to that goal," said the former senior employee, referring to the Nobel prize. "That's why we were positioning in the media and PR as we did. It boiled down to—the foundation is here to save the world, every life has equal value, and Bill is the front man." Alex Reid, a spokeswoman for Gates Ventures, said, "There was never any goal or discussion about securing a Nobel Peace Prize for Bill or the Gates Foundation."

The unofficial campaign for a Nobel Peace Prize may have been one reason why Gates met with Jeffrey Epstein at least once in 2013, according to media reports. Between 2011 and 2014, the Gates Foundation ran a highly visible campaign about its polio-related grant-making. Eradicating polio had been one of Gates's biggest priorities and the foundation had partnered with Rotary International, the nonprofit that was leading those efforts. Foundation staffers were hoping their work would win them the honor. Epstein, who had cultivated a wide network of powerful people, told a former foundation employee that he could help the philanthropist win the award for his work to eradicate polio. In late March 2013, Thorbjørn Jagland, then the secretary general of the Council of Europe, a human rights organization, and chairman of the Norwegian Nobel Prize Committee, hosted a dinner for Gates at his official residence in Strasbourg, France. Gates had sought the meeting, Jagland said, to learn more about the European Pharmacopoeia, a body affiliated with the council that oversees quality control for medicines distributed across European markets. To Jagland, it seemed natural that the philanthropist would be interested in learning about the council's work, and to the extent he knew, there was no other reason why Gates wanted to meet. Jagland, a former prime minister of Norway, said no one had put forth a Nobel Peace Prize nomination for Gates or the Gates Foundation that year, but he was given to believe that the billionaire brought Epstein to the dinner. "I don't know why he brought Epstein with him, I was not informed in advance," Jagland said. Asked about the meeting, Reid said that Gates had not brought Epstein to "a meeting with Jagland. If he was there, he was not invited by Bill, nor did he arrive with Bill." Also present at the dinner were officials from the International Peace Institute in New York, an independent organization that sometimes works with the United Nations, and whose president, Terje Rød-Larsen, had had several interactions with Epstein. An influential Norwegian diplomat who played a central role in negotiating the Oslo Accords, Rød-Larsen was not at the 2013 dinner, but seven years later, he quit the peace institute after revelations that he had taken money from Epstein to support his work.[15]

High-profile individuals, such as celebrities, business and political leaders, and billionaires who maintain an active public presence, often hire public relations firms or pay staff to handle media queries. What's revelatory about Gates Ventures is the highly organized and intricately detailed plan that goes into shaping and sustaining its founder's public persona, and its evolution over time. The firm started as an entity called bgC3 LLC. The awkward name, made up on the fly by Gates's assistant, consisted of his initials, the number "3," which was a reference to his formal name William Gates III, and the letter "C" for "catalyst," a word that stood for Gates's belief that philanthropy was a catalyst for change. Today, it is a much more professional operation, with an office on the top floor of a building in Kirkland, Washington. Its severe marble, gray, and steel interiors are leavened with quirky touches—there is an installation of a periodic table in the lobby area—reflecting the sciencey interests of its founder.[16] More than two dozen of its roughly 100 employees work full time to constantly shape, monitor, and polish Gates's aura in the press, and fashion the positive aspects into a consistent, relatable brand across his various roles: entrepreneur, technologist, philanthropist, and family guy, or, as one former employee put it, "lovable nerd philanthropist." Other key elements include casting Gates as a practical problem solver of social ills and a strategic philanthropist who invented a new standard of rigor in the field. It is all part of a meticulously planned campaign to build "brand fidelity" across the Gates empire and "exploit" social media channels to create positive attributes around the Gates brand. It was also designed to build engagement and activism around Gates's pet causes and highlight the habits of his that fit in with the broader storylines essential to the marketing of his brand. By now, the public knows that the philanthropist is a prodigious reader and thinker. Gates always travels with a book bag containing his current reading, carried at a respectful distance by his security detail. One person formerly in Gates's circle remembers having a discussion with him on meteorology, which the billionaire was trying to understand to aid the foundation's agricultural efforts in Africa; he later happened to peek into Gates's book bag to find three books on the subject. He has been known to spend at least a couple of hours walking on a treadmill while reading up on subjects like astrophysics. He reads *The Economist* magazine from cover to cover every week. The specific details might not make their way to the wider world, but the habits are valuable raw material for his media handlers. Gates's deep insight into technology and science, and his innate ability to map out the future, has also meant selling him as a prophet and seer with a polymathic brain. When Gates talks about artificial intelligence as the next leap in technology, his media handlers want to promote those aspects. "All the problems I take on require a lot of participation, whether it's scientists, or governments, or brilliant people in the field," Gates told *The Wall Street Journal* in 2019, reflecting on his high visibility.[17] "They won't succeed unless you can talk to broad audiences and shift perceptions." It has become less uncomfortable—but no easier—for Gates to deal with people in public settings, according to people who have dealt with him. Yet the decades-old mainstream media narrative about him as an awkward, sometimes robotic man unable to connect easily with an audience hasn't faded, and his team is constantly seeking to counter that storyline.

The rise of social media platforms gave Gates a direct way to communicate with his fans. In 2010, Gates launched his blog, *GatesNotes*, extending a tradition he had started the prior year of writing an annual letter for the foundation. The letter, which Gates began writing at the encouragement of Buffett, whose own annual letters to shareholders of Berkshire Hathaway have become a treat for investors, became very popular with readers. *GatesNotes* is a more casual platform for his musings, book recommendations, and updates on his work and thinking, typically written with a staff member. The posts are written in an accessible and engaging style, often laced with humor. Gates Ventures employees commission polls and surveys, usually called "sentiment analysis" in the public relations industry, to gauge what people wanted to hear from Gates about on *GatesNotes*. The *GatesNotes* blog was built to "dimensionalize" him, to give readers a better sense of his personality and make him appear more well-rounded, according to one person who worked on these strategies. Once, Gates posted an item in August 2022 about his tips for solving Wordle, the popular word puzzle, but said that in the end, he preferred Nerdle, which calls for a player to solve equations by guessing digits instead of letters. Typically, one of the blog's writers will put together a post and send it to Gates, who reads it in his spare time—sometimes on flights, or in between books—and sends it back with his annotations. His book recommendations, often posted on *GatesNotes*, have become so influential that in 2016, *The New York Times* labeled Gates the "billionaire book critic."[18] Gates has even launched a podcast and video channel called "Unconfuse Me with Bill Gates," in which he invites guests whose expertise helps him understand a topic better. In August 2023, he invited Questlove, the musician and entrepreneur, to discuss the future of food; earlier guests included the comedians Seth Rogen and Lauren Miller, who discussed the role of humor in raising awareness of diseases like Alzheimer's.

Gates is also a star on Reddit, the online community where people discuss everything from stocks to news to sports. He has participated in at least 10 of Reddit's "Ask Me Anything" sessions, which involve an online Q&A between Reddit users and persons of interest and stature. The AMAs, as they are known, have provided everyday fans with a level of accessibility to the billionaire that might never happen otherwise. Gates has answered questions about the cellphone he uses (a Samsung Galaxy Fold 3), what his favorite snacks are (he doesn't snack much because if snack foods were lying around he would eat them), if he ever makes himself a peanut butter sandwich (he makes tomato soup sometimes, but isn't much of a sandwich man), is he a beer drinker (no, he only drinks light beer at baseball games to "get with the vibe"), and so on and so forth. There are questions about his views on climate change and whether he reads philosophy. It's a digital version of a king holding court with his people.

The unceasing rhythm of spit-and-polish has helped Gates sustain a media voice that is earnest, curious, playful, serious, and relatable. In speeches and articles, he communicates with an unshakeable, almost child-like faith and optimism, studded with scientific facts and figures. It's a distinct "here's what I learned today, let me share it with you" approach. He is very much the socially conscious, civic-minded billionaire, but also the goofy elder statesman who dresses as one of Santa's elves putting books in the mail for his friends. He appears in carefully edited YouTube videos, such as the one in which he learns how to make baked chicken from Seattle's teacher of the year in 2019. For Buffett's ninetieth birthday in 2020, Gates's team shot a video of him baking an Oreo cookie cake for his friend. There was enough of the dorky personal stuff to make him an everyman (but a star), accessible (but only via social media), and grandfatherly (beyond reproach). In 2022, he appeared on his Instagram account with a festive holiday scarf wrapped around his neck, dropping off five of his favorite books of the year in free libraries around the world. Some of the downright silly videos were produced by Gates's media team to "humanize the guy," one person said, although some people on the media team aren't quite sure that they worked.

He also displays flashes of dad charm in interviews, talking about how his three children get frustrated that he still uses email as a primary form of communication, and that he is so large-screen focused, and how he must remind himself to check Instagram and WhatsApp because each child prefers to communicate via a different platform. When his elder daughter, Jennifer, who got married in 2022, gave birth to her first child in 2023, his social media feed carried photos of him holding his first grandchild. In his 2022 annual letter, he talked about how typing the words "I'll become a grandfather next year," made him "emotional"—a word that people rarely, if ever, associate with Gates.[19] Not long after, Gates showed up in an Instagram video post made by his team, where he is looking through a stack of made-up children's book titles. Among them: *Robotics for Babies*, *Climate Change for Babies*, and *Pandemics for Babies*. "Deciding first book to read to my granddaughter," the caption reads. In the end, he picks *I Am a Bunny* by Richard Scarry and looks at the audience with a smile. The journalist Theodore Schleifer, musing about the damage to Gates's image after the bad press that followed his divorce, wrote in 2021 that much of the philanthropist's "soft power" came from his "seemingly unimpeachable profile."[20]

Gates's political views and leanings are rarely part of the public sketch. That's partly because he frames issues through a technological and scientific lens, but also because it is essential to the foundation's work that he be seen as above politics. In interviews, Gates has described himself as a centrist who has steered clear of party politics partly because it would hurt his philanthropy. He has made the occasional donation to political causes in his home state of Washington. In 1993, he publicly opposed propositions to curb state spending, allying with teachers and healthcare officials and contributing $80,000 to the campaign. When he has taken a position on fraught or politicized topics, he often uses carefully considered words and only occasionally uses the digital town square of X, formerly known as Twitter, to advertise his views. He has said he supports higher marginal tax rates for the wealthy and that a lower capital gains tax rate is not ideal. He took aim at the Trump administration's response to the coronavirus pandemic. Before the Supreme Court struck down *Roe v. Wade*, reversing the constitutional right to an abortion, Gates said it would be devastating for the country, adding that he supported a woman's right to make her own decisions about her healthcare.

Each year between 2014 and 2019, Gates was the "most admired man in the world," according to YouGov polls. (He was replaced by Barack Obama in 2020 and 2021.) As of the first quarter of 2023, Gates was as famous as President Joe Biden on YouGov's list of public figures and ranked just below Biden in a measure of popularity. Such polls were often moments of celebration among Gates Ventures employees, worth flagging to Gates himself. In a 2021 survey of billionaires during the pandemic, 55 percent of Americans told the news publication *Vox* in a poll that they had a positive opinion of Gates. That was far higher than any of the other billionaires the survey identified as popular and having total recall in the public mind, including Musk, Bezos, and Zuckerberg. Gates's image transformation to optimistic, populist billionaire was complete.

The Reign of Janus

Every year, Gates—and, until she left, French Gates—would hold multiple meetings with executives of the Gates Foundation to approve plans and budgets, and review strategies. One of the highlights was the annual strategy review meeting, where the two of them listened to employee presentations about how well a program was working and whether adjustments needed to be made to improve their chances of success. For many, the meeting might be the only direct opportunity to interact with, and impress, Gates and French Gates. Employees also felt the pressure at these meetings to showcase their accomplishments so that they could defend their budgets. Several former senior executives who attended strategy review meetings recalled how, in the days leading up to them, the office atmosphere felt almost carnival-like, but suffused with dread. Employees rushed around preparing presentations frantically, reviewing their work and readying themselves for a possible inquisition by Gates.

The meetings themselves were spectacles, some attendees recalled; one described them as "almost comical." They were usually held in a big room with a seating pattern. Strict etiquette was followed. One former senior executive who participated in many of the meetings said they had the feel of a king holding court, as though Gates were Louis XIV and the employees were courtiers bowing and scraping before him in Versailles, hoping to earn their ruler's favor. Another recalled how, as executives were called upon to present to the former couple, highlighting what their team had done the previous year and how closely their work hewed to the strategies and priorities of the foundation, people would scrutinize Gates's expressions. The slightest hint of a smile or a nod could mean that he approved; an impassive face could mean he didn't. Gates and French Gates followed the presentations closely, usually saving questions for the end. Once the meeting ended, and people went back to their offices and desks, they would dissect Gates's questions and expressions for days, often celebrating if they concluded that they had impressed their boss, a third former attendee said. To this person, it seemed that many employees were motivated more by Gates's praise—sometimes, even the absence of opprobrium was seen as validation—than by the success of their grant-making. "Sometimes, the interpretation of what Gates wanted could take up hours of back and forth among the directors and teams," this person said. "I felt we were spending more time managing up than working to meet the needs of the people." Criticism was not valued in a place "where personal stakes are too high for anyone to stick their necks out."

More than two decades after its founding, the internal culture of the foundation remains one of deference, where hundreds of employees tiptoe around Gates, afraid to disagree and eager to do his bidding. If anything, its deferential culture has become ossified along with the multiple layers of bureaucracy and processes. People who left more than a decade ago describe a place not too different from those who left within the last two years. One recently departed employee observed that people at the foundation fall into three types: consiglieres who bow to Gates; young aspirants who are awed by him; and the skeptics who find Gates domineering and eventually leave. After the divorce, one person who advises the foundation on media strategy said that there were instead two power centers—Gates and French Gates—and employees were increasingly torn between the two. The former couple sought to maintain a professional relationship, giving themselves at least two years to see if they could work together, with the understanding that French Gates would leave if they couldn't. In May 2024, she cut her ties to the foundation, saying that she wanted to chart her own course in philanthropy.

Gates can be imperious in strategy meetings with small groups of senior executives, launching into a topic at length without seeking their input. He might be censorious, say, of an employee who didn't cite the source of a statistic in a document provided to him. It's not surprising that leaders of governments and companies and large entities have large staff paid to deliver things just as their bosses would like—no tomatoes in a sandwich, double-spaced briefing documents, no phone calls after 8 P.M. "Gates and Melinda weren't unique in how they were handled," said one outside public relations professional who has worked with the foundation. "A lot of clients get treated like royalty. It's like *Succession,*" the person said, referring to the hit HBO show about a scheming media mogul and his children. "People scurrying around with clipboards, but also that these guys are really busy, and you're given a meeting spot, so you have to know going in what your meeting is about."

What comes through about Gates for many is the fear he inspires for a number of things: for the fact that he and French Gates ran an organization without accountability to outside shareholders or other stakeholders; for the fact of his brilliance and fame that many find intimidating; and for the type of arrogant behavior that colleagues of Gates from his Microsoft days might find familiar, but that terrifies those who work for him. Those who have worked for Gates at both Microsoft and the foundation point out that Gates's behavior hasn't changed much, but it was more acceptable in Microsoft's competitive culture; the foundation is full of people from the more genteel and collegial culture of the international development and academic communities. This dissonance between his public image and private persona led many foundation employees to remark in private that outwardly, Gates is a global statesman and inwardly, he is an absolute monarch.

"He's the scariest person in the world to provide a recommendation or briefing to because he scans a page and comes back at you saying something like, 'what you say in the footnote on page 9 does not match with the foot-note on page 28,'" one former foundation employee said. The low hum of fear was a constant presence inside the foundation, in case an email came in from the boss asking about a grant application, or he pointed out something in your field of expertise that you had overlooked. If Gates sent an email asking for something to be done, there might be a flurry of as many as 100 emails among employees—after taking him off the chain—trying to deci-pher what he meant, why he meant it, and how they should follow through. "Something that was a foregone conclusion to him required a lot of back and forth to understand," said another employee, who found it almost laughable that people walked around on tenterhooks. Because of his bias toward num-bers, Gates often wouldn't greenlight projects that didn't have enough data to support a use of funds, creating a conundrum for employees and, in the eyes of one former executive, reducing the ambition of philanthropy.

There was no handbook for how to deal with the foundation's cofound-ers, especially with Gates. Those who know Gates better said that the billion-aire respects people who come in doing their homework and hates it when people waste his time. A person who repeats information from a document already sent to Gates at a meeting will be the target of his ire. But Gates is also known to respect a good argument that a person could defend. He is somewhat mellower now, and people who have engaged with him more recently said that both French Gates and Buffett had a hand in showing him that it was possible to be a strong leader and be cordial. Still, many people spent years bristling at Gates's approach. Ultimately, it came down to an individual's level of tolerance. Some brushed it off. Others tried to outargue Gates or couldn't stand him. And there were yet others who kept their mouths shut but seethed silently. It was particularly challenging for those who joined the foundation at the peak of their careers, hired for their expertise—the very expertise that Gates appeared to disregard and enjoy outsmarting someone on. Often, during a meeting, he would keep probing about why a suggested solution was the best one, to the point that it frus-trated senior executives. One former senior employee compared the style of discussion to the Socratic method, often used in law schools by professors who push students to reasoning through dialogue. But while professors are great at asking questions in a thought-provoking way, Gates was far less polished in his delivery, and as a result, conversations with him could be an unpleasant experience, the former employee said. "It's like using the Socratic method . . . with an autocrat."

Chapter 5

Besties with Buffett

An Unusual Friendship

Bill Gates, dressed casually in pale-yellow sweater and slacks, told the cheering audience that he had been a paper boy in his youth. He knew how to toss a paper. But almost immediately after he had picked up a hefty 36-page edition of the *Omaha World-Herald* and begun folding it, he changed his mind. The pre-folded paper lying next to it looked easier.

"Is this fair?" Gates asked the onlookers. He aimed for the porch of a model manufactured home that was set up inside the CenturyLink Center in Omaha. It was the first weekend of May 2015, and the basketball court inside the giant venue had been transformed into a showroom displaying the wares of dozens of companies owned by Berkshire Hathaway. The jamboree known as the Berkshire Hathaway annual meeting was underway, and Gates and his friend Warren Buffett, the chairman and chief executive of the giant conglomerate, were slowly making their way through the throngs of adoring Berkshire shareholders, including dozens who were visiting from China.

Gates hoped to land his paper on the bull's-eye marked on the front of the home, 35 feet away. Instead, the paper sailed in the air to the right and landed outside the porch. "That's a [customer] complaint," said a representative of Berkshire Hathaway Media Group, the company that housed the Omaha paper, which Buffett had bought in 2012.

"It's easier without the steps," Gates complained. "They do some homes without the steps."

Buffett, who claimed to have delivered 500,000 papers as a kid, fared just as poorly. He threw a few papers, but they landed off the bull's-eye. The two men moved on, posing for photos with eager shareholders, shaking hands, and strolling through the Berkshire empire on display.

Theirs was an unusual friendship. Buffett was folksy and outgoing, and never passed up an opportunity to crack a joke. He liked to speak in aphorisms. He enjoyed breaking down complex investing principles into simple nuggets that anyone could understand. When he met a new person, Buffett would be genuinely curious about their background. He asked them questions and listened intently, eyebrows furrowed, to the answers. Banter came to him easily. But Buffett was averse to conflict.

Gates, 25 years his junior, had a far different public persona. Everyone interviewed for this book who interacted with him—whether at a gathering, in the office, in small group settings, or during interviews—said he can be charming and engaging in the moment, but small talk and repartee are not his forte. He isn't immediately interested in the person in front of him, but if you asked him a question, he might go on for minutes. Courtesies are lost on him. The journalist Ken Auletta likes to tell the story of how he paid a visit to Gates's office once. Deep into the conversation, Gates reached into a mini fridge to grab a Diet Coke. He didn't think to offer Auletta one.

Buffett and Gates had been friends since the summer of 1991, when they were introduced at a Fourth of July weekend gathering organized by Gates's mother, Mary Gates, at Hood Canal. The family had long vacationed at the scenic, outdoorsy location with natural waterways and hiking trails about two hours from Seattle. Buffett was the guest of a friend, Meg Greenfield, then the editorial page editor of *The Washington Post,* in which Berkshire Hathaway was an investor at the time. Buffett was also close to Katharine Graham, the publisher of the *Post* and another friend of the Gates family.[1] Mary had convinced her son to take time off his schedule to pay a visit. Planning to spend no more than a couple of hours, Gates came out by helicopter. When his mother wanted to introduce him to Buffett, he replied that he didn't want to meet a "stockbroker." But the two men hit it off immediately.[2] Settling into a patterned couch, Buffett dressed in a red polo shirt and dark trousers, his left foot propped up against the coffee table, and Gates in a tennis outfit—shorts and a white shirt, his white socks coming up to mid-calf, his mop of hair tousled—they talked for eleven hours straight at that first meeting.[3] Gates was surprised by the penetrating questions Buffett directed at him about the software business, and found himself warming to the avuncular midwestern billionaire. Each found the other's view of the world "fascinating." The other guests had to tear them apart. Once, recounting the story to students at the University of Nebraska, Lincoln, Gates called it an "unbelievable friendship." Buffett quipped: "The moral of that is, listen to your mother."

Despite the difference in ages, backgrounds, and lifestyles, the two billionaires forged a bond based on free-flowing conversation and a mutual love of bridge, business, problem-solving, and philanthropy. It was not unusual to see them golfing together at the annual Sun Valley conference. A few times a year, Gates would fly into Omaha on his private jet, making the pit stop on his way somewhere else to spend a few hours with his friend, who sometimes drove to the airport to pick Gates up. Gates, whose schedule was so tightly packed that he held meetings in five- and ten-minute slots, would block off time on his calendar to play online bridge with Buffett, whose days were far more fluid. One person with insight into their friendship said Buffett was enamored of his friend, viewing Gates in some ways as his intellectual heir, although to another person the friendship seemed "lopsided," with the younger man eager to earn Buffett's praise.

Buffett's life has relatively few billionaire trappings. In response to a question about his wealth posed by this reporter in 2015, Buffett wrote: "In addition to the house in Omaha, I bought a house in Laguna Beach in the early 1970s for about $175,000. The entire family used this annually until Susie Sr.'s [Susan Thompson Buffett, his first wife] death; now used primarily by Susie Jr. [Susan Alice Buffett, his daughter] and friends. Last year I bought a $60,000 pontoon boat from Forest River [a Berkshire company] to be used by the family at Susie's house at Lake Okoboji. I have a 6.25% interest in a Falcon 2000 operated by NetJets [another Berkshire company], having been a NetJets customer myself and for my family for about 20 years. And that's about it."[4] Buffett has since sold the Laguna home. By contrast, Gates has a more traditional billionaire's lifestyle, with multiple homes, planes, expensive art, and a big personal staff to oversee it all. The essence of their friendship, for Gates, was captured in a black-and-white photograph that sat in his office at his private firm Gates Ventures, a person who worked there recalled. Buffett is clearly in the middle of delivering a joke, and Gates has his head thrown back in laughter. Not an especially emotive person, his "laugh out loud" moments were often when he reacted to a Buffett joke, shrieking with joy.

In 2004, Gates joined the board of directors of Berkshire Hathaway, which Buffett described as an "act of friendship."[5] To do so, Gates had to step down from the board of Icos, the biotechnology company that developed Cialis and the only company other than Microsoft whose board he had been on. In his resignation letter to the Icos board, where he had been a director since 1990, Gates wrote that his decision had to do with "my interest in helping out in any way [Buffett] ever asks." By then, Gates had stepped down as chief executive of Microsoft, although he remained its chairman. In March 2020, Gates said he would step down from the boards of both Berkshire and Microsoft to focus more on his philanthropy.

The performative aspects of their friendship, like the newspaper tossing contest in 2015, long delighted Berkshire shareholders, who made their pilgrimage to Omaha from around the world for the conglomerate's annual meeting. One year, the duo handed out soft-serve ice cream from Dairy Queen—another Berkshire company—to shareholders. Sometimes, they played Ping-Pong or drove around in a golf cart. They usually walked side by side, Buffett in a suit and Gates in one of his trademark sweaters, mingling and chatting with shareholders. As attendees thronged Buffett, asking for selfies and autographs, Gates could often be seen standing off to the side, hands tucked under his armpits, happy to let the spotlight shine on his friend. Fans of Gates also couldn't get enough of their friendship, and his media handlers used the opportunity to post short videos of the billionaire duo's antics on Gates's blog.

For decades, Buffett would host a brunch for a group of Berkshire friends and family, including shareholders, on the Sunday of the annual Berkshire meeting weekend. The venue was the Happy Hollow Club, a private country club started by a group of Omaha businessmen in 1907, with landscaped gardens, a golf course, tennis courts, and a dress code. In the 1990s, the group of invitees was small, about 60 or so people. Over the years, it swelled to about 300, nearly filling the club's capacity. The attendees included a mix of Berkshire shareholders and executives, leaders of various companies, board directors, and other Buffett family members. Guests would pile up their plates with eggs, waffles, and bacon and walk over to find a table to sit at, mingling with others and waiting for a chance to say hello to Buffett.

One year, Lawrence Cunningham, a corporate governance expert and longtime Berkshire shareholder who regularly attended the brunch, found himself face-to-face with Gates. In 2016, Bayer, the pharmaceutical giant, had announced its intention to buy the agrochemical company Monsanto for $63 billion, and the acquisition had caught the attention of the financial and science press. Knowing his interest in agriculture given that it was one of the Gates Foundation's focus areas, Cunningham brought up the deal. He could tell Gates was immediately engaged, launching into a discussion about the merits of agricultural equipment and seeds, and the social versus economic value that the companies contributed. "He's a wonky dude, small talk is not his thing, but if you can get him engaged in an intricate business discussion, then he's all over it," Cunningham said. "You see it in his stage personality as well. He's a software guy, an introverted personality, he'd rather sit and read. Warren is a stage performer, he's sold everything, including the concept of Berkshire as an institution. Warren is the introvert's dream because under his halo it's safe."

Philanthropic Earthquake

The New York Public Library stands in midtown Manhattan, a national historic landmark in front of which tourists linger, awestruck, even as office workers scurry by, inured to its majesty. Built in the Beaux arts style, with its tall columns and iconic lions sculpted out of pink Tennessee marble, the library opened in 1911. But on the morning of June 26, 2006, an unremarkable summer's day in New York, the 200 or so philanthropy executives, reporters, and others gathered inside the marble-lined main hall of the library were riveted less by the building's quiet magnificence and the striking murals on its ceilings than by the moment they were about to witness.

For days leading up to the event, the media had been buzzing. Invitations sent by Gates Foundation staffers had been cryptic, saying only that Buffett, along with Gates and French Gates, would be making an announcement. The day before, the journalist Carol Loomis, a longtime friend of Buffett's, revealed a little by publishing an article in *Fortune* magazine explaining what the Omaha billionaire planned to do with his enormous fortune. Now, the audience was about to hear from Buffett himself. Shortly after 11 A.M., Buffett, who had flown in from Omaha for the press conference, dressed in one of the boxy suits he favored, got straight to the point. He had always intended to give 99 percent of his fortune, then estimated at $44 billion, to philanthropy, during his lifetime or upon his death. Now, he had identified the Gates Foundation as the biggest recipient of his generosity during his lifetime.

The world's second-richest man at the time was handing over his money to the world's richest man, entrusting him with the challenging, fraught, and complicated work of finding the right causes to give to. The symbolism of the location they had chosen for the announcement could hardly be overlooked. The New York Public Library has long stood as a testament to the harnessing of private dollars for the public good. It was built with contributions from the Astor, Tilden, and Lenox foundations. Later, the nineteenth-century steel magnate Andrew Carnegie would donate $5 million to set up a branch system around the main library. Today, its flagship midtown Manhattan building is named after Stephen A. Schwarzman, the billionaire cofounder of private equity behemoth Blackstone, who gave $100 million to the institution in 2008.

Years before their announcement, Buffett had presented his young friend with a copy of "The Gospel of Wealth" by Carnegie. In the essay, originally published in 1889 as a pair of articles in *The North American Review*, Carnegie explained that it was the duty of a wealthy man to give back to society. In the first article, Carnegie provided a moral defense of the wealth created by capitalism by arguing that everyone is better off under a market-based economy. A society in which individualism, private property, wealth accumulation, and competition are preserved is the "condition of affairs under which the best interests of the race are promoted, but which inevitably gives wealth to the few," Carnegie wrote. In other words, unequal outcomes are the natural byproduct of the laws of capitalism, and even if it appeared unfair to individuals, it had to be accepted because it was beyond the power of people to alter, and because it was better than everyone being equally poor. After establishing his defense of capitalism and equating it with "civilization," Carnegie turns to the question at hand: What is the proper mode of administering the wealth that has landed in the hands of a few?

He argued that to leave a fortune to one's children is to "leave to my son a curse as the almighty dollar," because it would destroy them. And to leave it to public use upon death is just a means of disposal and not an active use of the funds by the generator of the fortune. Carnegie thought it was a disgrace for a man to die rich. Instead, he wrote, it was the duty of the wealthy man to give back to society during his lifetime—not through taxes, not by making less, but through personal philanthropy. The "true antidote for the temporary unequal distribution of wealth, the reconciliation of the rich and the poor—a reign of harmony" is for the wealthy man to disburse his fortune. "They have it in their power during their lives to busy themselves in organizing benefactions from which the masses of their fellows will derive lasting advantage, and thus dignify their own lives." He warns that giving money away indiscriminately or thoughtlessly would be akin to "almsgiving." Rather, the benefactor must give money to those who would help themselves and in a way that uplifts the general condition of people.

"Thus is the problem of Rich and Poor to be solved," Carnegie wrote. "The laws of accumulation will be left free; the laws of distribution free. Individualism will continue, but the millionaire will be but a trustee for the poor; entrusted for a season with a great part of the increased wealth of the community, but administering it for the community far better than it could or would have done for itself. The best minds will thus have reached a stage in the development of the race . . . thoughtful and earnest men into whose hands it [the wealth] flows . . . by using it year by year for the general good."

His proposals caused a stir at the time because they were considered radical, but more than a century later, *The Gospel of Wealth* became the intellectual bedrock of much of the philanthropic giving by the wealthy. Carnegie put his own thinking into practice, donating not only to the New York Public Library, but also founding think tanks like the Carnegie Endowment for International Peace, one of the earliest examples of a modern private institution built for the public good.[6]

Although Buffett had long believed in the ideas of Carnegie, he had little interest in overseeing the disbursement of his own wealth. He liked to stay within what he called his "circle of competence," arguing that a person shouldn't assume that, because they're good at one thing, they are good at everything. Rather, Buffett had hoped to leave the Berkshire fortune to his first wife, Susan, an abortion rights activist who ran their foundation, to give away, expecting that she would outlive him. But when Susan, who had been diagnosed with cancer, died suddenly of a stroke in July 2004 at the age of 72, Buffett, bereft and blindsided, was forced to revisit his philanthropic plans. His three children, Susan (known informally as Susie Jr.), Howard, and Peter, each had a foundation, but the entities were fledglings. The foundation that his deceased wife had run—called the Buffett Foundation before he renamed it the Susan Thompson Buffett Foundation in her honor—was bigger, but not prepared to handle the billions of dollars he was ready to give away. At the same time, Gates had been paying more attention to the shape and structure of his philanthropy after quitting his job as chief executive of Microsoft in 2000. Buffett watched as his friend built an organization from the ground up that had already begun to reshape global philanthropy. By 2005, when he reflected on his own mortality in his annual letter to Berkshire shareholders and told them about his intention to give every Berkshire share that he owned to philanthropies, the solution to his conundrum was obvious, even if his decision was impulsive, according to several people who witnessed the events at the time. Once he had made up his mind, Buffett held multiple conversations with both Gates and French Gates about their work, their ambitions for the foundation, and whether they would be able to build out the infrastructure necessary to support the billions they would have to give away because of his annual gifts. It was only after he was satisfied with their long-term goals that Buffett took the momentous step. In doing so, Buffett was repurposing his business strategy to his philanthropy: Just as he picked businesses and investments for Berkshire based on the quality of the managers running them, Buffett was picking Gates to run his philanthropy for him. "What Warren has always done is find out who is the best at doing this, that, and the other, and get them to do it," said Cunningham, the Berkshire shareholder and a professor emeritus at George Washington University. "When it came to philanthropy, that's what he did too." Cunningham described Buffett's position as "I don't know anything about malaria and I'm not gonna find out."

That morning at the New York Public Library, Buffett outlined a complicated plan, which was premised on his faith that the value of Berkshire, the gigantic conglomerate he had built and whose success had made him an investing legend, would only keep rising. Rather than hand over his fortune all at once, Buffett created a formula that would allow him to give away far more over time, until he died. He explained clearly and methodically how it would all work. Berkshire had two classes of shares, A and B, and Buffett's wealth was tied up in A shares. (At the time, a single A share was equal to 30 B shares, but following a stock split in 2010, one A share became equivalent to 1,500 B shares. The A shares can be converted to B shares, but not vice versa.) Buffett had earmarked 10 million B shares for the Gates Foundation, and smaller amounts for the four family foundations. In the first year, he would give the Gates Foundation five percent of those earmarked shares. Each year thereafter, the foundation would get five percent of the remaining shares. The bet, Buffett explained, was that even though he would be donating a diminishing number of Berkshire shares each year, they would appreciate enough over time that their dollar value—and thus the amount going to the foundation—would increase. Buffett was right: One A share of Berkshire traded on average at $95,000 in 2006. In 2023, a single A share was valued at more than half a million dollars—almost three times the median net worth of American families in 2022.[7]

Buffett's gift to the Gates Foundation came with three conditions: One, that either Gates or French Gates would remain an active participant in the foundation. Two, that the funds that came from him each year had to qualify as charitable dollars rather than gifts, which are taxed differently. And three, that the value of his annual contributions had to be given away within the year, rather than sitting in the foundation's endowment, in addition to the five percent of net assets that foundations are required to give away under tax law. Between 2006 and 2023, Buffett had given more than $39 billion to the Gates Foundation. By comparison, Gates and French Gates gave $39 billion between 1994 and 2022, including $22 billion to get their foundation going in 2000. In some years, the former couple gave the foundation less than half a billion. In 2021, they pledged $15 billion to the foundation's endowment, and the following year, they transferred that money, as well as another $5 billion Gates contributed. "There is one not-very-well-known but incredibly important reason why the foundation has been able to be so ambitious," Gates wrote on his blog in 2022. "Although it is named the Bill & Melinda Gates Foundation, basically half of our resources to date have come from Warren Buffett's gifts."[8] As of 2023, the foundation's annual activities had been funded in large part by Buffett's gifts.

In the hoopla surrounding Buffett's announcement in 2006, an important detail of his plan escaped attention: Although the investor had pledged 99 percent of his wealth to philanthropy, his commitment to the five foundations would stand only as long as he lived. Buffett, then seventy-five, said he would make separate plans for how to distribute the shares that remained after his death. Some months later, Buffett told Berkshire shareholders in his 2006 annual letter that he had stipulated in his will that all Berkshire shares that remained in his pocket when he died would have to be used for philanthropy within a decade of his death. (In 2021, two months shy of his ninetieth birthday, Buffett said he had reached only the midpoint of giving away all his Berkshire shares.) Only decades later would the broader implications of that lifetime pledge become an issue of significance for future funding at the Gates Foundation, the four Buffett family foundations, and the responsibilities of his three children. It would also come to strain Buffett's friendship with Gates.

But on that summer's day in 2006, as the journalists, nonprofits, philanthropists, television pundits, and academics discussed how the Gates Foundation would begin to spend those billions, the trio had already orchestrated a media blitz. They took out a front-page ad in *The New York Times.* They held another press conference at the Sheraton New York Times Square Hotel. That evening, they went on the *Charlie Rose* show. At these appearances, Gates was by turns excited and enthusiastic about the possibilities the Buffett gift had unleashed. "We're going to do our best to make sure it's well spent," he said, responding to questions from reporters on how the foundation planned to disburse the money. "We want to show people that philanthropy can be a lot of fun and it can have a lot of impact." When Rose asked Buffett how he arrived at his decision, the billionaire said his thinking was straightforward. Wealth had no meaning unless it was translated into something, he said. Money had more utility to others than to him, so giving it away was the only logical option. "In big-scale philanthropy, it's not the batting average that counts but the slugging percentage," he said, borrowing from baseball terminology. A big foundation should aim for a high slugging percentage, meaning that it should gauge its success by the impact it makes rather than the number of projects it funds. Gates and French Gates were ideal leaders, he told Rose, because they had the stature and eloquence to inspire others into action. "Giving money away is easy, giving time is not," Buffett said, adding that the duo's hands-on approach went well beyond the involvement of Carnegie and Rockefeller in their philanthropic endeavors. Although Buffett wouldn't be involved in the day-to-day decisions of how the money would be spent, he would join Gates and French Gates as a trustee. Until he stepped down from that position in 2021, he typically only attended the foundation's annual meeting, but he served both as a silent partner and sounding board for Gates. After all, their legacies were forever intertwined.

A Foundation on Speed

When the Gates Foundation got its start in 2000, even Gates would probably not have told you that nearly a quarter of a century later, he and French Gates would have created an entity that can claim to have saved millions of lives, shaped the global public health agenda, and propelled the Microsoft cofounder to a level of renown and respect typically reserved for Nobel Peace Prize winners. Founded on the animating principle that "all lives have equal value," a phrase dear to the former couple, the mission of the Gates Foundation is to fight poverty, disease, and inequity around the world, and "to create a world where every person has the opportunity to live a healthy, productive life." Gates and French Gates called themselves "impatient optimists." By 2005, the year before Buffett's announcement, the foundation was already the world's largest philanthropic organization of its kind, with an endowment of about $22 billion coming from Microsoft stock. But its framework and their ambitions—which the Buffett money would help unleash—were still in the making. In the years following the Buffett gift, the foundation scrambled to build a far bigger chassis that could accommodate the giant waves of money that were about to hit their shores annually and effectively give away many more billions of dollars. In 2006, it gave away about $1.6 billion; by 2009, it projected it would have to make $3.2 billion worth of grants per year.

In 2008, Gates gave up his day-to-day role at Microsoft, although he remained chairman of its board until 2014. And with their children going to school, French Gates had more time on her hands to get involved in the foundation's affairs. Suddenly, the two of them were walking around the foundation's offices several days a week, taking a much deeper interest in the various programs that it was making grants to, and directing its next phase of growth. Their hands-on involvement at least partly reflected the tremendous pressure Gates and French Gates felt to live up to the faith that Buffett had placed in them. Between 2007 and 2010, the Gates Foundation had the messiness of a rat's nest and the pace of a weed's growth. It hired people at a frenetic pace; the employee count went from 300 to roughly 1,500. Its new hires included academics, policymakers, experts in international development, and communications advisors. They joined to expand the foundation's programs, defining new strategies and foci in global health, agriculture, and development.

Prabhu Pingali, a professor at Cornell University, joined the Gates Foundation in 2008. Pingali, who worked at the United Nations Food and Agricultural Organization in Rome at that time, recalled a visit from foundation executives who wanted a crash course on agriculture, and to see if there was a unique role for philanthropy in farming. He ended up providing an overview of the dynamics of global agricultural development, including food prices, biotechnology, farming practices, and more, and eventually moved over to the foundation. When he joined the agricultural development team, there were 15 people, Pingali said. When he left in 2013, there were 80. Mark Suzman, a former journalist and official at the United Nations, also joined the foundation around 2007 to build out its global development program and set up offices around the world. In 2020, Suzman became the foundation's fourth chief executive. Many experts who joined during that burst of growth said that a big part of their job, in addition to determining programs and strategies, was to educate the former couple about the complexities of international development, education, financial literacy, and agriculture. These were relatively new areas of focus where data was often patchy, and knowledge of local contexts was essential to understanding why philanthropic approaches needed to be more flexible and fluid from region to region.

To house the new hires, the foundation, which had been operating out of a patchwork of five office buildings, began constructing a new campus in 2008. The campus, which became operational in 2011, is built on what was once a contaminated, 12-acre parking lot. Located across from a cluster of Seattle attractions including the iconic 605-foot Space Needle building, and a museum and garden that house Dale Chihuly's vivid glass sculptures, the campus has 900,000 square feet of office space. It was built at a cost of $500 million, $350 million of which came from the Gateses' personal account. Its two boomerang-shaped office buildings, which house about 1,800 people, are visible from atop the Needle. The foundation takes pride in the buildings' energy-efficient construction; each building has a green roof with mechanisms to harvest more than one million gallons of rainwater. The original plan was for there to be three buildings, but they settled on two after Buffett advised restraint, one former employee who was present during that time said. The foundation had come a long way from its early days, when it operated out of a small, one-room office above a pizza restaurant with about a dozen people.

The media scrutiny was intense. Senior reporters and columnists, curious about the foundation's plans and its frenzy, began calling. The work had become overwhelming for the handful of people on the communications team, who often took days to clear up the backlog of reporter calls. Initial publicity efforts were piecemeal and more reactive than strategic, and geared toward highlighting the work of its grantees. But with all the changes, it became evident that the foundation needed a clearer and more proactive communications strategy. Over a two-year span, the number of media professionals increased from around eight people to about 80. They set about commissioning polls to get a sense of the best approach. It appeared that people wanted to hear from Gates rather than from program officers who were overseeing individual strategies, or the nonprofits on the ground who received foundation grants. That did create some frustration among people inside the foundation who felt that their programs, which needed their own communications to help get the word out, were starved of attention because of the focus on the two individuals, and because Gates and French Gates didn't have the time to promote every line of activity the foundation was working on.

Today, the foundation's resources dwarf those of the Ford Foundation, the Robert Wood Johnson foundation, the Wellcome Trust, and other big global foundations. Its annual budget exceeds that of the World Health Organization (WHO). Not unlike an undulating octopus, the Seattle-based organization has its tentacles in a variety of global issues, from vaccines and public health to agricultural development and food security, from poverty alleviation and sanitation to gender equality and digital accounts for the unbanked. With offices scattered across the globe and a presence in 130 countries, it has built an enormous—and sometimes invisible—network of ties with governments, multilateral institutions, corporations, countries, universities, and nonprofits. That allows the foundation to act as an influential go-between among various parties. The foundation has largely decided to shoulder the burden of sustaining and improving the sometimes chaotic global infrastructure of public health and development, by creating new alliances and propping up old ones, providing funds for research into cures for overlooked diseases, and lending its experts to help shape policy. Its way of doing things has cemented "big" or institutionalized philanthropy as distinct from the passive and ad hoc charitable giving long practiced by individual wealthy donors.

In 2019, the foundation—whose influence, size and practices had already invited criticism—took an even bigger hit to its reputation when the news emerged, just weeks after Jeffrey Epstein was found dead in his Manhattan jail cell, that Gates had met with the convicted sex offender and pedophile several times. Gates clarified that he had met Epstein purely to discuss philanthropy, and that he was sorry for his poor judgment. Less than two years later, in May 2021, Gates and French Gates announced their divorce. The following month, Buffett said he would step down as the third co-trustee of the Gates Foundation, adding that there was no reason for him to stay in the role but that his pledged gifts would continue. "My goals are 100% in sync with those of the foundation, and my physical participation is in no way needed to achieve those goals," he said in a statement. Buffett added that Suzman, who had been appointed chief executive in 2020, was an "outstanding recent selection who has my full support." In July 2021, Gates and French Gates made their $15 billion commitment to the foundation's endowment. In January 2022, the foundation created a new board of trustees to improve its corporate governance practices, and to bring fresh perspectives that would inform the next phase of its growth. In a blog post that year announcing that the Gates Foundation would spend $9 billion a year by 2026, Gates expressed his gratitude to his friend. "Warren, I can never adequately express how much I appreciate your friendship and guidance as well as your generosity."[9]

Although civil, the public statements, taken together, contained a sense of an ending, as though viewers of the long theater of a friendship and a world-changing philanthropic partnership were witnessing the final act. And Buffett was, in fact, reminding the world—and in particular the employees and new trustees of the Gates Foundation—that the lifetime pledges he had made in 2006 could come to an end anytime given his age, and that they shouldn't count on Berkshire billions in making long-term funding plans, according to several people with knowledge of Buffett's motives. During Thanksgiving week in 2022, as many Americans scattered across the country for the annual feast with family and friends, Berkshire Hathaway put out a regulatory filing

disclosing that Buffett would donate more shares to his four family foundations. He had already increased his gifts to his children's foundations once
before, in 2012. The following Thanksgiving, Buffett put out a news release
announcing another round of gifts to the four entities. "They supplement certain of the *lifetime* pledges I made in 2006 and that continue until my death
(at 93, I feel good but fully realize I am playing in extra innings)."

He also spelled out the plan for the Berkshire shares that would be impossible to give away during his lifetime, given that he had only hit the
midpoint in 2021. Valued at around $100 billion in 2023, those shares
would be placed into a trust. His three children would be the co-trustees,
and they would have a decade after their father's death to disburse those
funds to charity. There was no mention of the Gates Foundation. Buffett's
children are unanimous that none of the remaining shares will go to the
Gates Foundation, according to people aware of their thinking. Always deliberate with his language, Buffett emphasized the word "lifetime" to avoid
any miscommunication or confusion about which philanthropies stood to
get his money, partly because there was a longstanding assumption within
the Gates Foundation that it would always get Buffett's money, three of the
people said. In a footnote to its combined financial statements for 2022 and
2021 that was released in May 2023, the Gates Foundation Trust, which
manages the endowment for the foundation, noted for the first time that the
Buffett money would no longer come in after his death. "As this gift is con-
ditional and applies only during his lifetime, its receipt cannot be assured in
advance of each year's installment of the gift," the note said. "After his death,
Mr. Buffett's executors will direct the disposition of his assets."

There were other factors that strained their friendship. For more than a
decade, Buffett—known for his love of lean and efficient operations free of
bureaucracy—had been bothered by what he saw as the foundation's bloat
and inflated operating costs, a fact that was well-known in the philanthropic
community. The foundation had settled into a groove and even become com-
placent, he told staffers, which reduced its appetite for taking the kinds of
risks that could lead to more effective philanthropy, and that he had hoped
his donations would be used for. He was also upset by comments relayed

to him by others who had found Gates rude and condescending, according to multiple accounts. Buffett had long offered Gates advice on how to be a friend. Be aware of how your closest friends think of you, Buffett would tell Gates, and be good to them. When this reporter suggested to Buffett in April 2024 that Gates's "genuine 'laugh out loud' moments are when he's around you," Buffett chose to reply in the past tense: "We have had a huge number of laughs together and he has a keen sense of humor," he wrote. At the same time, Gates, who has posted at least one goofy video of him and Buffett every year on his *GatesNotes* blog since it launched in 2010, did not write a single entry solely about his friend in 2021, 2022, or 2023. In previous years, his team would also post at least one video of the two from the Berkshire annual meeting or other events where they spoke together. In his last post dedicated to Buffett, in 2020 during the pandemic, Gates filmed himself in an apron baking an Oreo cookie cake for his friend's ninetieth birthday. The two remain friends and talk on the phone—Alex Reid, a Gates spokeswoman, said that they speak "as frequently (if not more frequently) than they ever have"—and Gates still visits Buffett in Omaha occasionally, but Buffett typically does not initiate the outreach, two of the people said, although they added that Buffett has minimized all his interactions given his advanced age. Speaking of the friendship between the two, another person said: "All tea leaves point to disturbance in the mythology."

Pledging for Publicity

Ted Turner was a bit of a public scold in the 1990s. At the beginning of that decade, the brash and outspoken media mogul and billionaire founder of CNN had embraced philanthropy in a big way, starting with the creation of the Turner Foundation in 1990. In September 1997, the United Nations Association of the United States of America, a nonprofit tied to the U.N., recognized his contributions by honoring him with their global leadership award. The U.N. had been under enormous financial strain for some time, and it was on Turner's mind when he announced at the event that he would pledge $1 billion to the multilateral organization to support its various programs, from cleaning up land mines to helping refugees. As one of the largest donations from an individual at the time, Turner's move made front-page news. That evening, Turner also vowed to raise more funds for the international agency. And he used the pulpit to bully other mega-rich individuals into giving more to charity. "Everyone who's rich in the world can expect a call from me," he told the black-tie crowd gathered at New York's Marriott Marquis hotel.[10]

It wasn't the first time Turner had tweaked other billionaires for not doing enough on the philanthropic front. In 1996, he proposed creating an "Ebenezer Scrooge Prize" for the most tight-fisted billionaires. In particular, he picked on Gates and Buffett, then the richest and second-richest individuals in the world, calling them "skinflint" billionaires for not giving their money away. "They are fighting every year to be the richest man in the world," he told the *New York Times* columnist Maureen Dowd. "Why don't they sign a joint pact to each give away a billion and then move down the Forbes list equally?"[11]

In the summer of 2010, Gates and Buffett went one step further, inviting other billionaires to commit publicly to giving away at least half of their wealth to charitable causes during their lifetimes or in their wills. The highly publicized pressure campaign, called the Giving Pledge, was meant to get the billionaire class thinking more deeply about philanthropy. The idea had come about after a small group dinner for about seven couples in 2009 hosted by David Rockefeller.[12] As they went around the table, each guest or couple talked about their philosophy of giving. Many in the group knew each other only glancingly, but they took comfort in their shared status and spoke in a spirit of candor, sharing stories about their families, how their parents had influenced their attitude toward charity, and the problem of how much to leave their heirs. It took two hours to go around the table.

Even before the Giving Pledge, the tie-up between Buffett and Gates had already roused a lot of interest among other billionaires, many of whom reached out to the foundation wondering if they too could give their money to its endowment. Inspired by the chord they had struck, the trio, including French Gates, tossed around ideas of how they could get the broader billionaire community to make better plans for their philanthropy. In particular, Buffett, who would soon enter his eighth decade, wanted to get more people thinking about how to give their money away when they were younger and their thinking was clearer, rather than toward the end of their lives when their decision-making abilities might be diminished.

Gates and Buffett borrowed heavily from the philanthropic ideas of Charles Feeney, an Irish American who had made his fortune building the global network of Duty Free Shoppers (DFS), the airport stores where passengers could buy Scotch whisky, a Swiss watch, or a bottle of French perfume while waiting to board an international flight. Feeney, who had set up his foundation, the Atlantic Philanthropies, in 1982, had popularized the concept of "giving while living." When the world came to know about his philanthropy in 1997, scorekeepers of wealth had to revise their estimates quickly; the man whose net worth they had pegged in the billions had assets of about $5 million.[13] It wasn't that their calculations were wrong. Feeney had indeed been a billionaire once. But since 1982, he had been stealthily and steadily climbing down the ladder of wealth by earmarking more and more of his DFS shares for charity. There were no press releases announcing his donations. His name wasn't on the door of a building. He made grants through the Atlantic Philanthropies, to which his name was not publicly tied. Universities and nonprofits that received his money were often told the gifts came from a group of wealthy clients. He established General Atlantic, a private equity firm, to manage his investments and fund his philanthropic activity; as a so-called limited partner in the firm, he could cloak his identity. Anonymity was so important to Feeney that his representatives sometimes paid by cashier's check. He set up his foundations in ways that would minimize regulatory disclosures. Feeney was required to reveal his philanthropic activities in 1997 when Möet Hennessy Louis Vuitton (LVMH), the global luxury giant, bought DFS. In 2002, Feeney said he would spend down his foundation's assets by 2016. By the time the Atlantic Philanthropies ended its grant-making that year, hitting its target, it had given out $8 billion. By 2020, it had shut its doors. Feeney, then 90, had achieved his goal of "giving while living." He died in 2023. Gates has said of Feeney: "Chuck has been a beacon to us for many years; he was living the Giving Pledge long before we launched it."[14]

Buffett and Gates conducted what was essentially a get-out-the-vote campaign to mobilize other billionaires to sign the pledge. Buffett encouraged people to write letters addressing how they had arrived at their decision, arguing that written pledges were important for the historical record, and because they might inspire future generations to think about philanthropy the same way Carnegie's *Gospel of Wealth* had inspired him and Gates. To those who were resistant, he gently suggested that there was little point in taking their money with them to the coffin. The software billionaire Larry Ellison said he took the pledge simply because Buffett had personally asked him to do so. Gates took a different approach to draw billionaires into the philanthropic circle. He and French Gates hosted dinners with small groups of wealthy people around the country, typically no more than a dozen, to gauge their interest in signing the pledge. If some seemed interested, Gates would follow up with a call and provide more details about the mechanics.

In talking about the pledge, Gates doffed his cap to Turner, although he cast philanthropy as "fun" rather than an obligation. "Ted Turner started that by scolding people," he said once. "We're trying to complement that by showing people how much fun it can be." If the intention of the Giving Pledge was noble, its timing was fortuitous. The financial crisis of 2008 had ravaged the economy, plunging it into the Great Recession. People were seething at Wall Street's greed, which they held directly accountable for the housing crisis and ensuing mess. Top earners had come in for personal attacks in a world that felt fundamentally inequitable, with rising student debt, out-of-control healthcare costs, and taxes that appeared to benefit the wealthy. The Occupy Wall Street movement was still a year away, but it would come to symbolize the growing frustration of people who had no way of holding the wealthy accountable for their actions. Against the background of that simmering resentment, the Pledge campaign scored some publicity points, even if others cynically called it little more than an image management stunt for billionaires.[15]

The initial group of 40 signatories included billionaires from around the country, with the majority coming from California and New York. By the end of 2010, 17 additional billionaires or billionaire couples, including Mark Zuckerberg and his wife, Priscilla Chan, had signed the pledge.

The pledge was originally limited to U.S. billionaires but opened to global billionaires in 2013. As of 2023, 243 billionaires had signed the pledge—a substantial number but still only a fraction of the world's 2,600 billionaires. A large number are from the United States, but there is a growing contingent from other countries with an emerging billionaire class, including India and China. There were a couple of years when the pledgers numbered more than two dozen, but on average, there have been 15 signatories a year. In 2023, there were only seven pledgers; in 2022, there were five—the lowest numbers since the campaign began.

Their letters, carefully worded and posted for all to see on a website dedicated to the Giving Pledge, follow a similar pattern, in keeping with the guidance Buffett had initially provided about the themes to address. Some billionaires describe how they got their start and built fortunes beyond their wildest dreams, and how they hoped to make the world a better place by giving it away. Others highlight the role of a good education, opportunity, and hard work in building their riches, and the responsibility they feel to give back to society. They express gratitude, underscore the importance of values, occasionally acknowledge their privilege, nod to those who helped along the way, reflect on what led to their decision and what they hope to direct their philanthropy to. Often, the letters are as humble as the talk is lofty. Some of the letters have the feel of an acceptance speech. Many of them speak in the jargon of business, of investing their dollars in innovative solutions and building platforms for giving. There are sprinklings of billionaire hubris— the idea that they have been handed gifts of talent that should be used to improve the lot of others. Many letter writers strike a self-aggrandizing note when describing their generous intentions; Taylor Swift may as well have been referring to them in her song lyric, "Did you hear my covert narcissism I disguise as altruism like some kind of congressman?" They call philanthropy fun, fulfilling, worthwhile, and an experience of pleasure unlike any other.

"Everyone is dealt a group of cards at birth," Nicolas Berggruen, the investor once known as the "homeless billionaire" because he had no fixed address, wrote in his six-sentence letter. "What one does with them is up to each one of us; and the sum of those choices, constitute our lives." In his letter, David

Rubenstein, a cofounder of the private equity giant Carlyle, wrote that he had already committed to giving most of his wealth away before Gates talked to him about signing the pledge. He agreed to sign it, Rubenstein wrote, because he hoped that the publicity around it would encourage all Americans—not just the wealthy ones—to give more. "And if every person with the ability to make some philanthropic gifts does so, the country will be much better for these gifts, and the donor will surely feel much better about himself or herself," Rubenstein wrote, with patriotic flourish. Many other Wall Street billionaires also took the pledge. Bill Gross, the bond fund manager who cofounded PIMCO, wrote his 2020 letter by hand, explaining how he initially resisted signing, but his thinking had evolved over time. "I have evolved/aged." Feeney, whose philanthropy had served as an inspiration for the Giving Pledge, wrote a letter in 2011 although he had already given much of his wealth away by then. He encouraged billionaires not just to give money away, but to also "fully engage in sustained philanthropic efforts during their lifetimes." Turner, also among the original group of signatories, wrote about how his father's actions, including supporting the education of two African American students at his alma mater in the 1950s, instilled in him the value of charitable work. Turner then claimed a bit of the credit for, as he wrote, "putting other people on notice" when he first called on others to give more, way back in 1997.

Taken together, the letters provide a collective view of how billionaires would like the world to perceive them as philanthropists: thoughtful, grateful, and generous. Not a single letter mentions the tax benefits of charitable donations, or the reputational bump provided by highly publicized giveaways. For the most part, the letters don't address questions about systemic inequalities that create hurdles to achievement, or the conditions that allowed them to accumulate so much wealth in the first place, focusing instead on the role of individual opportunity, good education, and hard work.

"The explanations recorded remain within a realm of what signatories may consider a socially desirable account of their generosity," Hans Peter Schmitz and Elena M. McCollim write in their 2021 study of the Giving Pledge letters.[16] The authors call it a tale of good intentions with no ability for others to follow through on whether anything has been delivered.

In the more than thirteen years since the Giving Pledge was launched with much fanfare, the public conversation around economic inequality has only become more trenchant and the exponential increase in billionaire wealth has come in for particular scrutiny. The biggest question is whether the achievements of the pledge—essentially a movement by the wealthy for the wealthy—should be assessed, and if so, how. From the beginning, Buffett, Gates, and French Gates clarified and defended the pledge as no more than an ethical and moral commitment, the goal of which was to prompt billionaires to think more systematically about giving and engage with their ilk to learn about approaches to philanthropy. The website of the Giving Pledge underscores that it is not legally binding, and it is not a platform that holds people accountable to their words. The campaign is also clear that it does not track whether billionaires have in fact given their money away. Its deliberately fuzzy and open-ended nature has invited criticism for leaving pledgers with a lot of wiggle room. (Notably, Buffett is one of the few billionaires who laid out his plan in full detail.)

The pledge deserves scrutiny at the very least because of the free publicity it generates for billionaires who sign on, with no way to test if they have followed through on their commitment or assess its impact on the ground, even as it has become something of a rite of passage for billionaire philanthropy. For starters, the pledge does not specify whether "half of one's wealth" should be measured at the point when a billionaire wrote their letter, or when the person starts to give money away, or if it's an average of the two, or a changing target. The question becomes meaningful given the rise of billionaire wealth. At the end of 2022, the collective net worth of the top 10 American billionaires who had signed the pledge was more than $720 billion. Collectively represented, the net worth of the same 10 individuals at the time they signed the pledge was roughly $150 billion. In other words, the amount billionaires pick to give away would differ significantly based on what the cutoff point for net worth is.[17]

Buffett addressed the issue in 2021 when he announced that year's gifts to the five foundations. The total amounts he gave to philanthropy, at the moments he chose to give them over the years (with instructions that the money be spent in short order), added up to $41 billion. Had he waited until June 2021, when he wrote the letter, to give the same money away, it would have been $100 billion.

"Would society ultimately have benefitted more if I had waited longer to distribute the shares?" He acknowledged the complexity of the question but said those were decisions each donor had to make individually. "Deciding when to switch from building philanthropic-destined funds to depleting them involves a complicated calculation based on the nature of the assets involved, family matters, the seldom-confessed instinct to not 'let go' and a host of other variables. One size definitely does not fit all."[18] It is also a rich irony that despite the billions of dollars that many have earmarked for philanthropy, many have not slipped down the billionaire list; their money is coming in much faster than it is going out the door.[19] The rise in wealth has invited more incisive criticism.

Wealth-X, which tracks the wealth of the world's richest people, has estimated that $600 billion had been pledged as of 2020. That might sound like a lot, but headline numbers like that can be misleading because there is very little public data—not to mention scant details in the letters—about how much of those earmarked funds have made their way to the nonprofits and other direct recipients that can immediately put the money to work. Foundations are required to give away at minimum 5 percent of their assets every year to maintain their tax-exempt, charitable status. Dollars directed to a billionaire's private foundation are counted as philanthropic dollars for tax purposes. Many billionaires also put money into donor-advised funds, which allows the giver to get the charitable tax benefits immediately, without imposing a time frame within which the money has to be disbursed, allowing money to sit in foundation endowments and donor-advised funds in perpetuity, doing little good in the world.

Aaron Dorfman, who leads the National Committee for Responsive Philanthropy, a watchdog organization, said that's exactly what has happened; to the extent that dollars can be traced from a pledger to the nonprofit world, not much of it has actually moved. Instead, a big chunk of the money pledged is lodged in foundations or inside donor-advised funds, he said. An outspoken critic of the Giving Pledge, Dorfman allowed for the fact that the practice of philanthropy has gotten more sophisticated in the past decade or so. But he took the view that the Pledge campaign, in a sense, has acted as a "release valve" for pressure that might otherwise result from public policy changes that would prevent people from getting wealthy in the first place. "If we have this sense in the society that most billionaires are going to give money away, then we don't have to change policy to get them to do it."

A 2020 study of the Giving Pledge by the Institute for Policy Studies, a progressive think tank, pointed out another loophole: As billionaire wealth has grown, the charitable deductions billionaires can take has also increased in absolute dollars. Hypothetically, the study said, that could represent a hole of hundreds of billions of dollars of lost tax revenue for the government, which would have to be filled by the rest of the country's income earners.

Pledge or not, the massive wealth accumulation has created another problem: How to give? Giving money away takes time, work, and creativity. It's one thing to set up a foundation and quite another to build the infrastructure and carry out the due diligence to give the money away wisely and effectively. David Friedman, who cofounded Wealth-X, a platform that sells data to companies that target the ultrawealthy, said that when the Giving Pledge was announced and a lot of people committed to it, they didn't really think about the implementation side of things. As a result, Friedman said, the Giving Pledge is "basically stalled."

Signatories of the pledge whose donations can be tracked appear to have given much of their money to traditional causes, including university endowments and research, rather than toward big transformative social change. Some of the richest Americans, including Bezos, Ballmer, Page, and Brin, had sidestepped the Giving Pledge as of 2023, although each engages in some philanthropy. Nike's Phil Knight and Starbucks' Howard Schultz were also among those who didn't feel the need to join the club, or have Gates tell them to give their money away, according to a consultant on philanthropy who has direct insight into the matter. Yet others intend to be charitable, but don't want to be held accountable by signing the pledge, in case they change their minds. Thus, the loopholes of the Giving Pledge are so numerous as to make it almost meaningless.

Those more sympathetic to the impetus for the pledge say it should be measured not in terms of the actual philanthropic outcomes, but rather on the fact that it shone a spotlight on the need for giving and caused people to think about what they wanted to do with their wealth. Buffett's message that it was better to give money away during your lifetime than leave it all to your children resonated with a lot of potential donors. It also resonated with multimillionaires—the thousands of people with tens or hundreds of millions sitting around.

The Giving Pledge has fed the growth of the philanthropic advisory industry in the past decade or so, because many wealthy people who want to be generous and think beyond donating to their alma maters or hospitals and research centers don't know where to start. Philanthropic advisors and those who manage the investments of billionaires through private firms called family offices, say their industry has gotten much better at helping people understand how to do a better job of giving money away. They say they are providing a professional service that helps the wealthy build foundations and identify the best-run nonprofits where their donations can make the most impact.

"I was skeptical about how much the Giving Pledge would do, but it has fostered collaborative giving," said Joel L. Fleishman, the Duke University professor who has studied the campaign closely. "Those who have signed the pledge have regular meetings, not only with other principal donors but also their children," he said. "Other institutions such as Indiana University tried to bring wealthy individuals together for confidential sessions but never succeeded in doing it. The few members of the Giving Pledge I know have told me with considerable enthusiasm that they get to talk with the big givers, and they value it."

Over time, the pledge has become a resource for billionaires looking for ways to "do" better philanthropy. There is an annual two-day conference hosted by the organization that was set up to run the Giving Pledge campaign, at which billionaires and their representatives come together to discuss themes, exchange ideas, and strategize with philanthropy experts about the most effective methods of giving. Signatories also attend group meetings where they can build new networks and exchange ideas and tips on what has worked and what has failed. In 2022, Gates and French Gates both attended the conference—held in Ojai that year—and reaffirmed their commitment to philanthropy.[20] At learning sessions held throughout the year, pledgers are schooled by experts on poverty alleviation, education reform, and other potential areas of giving. Pledgers have even visited the White House to discuss ways in which governments and philanthropists can collaborate.

One person who has attended these meetings on behalf of a Giving Pledge signatory said the gatherings felt like events where billionaires could discuss problems specific to their class without fear of being judged. The topic of how much money to leave one's children came up frequently. But billionaire participants also shared tips about juggling multiple homes, maintaining staff, and coordinating the lives and schedules of family members as they crisscrossed the world for work and leisure. Those in the philanthropic advisory business also say that the Giving Pledge has had a bigger impact on billionaires outside the United States than they expected. Melissa Berman, who launched Rockefeller Philanthropy Advisors, a nonprofit, in 2002 and stepped down from it in early 2024, observed that many of the international givers saw the pledge as part of a global club they wanted to belong to, a certain signaling comparable to being a regular at the World Economic Forum in Davos, or at the ground level, the way people might wear a sticker that said, "I donated blood." She has even encountered those who would exaggerate their net worth to be able to sign the pledge. The most measured assessment of the impact of the Giving Pledge came from Buffett himself. "There's been more money that has been contributed by the members than they otherwise would have contributed though this is impossible to measure," he wrote via email. "Bill has helped materially to change the culture of giving in many countries and continues to do so whenever he travels. I did my share the first couple of years but Bill has carried the load ever since." Although there was no grand plan when he, Gates, and French Gates launched the initiative, Buffett said, "it has worked out better than I anticipated and has made a definite contribution to philanthropic thinking around the world."

Chapter 6

Melinda without Bill

A Feminist Identity

Melinda French Gates had been seething for a long time. She had been seething about the unequal nature of her marriage to a man heralded globally as a technology genius and trailblazing philanthropist. She had been seething about his infidelity. She had been seething about her yearslong slog to establish a foothold at the top of the foundation that, until 2024, bore her name. And she had been seething about the plight of women around the world, seeing in their vulnerability something of her own.

"I have rage," she wrote in her first book, *The Moment of Lift*, adding that it was up to her to metabolize that rage into fuel to spur her philanthropic work. Published in April 2019, the book is a mashup of memoir and manifesto, a sort of coming-out party for French Gates, cementing her identity as a feminist and an empathetic advocate of women's rights and gender equality. Written in unadorned and accessible prose, the book is a summary of the themes she has spoken about over the years. Its central argument is that the uplift of women is good for all of society. She also uses the platform to recount her journey from trying to fit in to living her values, share stories about the experiences of women she had met during her travels, highlight the female friendships that sustained her, and state her commitment to correcting gender imbalances. Gates called her book "wise, honest and beautifully written."[1]

Just over two years after the book's publication, on May 3, 2021, she and Gates announced their divorce, citing "irreconcilable differences." French Gates crafted a masterful narrative about the unraveling of her marriage, about how she had given it her all, only to be disappointed by a pattern of behavior by Gates that led to a breakdown of trust and pushed her to seek a divorce. She said as much as she left unsaid, implicating her ex-husband through her silence. Her voice, although vulnerable, was not one of victimhood. It was one of empowerment, strength, and dignity that turned personal history into feminist idiom. Cicatrizing in the public eye was part of the plan.

Marriages are phantasmagorias. They change shape, they confound, they bewilder. Sometimes, they start out sturdy as a tree trunk and end up fragile as splinters. At other times, they are stitched together for convenience, with the seams showing. People enter marriages hoping that the formal bond will seal existing cracks in relationships. Many in the Gates universe—those who knew Gates in his bachelor days, those who were guests at the wedding, those who worked individually with Gates and French Gates at the foundation, and those who had the opportunity to discuss aspects of the relationship with the two central characters—suggest their marriage existed in the somewhat indeterminate spaces between those possibilities. An uncoupling surprised few of them.

Celebrity divorces have always captivated people, especially as tawdry details tumble out of the closet, but billionaire divorces have become their own category, partly because of the high-profile nature of some of the people involved but also because of the sheer enormity of the assets at stake, the wide-ranging implications for the companies they founded, and for philanthropy. The 2019 split between Bezos and his wife of 25 years, MacKenzie Scott, happened amid a scandal involving the Amazon founder and his girlfriend, Lauren Sánchez, whose brother had leaked the story of their affair to a tabloid. Amazon shareholders may have been titillated, but they were more concerned about the implications the divorce had on the company's shares, worried that the division of assets could affect Bezos's control of the company. The former couple held about 16 percent of Amazon, worth about $140 billion at the time of the divorce, and Bezos was its largest shareholder. He now owns under 10 percent, while Scott left with a 4-percent stake. Since the divorce, Scott has emerged as one of the world's most prolific philanthropists, taking a low profile and unfussy approach to grant-making. When the casino mogul Steve Wynn divorced from his wife Elaine Wynn in 2010, they each retained an equal stake in Wynn Resorts, but the split—which started out amicably—turned acrimonious when Elaine was pushed off the board. Bill Gross, the bond fund manager, fought his ex-wife Sue for ownership of their Picasso and their three cats. He lost. When Ken Griffin, the billionaire hedge fund manager, got divorced from Anne Dias Griffin, the two fought in court over the details of their prenuptial agreement and the custody of their children. In a sign of how much billionaire divorces had caught the public imagination, Apple TV ran a comedy series in 2022 called *Loot*, in which the actress Maya Rudolph plays Molly Novak, a 45-year-old woman whose divorce has left her with an $87 billion fortune. She stumbles around at first in a whirl of self-loathing, but eventually finds a role for herself at the charitable foundation set up in her name, also finding herself in the process. Putting aside the shortcomings of the plot, *Loot* caricatures the mega-rich and has a topical, ripped-from-the-headlines feel, given the rise to philanthropic prominence of Scott and French Gates.

But the breakup of Gates and French Gates went far beyond assets, or the fate of a single company. They were the twin suns around which not just the Gates Foundation, but much of the philanthropy world, orbited. Their coupledom was woven into the origin story of the foundation, a multimedia version of which is permanently displayed for visitors to the Seattle campus. In 1993, as a young couple engaged to be married, they took a safari trip to Africa. Gates didn't believe in vacations in those years but his wife-to-be forced him to take one. A widely shared photograph of that first trip shows the two sitting in a safari van, Gates in a black T-shirt with his oversized glasses and floppy hair and French Gates dressed in neutral colors. Both are smiling. However, the bleached gold of the savanna and the crystalline blue waters of Zanzibar would soon lose their allure as they encountered the region's extreme poverty. The level of destitution was unfathomable to two young Americans who grew up in cloistered upper-middle-class homes—especially for Gates, who until then had paid little attention to the world beyond Microsoft. They were dumbfounded to learn that thousands of people in developing countries died each year of easily preventable diseases because they didn't have access to vaccines. They were appalled after reading health data cited in the 1993 World Development Report, which contained the global statistics on poverty and other data on the plight of the world's poor that provided written proof of what they had seen. Another piece of the foundation's origin story, documented on its website, is a PDF of an article Gates sent his father, Bill Gates Sr., in 1997 about water-borne illnesses, accompanied by a seven-word note saying, "Dad, maybe we can do something about this." Gates and French Gates often talked about these early experiences and how, as they read about preventable illnesses like diarrhea and rotavirus that killed scores of children in poor countries, they began to see an opportunity for their money to make a difference.

Over the decades, they portrayed themselves as a complementary pair—he the technical maven, she the intuitive counterpoint. If Gates spoke in statistics and numbers, she conveyed the emotional sucker punch of seeing destitution firsthand. Each also spoke about the other in the press periodically, bewitching audiences with carefully selected tidbits. French Gates often talked about how she insisted that Gates and their children help with the dishes, or how her ex-husband set an example for other dads by driving their children to school. Polls regularly listed them among the most powerful, the most inspiring, and the most admired couples in the world as they moved about like royalty in their philanthropic quests. Their relationship was so important to the stability of the foundation and the wider nonprofit world that the duo kept their "couple" image intact in the media until the moment of their divorce announcement. On Jan 1, 2020, French Gates posted on Instagram: "New Year's Day will always be extra special to me—marking both a fresh year and an opportunity to celebrate being married to @thisisbillgates. Today makes 26, and I'm still marveling at just how full a heart can get. Happy anniversary to the man who keeps me dancing through life." By then, she had already been consulting with divorce lawyers.[2] Even if those with insight into the divorce had been aware of the rough storm of their marriage, its announcement caused consternation at the Gates Foundation, as many of its roughly 1,800 employees suddenly found themselves wondering about the future of their employer and their own livelihoods. There had always been informal rivalry between those who worked closely with Gates and those who worked with French Gates, but now, the "Team Bill" and "Team Melinda" camps acquired, if not the rabidity of sports fans, at least some of their energy. Uncertainty also rippled through the wider nonprofit world, where hundreds of recipients of grants from the Gates Foundation, in dozens of countries, were gripped by fear and uncertainty as some were told that their funding, which was already under scrutiny as the pandemic shifted priorities, would be put on hold until the foundation had sorted out the implications of the breakup. Although the impact lasted only a few months, it made people panic because so many grantees depend on the foundation for a major chunk of their funds.

"The divorce had a disquieting effect on the nonprofit world," said Michael Thatcher, a former Microsoft employee who runs Charity Navigator, a nonprofit organization that evaluates other nonprofits to help people direct their giving. Charity Navigator had been receiving grants from the Gates Foundation for several years. When the divorce was announced, the foundation's grant officers reached out to say that they wouldn't be able to approve Charity Navigator's grant renewal proposal for a while. The divorce had temporarily upended the foundation's planning and approval processes, but during this period of upheaval, the foundation provided Charity Navigator with a bridging grant, and came through with additional funds in 2022. "We were not left high and dry," Thatcher said. "They took care of their regular recipients but weren't able to do so for a while." By the time French Gates left the foundation in 2024, three years after the divorce, it was fully set up for its next chapter.

When Gates and French Gates started their foundation in 2000, Gates was already one of the world's most recognized businessmen. She, by comparison, was an enigma. The press treated French Gates as sort of a curiosity, partly because she guarded her private life fiercely, requesting that those in her circle not talk about her.[3] She made public appearances occasionally, but rarely gave interviews. When she gave speeches—usually on causes dear to her heart, such as the importance of educating girls—she picked low-profile settings like local clubs and community colleges. She was involved in a few local outside efforts and took her first director position in 1999 when she was named to the board of Drugstore.com, one of the early online pharmacies. She served on the board of the Washington Post Company from 2004 to 2010. She also served for a time on the board of trustees at Duke University, her alma mater. When Gates stepped down as the chief executive of Microsoft in 2000 and trained his eyes more closely on his philanthropy, French Gates got involved too, although early foundation employees weren't made aware of what her contribution would be. However, she had always envisioned a bigger role for herself at the foundation, and as the couple's three children grew older, she started showing up more and began to embrace publicity. Still, French Gates largely remained a presence by her husband's side, both inside the foundation and in public. The two portrayed themselves as equal partners, but it was clear that Gates drove the foundation's direction and priorities, and that he was its chief spokesman.

In 2004, French Gates appeared on *Good Morning America*, one of her first solo media appearances. (It was her first live television interview, according to a transcript with Diane Sawyer.) Her motto, according to Sawyer, was to "laugh often and to love much in life."

Two years later, in the swirl of television interviews and press conferences that followed Buffett's decision to bequeath the bulk of his fortune to the Gates Foundation, French Gates spoke with passion about the uplift of communities that philanthropic dollars could deliver. She spoke of the need to empower women and use their agency to aid development, rather than labeling them as a category that things had to be "done to." It was one of her first public events on behalf of the foundation, and her early efforts to build a more visible media profile. Part of the reason, she said, was to be a role model for her two daughters.[4]

In the years immediately following the Buffett gift, as media interest in the foundation revved up, its communications team built a strategy around the former couple. As the two faces of the entity, they were thrust into the spotlight regularly, both together and separately. The idea was to put Gates and French Gates in front of different audiences, according to people involved in developing the strategies. Gates, who was a familiar figure in the traditional business and technology press, was now being positioned as a "thought leader." The aim was to put him alongside policymakers, world leaders, and corporate decision makers. To do that, the foundation's communications team pushed him to appear at TED conferences, the World Economic Forum in Davos, fireside chats, and television interviews on specific topics, as well as to pen opinion articles and an annual letter. In 2008, he became the first nongovernment leader to speak at Davos.

At the same time, foundation staffers developed a two-pronged strategy around French Gates. First, they would introduce her to a general mainstream and business audience. In 2008, *Fortune* magazine wrote one of the first big profiles of French Gates, putting her on the cover. The second part of the strategy was to push French Gates as the foundation cochair who spoke about the challenges and successes of delivery mechanisms in public health or education, two early areas of focus. Gates was—and would always be—the data guy. But she could be what the communications team called the "other side of the mat," putting a vivid and human spin on the foundation's work through stories of the difficulties that people in poor countries had in accessing basic healthcare services. It was a struggle to emerge from under Gates's shadow because her profile was closely intertwined with her husband's profile, and his focus on global public health. Unlike Gates, who by then was used to extreme media scrutiny, she was a newbie. But people who worked with French Gates to build her public persona found her determined and receptive to their suggestions. She was ambitious and "very interested in being seen as Bill's equal," said one person who worked closely on building her image. She welcomed media training and run-throughs of speeches and interviews. She requested intensive briefing documents and asked a lot of questions about the material.

French Gates sought to build an identity that was separate from that of her ex-husband, both internally and externally. She gradually felt her way around the chaotic belly of the foundation, scouting out a role for herself and potential perches she could call her own. At the very beginning, French Gates didn't want to focus on gender because it would have been the obvious choice for a female philanthropist. But with Gates so focused on public health, as she went on trips and saw more of the world, French Gates realized that gender issues were an opportunity. She didn't have to follow her husband's interests, but could instead build her own point of view, according to one former employee of the Gates Foundation who worked directly with French Gates. She messaged her vision differently; as opposed to advocating for women to have equal rights, she made the point that if women have rights, everybody is better off, this person said. "It shows a certain savviness."

Around 2010, French Gates started pushing for the foundation to create strategies to address women's rights and empowerment. She not only sought to build gender issues as an area of focus but also tried to include a gender dimension across the foundation's work, according to employees and news reports.[5] Gates considered women's issues to be part of public health, according to people who worked at the foundation. French Gates argued that global development was its own category and should not be subsumed by global health. Still, women's rights remained more of an inclusionary aspect of broader program goals at the foundation. One study found that between 2013 and 2015, Gates Foundation dollars accounted for nearly half of the $3.7 billion that went to gender-related issues in developing countries, representing the largest single donor. But the Gates Foundation was not among the top 10 organizations that made such giving a priority.[6]

Eventually, French Gates became the public face for the foundation's work on family planning and gender equality. Those who worked with her on some of these issues identified the London Summit on Family Planning in 2012, where she called for voluntary access to family planning for women in the developing world by 2020, as a defining professional moment. In a 2016 announcement posted on the foundation's website about a new gender-related initiative, only French Gates is listed: "Melinda Gates commits $80 million over three years to collect data about how women live and work around the world," according to the press release. "The data will help jumpstart the foundation's work to help women and girls thrive."

The foundation has directed more money to areas French Gates directly nurtured. In 2020, it created a new gender equality division, focusing on women's empowerment and bringing a gender lens to all of its work. In 2021, it gave $90 million through that strategy, but in 2022, the amount of money the foundation disbursed to gender equality was far bigger at $747 million—partly because it moved some of its programs, including maternal and newborn health, into the division.

French Gates had to work equally hard to establish herself within the foundation. Given that employees were used to reporting only to Gates, she had to assert herself repeatedly before they began to account for her presence and preferences. Carving out a role for herself inside the foundation meant that Gates had to adjust as well. He was used to striding into a conference room and having meetings geared to what he needed. "He would walk into a meeting and to whoever is leading the meeting he says, let's go, it's right to 100mph," said a former foundation employee. "With Gates, there is no preamble, not much small talk, he tends to launch right in, and he likes efficiency." With French Gates in the room, "the meeting pace and style had to be adjusted to accommodate her questions as well. Both ask questions, but Gates can rattle off questions as you're speaking, while French Gates typically waits till the end, rather than cutting someone off."

Sometimes, he would cut her off too, and she would sit quietly, fuming. At other times, when he launched into a topic and threatened to go on for hours, French Gates would reel him in, saying "Bill, I think they get it." Gates found it difficult to take her advice in the moment, a tension that created awkward situations for the other attendees. One of those attendees, in describing a particularly contentious meeting, created a tableau: Gates speaking so animatedly that spit flew out of his mouth; his father, then a cochair of the foundation, asleep in his chair; and French Gates, staring into the distance, lips pursed and arms folded.

French Gates's book describes her ex-husband's reaction when she asked to cowrite the foundation's annual letter. Gates had become used to writing it on his own and quite enjoyed the process. When she suggested in 2012 that they write the next one together, his immediate reaction was: The process has been working so well, why change it? She held her ground. For the first two years after that, she wrote a section of the letter, and from 2015 on, they cowrote it until their divorce. Slowly, French Gates established her footing, partly because she insisted to her ex-husband in private conversations that she wanted—and deserved—to be treated as a principal. As Gates made room for her and she became a significant presence in the office, employees too began to adapt. The duo requested that they get the same briefing materials so that one didn't have an information advantage over the other, but they read them separately and sent back questions, making sure to copy each other on all communications. Gates would typically ask about the technical aspects of a program and the data to back it up, whereas French Gates would ask about the "interface" piece of it—or how easy or difficult it was for the end user. That contrast in approach was helpful to foundation employees because it allowed them to explain things in two ways.

French Gates also asserted herself at Cascade Asset Management, a private investment firm that managed the Gates fortune and the endowment of the foundation. At Cascade's annual meetings, in which employees shared the performance of the various portfolios, Gates tended to ask all the questions. French Gates was in attendance but far more reserved, according to attendees. But as she became more involved with the foundation's affairs, she also engaged more with Cascade, and the investment team began preparing a separate, more abridged set of reports for her so that she could educate herself on their holdings. She didn't ask too many questions, but "behind the scenes she was trying to understand, and over the years you could see progression, where she began to find her voice," one meeting attendee said.

Despite her insistence and hard work, sharing the platform with a celebrity husband could be tough. As French Gates wrote in her book, "I've been trying to find my voice as I've been speaking next to Bill . . . and that can make it hard to be heard." In the stories of women that she shares in her book, French Gates often seems to find echoes of the power imbalance in her own life. She had to fight for equality within the relationship; it wasn't going to be handed to her by her former husband. In her book, she also tried to connect with her audience by sharing her own story of being in an abusive relationship (before Bill), which she said killed her self-esteem and which she had never mentioned publicly until the book. "That, to me, is not that different than women in the developing world who lose their voice or have no decision-making power," she said in an interview about the book.[7] Its title comes from the idea of "lift," the moment when a rocket takes off. Her father was an aerospace engineer in the Apollo missions, and as children, French Gates and her siblings would go watch the rockets launch.

In 2015, French Gates founded Pivotal Ventures, a Seattle-based firm that seeks to empower women through investing, philanthropy, and advocacy. That effort initially came about as a "complementary philanthropic vehicle" to help her go further, faster, according to an interview that Haven Ley, a former Gates Foundation employee who became a key team member of Pivotal, gave to *Barron's*.[8] But in the following years, Pivotal became French Gates's launch vehicle as she claimed for herself a public role as a champion of women's rights. She pulled together a mostly female team, including several staffers like Ley from her personal office at the foundation. Communications professionals were tasked with shaping, sustaining, and burnishing her brand as separate and distinct not only from her husband's, but also from the foundation's. Gates never changed out of his uniform of collared shirts, sweaters, and slacks—he once offered fashion advice to Paul Allen's girlfriend, "basically, to buy all your clothes in the same style and colors and save time by not having to match them," Allen wrote in his memoir—but French Gates's wardrobe evolved over the decades. In the 1990s, she typically bought her own outfits at homegrown Seattle stores like Nordstrom, according to a buyer for the luxury department store, and often favored classic brands like Gucci and Prada. Her outfits are still understated, but in recent years, they have become a little edgier—although with none of the verve of, say, Michelle Obama. From her hair to her outfits, from her speeches to her public appearances, French Gates employed a slow but intentional rollout of her "new" self and new firm, but it wouldn't be until 2018, in the runup to the publication of her book, that Pivotal unveiled fully in the public eye.

In 2019, she penned an opinion piece in *Time* magazine about women and girls, committing $1 billion to promote gender equity.[9] In 2020, she penned another opinion piece for *The New York Times* to mark International Women's Day that was a riff on her core message about empowering women, urging readers to start a conversation about gender equality.[10] In the months leading up to the announcement of their divorce in May 2021, she was virtually impossible to miss, going on television, giving interviews to magazines and newspapers, and creating the conditions for her emergence as an independent feminist-philanthropist. By 2024, when she decided to leave the Gates Foundation to pursue her own form of philanthropy, that identity had fully taken hold. It was French Gates's moment of lift.

Scenes from a Marriage

Bill Gates married Melinda French in 1994 on New Year's Day on the seventeenth tee of a golf course in Lanai. Roughly 130 guests, including colleagues from Microsoft, close friends, and family, flew to the Hawaiian island. Once the site of pineapple plantations for the Dole Corporation, Lanai has only three hotels. Dirt roads crisscross the land and there are no stoplights. On that Saturday evening, the bride wore her hair down; the groom wore a white tuxedo, a gentle breeze ruffling his sandy blond mop. As the sun set over the bluffs, they set course on their 27-year marriage. The singer Willie Nelson entertained the guests. No reporters or photographers were allowed, but some came anyway for the wedding of the world's richest man, hoping to shoot a few pictures, catch a couple of quotes. As some of the guests began complaining about the intrusion, Katharine Graham, a friend of the Gates family and publisher of *The Washington Post*, who was in attendance, proclaimed, "freedom of the press!"

Gates had a security force chase them away, slapping them with no-trespass orders. Later, the overzealous security would cause trouble as reporters claimed harassment at being pushed away from public areas of the island, and even sued the billionaire. Ten days later, on January 10, the newlyweds held a reception in Seattle. The press release from Microsoft described the reception as "classic and elegant." It was held at a private home and included a formal sit-down dinner. Natalie Cole performed for the guests. French Gates's fur-trimmed dress caught the attention of antifur activists, the *Seattle Post-Intelligencer* reported.

Born Melinda Ann French on August 15, 1964, French Gates grew up in a close-knit family. The second of four children, she was valedictorian at Ursuline Academy of Dallas, an all-girls, Catholic prep school from which she graduated in 1982. She joined Microsoft in 1987 after graduating from Duke University with a degree in computer science and an MBA. Not long after, she made her boss's acquaintance when she sat next to Gates at a dinner. A few months later, they ran into each other again at the company parking lot. It was a Saturday afternoon and, as French Gates has recounted many times, he asked her out on a date two Fridays out. She responded that it wasn't "spontaneous" enough for her. Later that day, he called to ask if they could meet for a drink that evening: "Is this spontaneous enough for you?" The couple kept it quiet in the early years of their courtship. Family and close friends knew, but French Gates was particularly mindful of the optics of a junior executive dating the cofounder and chief executive of the company. She rose through the ranks at Microsoft, working as a product manager overseeing teams developing applications like Word and eventually becoming a general manager, but she initially found it difficult to fit into the company's culture. "It was just so brash, so argumentative and competitive, with people fighting to the end on every point they were making and every piece of data they were debating," French Gates wrote in *The Moment of Lift.* "It was as if every meeting, no matter how casual, was a dress rehearsal for the strategy review with Bill."[11] Women were mainly in the product management and marketing side of the company, and female engineers were hard to spot. After dating on and off for about five years, Gates and French Gates got engaged in the spring of 1993, when she was 28 and he was 37.

The news of the engagement made the front page of *The Wall Street Journal* under the headline: A MARRIAGE MADE AT MICROSOFT: WILL BILLIONAIRE'S UNION LEAD TO A COMPUTER DYNASTY, OR LESSEN HIS AMBITION?

People who worked with Gates at the time said that it was well understood that the Microsoft cofounder, consumed as he was by his company, had not factored marriage or children into his life. There were those in the computer industry who wondered what kind of husband and father he would make. For a time, he dated Ann Winblad, one of the technology world's early female entrepreneurs. A few years older than Gates, Winblad wanted to settle down and start a family. Hoping to plant the marriage seed in Gates's mind and introduce him to the joys of family life, she invited Mitch Kapor, the Lotus founder, his then wife, and their toddler for a visit to her cottage in the Outer Banks of North Carolina. Gates spent the entire weekend immersed in a biography of Henry Ford, although he did take a break or two—to ride a dune buggy.

Gates's mother, Mary Gates, was also pushing her only son to consider marriage. He asked friends and key confidantes about their views; coworkers, tired of his monomaniacal focus on work, joked that married life would slow him down. In the documentary *Inside Bill's Brain*, which aired in September 2019, French Gates recounted how she entered his bedroom once to find Gates writing a list of the pros and cons of marriage on his whiteboard. She also said in the film that their relationship had come to a point where they would either get married or break up. Gates decided to get married because, as he told *Playboy* magazine in 1994, French Gates made him feel like it, despite all his "past rational thinking on the topic."[12] He added that he liked women who were smart and independent. One former Microsoft executive who spoke directly with Gates at the time said that French Gates represented the kind of responsible, caring, and warm person that "mapped onto his mother"—someone with whom he could settle down and have children.

In the early 1990s, Gates had begun building a multistoried 66,000-square-foot mansion on a five-acre parcel of land in Medina, a suburb of Seattle on the rim of Lake Washington. With a population of 3,000, Medina is where some of the country's wealthiest have built a dense cluster of mansions nestled amid thickets of firs, maples, and alders, and 10-foot-tall hedges. Nearly every lakefront house has a yacht. It's not uncommon to see a Porsche 911 GT3 stop by the corner deli. Gates had originally conceived of the house as a man cave outfitted with the kind of hi-tech, futuristic accoutrements one would expect from a technology billionaire, but also as a showcase for his growing collection of valuable art and literature. In 1994, Gates paid $30.8 million for his prized Leonardo da Vinci manuscript, and pursuing his love of photography, he had also bought the Bettmann Archive, a gallery of historical photos. Built in the style of a Pacific lodge, with sloping roofs and rich, tan wood from hundreds of Douglas firs, the house earned the nickname Xanadu 2.0, after the over-the-top mansion built by Charles Foster Kane in the movie *Citizen Kane*. It included a movie theater and a trampoline room, a nod to Gates's old habit of jumping out of trash cans and over armchairs.[13] French Gates, horrified at the thought of moving into and raising children in a showy but soulless structure, hired Thierry Despont, the famed French architect and interior designer, to dab on some homey touches and create warm, intimate areas that could embrace the clutter of daily life.[14] Xanadu 2.0 took more than six years to build, and once the riot of construction ended, and the interior decorators had left, the couple moved in along with their baby daughter. In 2007, a Microsoft intern named Robert Smith had the chance to visit the house. "Going down Bill's driveway is like arriving at Jurassic Park," Smith wrote in a blog post.[15] He raved about the green carpet of land surrounding the house—"there's grass that looks like someone went at it with scissors"—and the movie theater, complete with "Now Showing" posters. French Gates occasionally took visitors on a tour of the house, pointing out the Douglas firs on the property and the swimming pool that was separated into outdoor and indoor sections by an underwater divider. A highlight was the estuary built on the compound, fed by a stream, where salmon, trout, and other fish came to spawn. Indoors, the walls of one study were plastered with award plaques and notes from world leaders the duo had received for their philanthropic work. Priceless objets d'art and museum artifacts were carefully placed around the house. Once, Despont commissioned an artist to create replicas of a 2,000-year-old gold-leaf vase Gates had seen in a museum in Italy that he supposedly wanted to buy—but that the museum would not sell to him. About a dozen replicas of the vase, which age had stained with a unique patina, were placed around the house as table-lamp bases. The couple loved F. Scott's Fitzgerald's *The Great Gatsby* so much that they even had their favorite quote from the book painted on the ceiling of their library: "His dream must have seemed so close that he could hardly fail to grasp it."[16] When they were dating, French Gates would leave a green light on in her office at Microsoft, which signaled to Gates that he could visit—an echo, perhaps, of the "green light" that Nick Carraway describes as he writes about Gatsby's love for Daisy Buchanan. Gates, who once got a speeding ticket as a young man in Albuquerque, indulged his passion for fast cars, building a collection of Porsches, Mercedeses, and other luxury cars. An underground garage with room for around 20 cars was tunneled into the property. Armed security guards kept a close eye on curious visitors, shooing away tourists sightseeing by boat on the lake when they came too close to the property.

Eventually, Gates eased into married life. Their three children—the eldest, Jennifer, born in 1996; the middle child, Rory, born in 1999; and the youngest, Phoebe, born in 2002—grew up in the Medina home. At school, French Gates registered the children under her maiden name to maintain privacy. Seattle residents would sometimes see French Gates, a practicing Catholic, during Sunday mass, kids in tow. As children who grew up in inconceivable luxury, whose lives could only be truly understood by the billionaire class, they indulged their passions, and continue to do so. Jennifer is a pediatrician, having graduated from the Icahn School of Medicine at New York's Mount Sinai Hospital, and a show jumper who owns breeding stables and horse farms, including in upstate New York. Married to a fellow equestrian, Nayel Nassar, a Stanford-educated Egyptian American, she operates in a rarefied circle of equestrians, including the children of celebrities and other billionaires, among them Eve Jobs, the daughter of Steve Jobs and Laurene Powell Jobs; Georgina Bloomberg, the daughter of Michael Bloomberg; and

Olympian Jessica Springsteen, the daughter of Bruce Springsteen and Patti Scialfa. In 2023, Gates and French Gates became grandparents after Jennifer gave birth to a baby girl. Rory, a graduate of the University of Chicago, retains a much lower profile than his siblings. The youngest, Phoebe, a Stanford University student and budding fashionista, wields considerable clout on social media where she posts a stream of content including videos of her dad being goofy and her mom's work in women's rights.

The view among many observers of the Gates marriage and its unraveling is that each held different notions about the meaning of a marital contract. Even though French Gates agreed to marry Gates, fully aware of his reservations about the institution of marriage, the two were very much in love, and her sympathizers said she genuinely believed that the fact of being married would make a difference because of her own deeply held belief in its sanctity. Those who are more accommodating of Gates observed that love and marriage can often mean two different things. One former associate of the Microsoft cofounder pointed out the difference between marrying someone and committing to exclusivity in that marriage, comparing it with the arrangement Buffett had with his first wife, Susan Buffett, who left him to travel and pursue a singing career but arranged for a companion for her husband. (They remained married, and "more than amicable," Buffett said, until Susan's death in 2004.) It was hardly a sparkless or joyless marriage, according to those who observed the former couple in private settings. There were plenty of moments of mirth and affection between the two. There were times when she reached for his hand. Yet, he was unfaithful to her over the years. "There's a duality in Bill," said one person who worked closely with French Gates. "He loves Melinda very much and [I] don't think he ever thought he would lose her." At the same time, "Melinda is wired to serious monogamous relationships."

Gates's years as a young man who liked to party and go to strip joints were widely known among Microsoft executives, as well as others in the still-small tech community of the 1980s. In *Hard Drive*, a 1993 biography of Gates by two investigative reporters for the *Seattle Post-Intelligencer*, the authors recount how the young Microsoft cofounder once flew by helicopter to a chalet in the French Alps for an international sales meeting, where they partied all night. At 5 A.M., as one of the attendees was leaving, he almost stepped on Gates, lying on top of a woman. Before his marriage, Gates was often "besieged" by women who wanted to date him, and he sometimes reciprocated their advances, the reporters wrote.[17]

The July 21, 1986, issue of *Fortune* magazine carried a cover story about how Microsoft pulled off its initial public offering that year. In the story, filled with details about the company's high-stakes negotiations with bankers and lawyers, the journalist David Kirkpatrick noted, in almost a throwaway way: "Gates, a gawky, washed-out blond, confesses to being a 'wonk,' a bookish nerd, who focuses single-mindedly on the computer business though he masters all sorts of knowledge with astounding facility. Oddly, Gates is something of a ladies' man and a fiendishly fast driver who has racked up speeding tickets even in the sluggish Mercedes diesel he bought to restrain himself."[18]

A person familiar with Gates's interactions with women said that until the Microsoft cofounder got married, there were women who hoped to catch their boss's eye, and Gates enjoyed the attention. Some women even wore MARRY ME, BILL T-shirts to office events.[19] A former senior Microsoft employee recalled being told by an office assistant to Gates that he was like "a kid in a candy store" in the company of women, if not restrained. In the early 1990s, when Microsoft was one the biggest clients of Goldman Sachs, which had taken the company public, Gates would sometimes hit on women at cocktail receptions arranged by the bank—including the spouses of senior bankers, recalled one person with knowledge of discussions Goldman executives had on the matter. It's unlikely that the bank took any action, given that Microsoft was its biggest tech client. Once, a female acquaintance of Gates who was planning to stay at his guest apartment called his office to ask for his home phone number, in case she had problems getting there. Gates's secretary hesitated. When the female acquaintance pushed the secretary for his number, she reluctantly told her that Gates's mother, Mary, did not let her hand out her bachelor son's number to girls.

Rumors about Gates and his gallivanting have long circulated inside Microsoft, the Gates Foundation, and Cascade, the investment firm that manages his fortune, according to people who have worked at each of the entities. Well into his marriage, it was not unusual for Gates to flirt with women and pursue them, making unwanted advances, such as asking a Microsoft employee out to dinner while he was still the company's chairman.[20] In 2000, Gates conducted an affair with a Microsoft employee. Nearly two decades later, in 2019, the woman informed the company's board about the relationship, which led to an investigation by a committee of the board that was aided by an outside law firm. The investigation led to Gates stepping down from the Microsoft board in 2020, *The Wall Street Journal* reported.[21] At the time, a representative for Gates acknowledged that the affair had happened but said that it had ended "amicably," and that the board's investigation had nothing to do with Gates stepping down. On occasion, Gates flirted with some of the interns at the Gates Foundation, putting them in the uncomfortable position of having to think about their career prospects while not wanting to be hit on by the boss, according to one person who was aware of his behavior. In one instance, a colleague chastised the person for sending a 22-year-old intern to Gates's office by herself: "She's too young and too pretty," the person recalled the colleague saying. More recent reports suggest that in 2010, Gates, an avid bridge player, also conducted an affair with a Russian bridge player, Mila Antonova, who was then in her twenties.[22] Gates's approaches were clumsy rather than predatory, according to people who knew about some of them, witnessed them firsthand, or reviewed flirtatious emails he sent to them; one labeled them "cringeworthy." At least three people who knew Gates at different points in his life, from the Microsoft days to the foundation, said that he did not prey upon female employees and seek sex with them in exchange for promoting their careers. "Bill was far from predatory," said a former Microsoft executive with direct insight into his boss's behavior. "That was never his problem." Gates was "not Harvey Weinstein," this person said, referring to the former movie producer and convicted sex offender who is serving a prison sentence. He could be "charming, respectful and just fun, so you start there. . . . I know of no real situation in which anyone got anything for sleeping with Bill." Gates displayed a certain naïveté in his interactions with women, occasionally mistaking an engaged conversation for mutual interest and pursuing it gently but dropping it if the other person didn't reciprocate, according to sympathizers. He enjoyed the adoration that came his way as a celebrity, especially at conferences and events where both women and men would form a throng around him, but couldn't always tell the difference between flattery and flirtation.

French Gates wasn't always happy with the script. The Microsoft billionaire's calendar would include blocks of time for what were ostensibly personal meetings into which few people had visibility, according to two people who directly knew about the events. More than a decade ago, Gates's longtime executive assistant was replaced, two people who knew about the action said; one of them said the change happened because the assistant was "enabling him to be places where [Melinda] didn't know he was at." There were other abrupt personnel changes over the years, including within Gates's personal security team, according to two people who knew about the changes and a third who was told about them. Reid, the Gates Ventures spokeswoman, said the security team was replaced for "compliance reasons," but declined to elaborate.

Gates occasionally sought freedom from his highly choreographed days, which were packed with back-to-back meetings, often in five- to ten-minute increments. He relished his time with Buffett, especially visits to Omaha where the two billionaires enjoyed meandering, freewheeling conversations that were in sharp contrast to the structured life he led with French Gates. Buffett once observed to a friend that Gates's visits seemed to him to be moments of respite from a tightly scheduled life, including personal time, largely organized and arranged by French Gates, which included family time. When Buffett asked Gates why he couldn't control his life and live it in a way he wanted to, Gates would simply shrug. "Bill **likes** to have a schedule; I don't," Buffett said in an email. Buffett, who is famously conflict-averse, stepped away from the troubling situation at the foundation after the divorce; that way, he wouldn't have to deal with any potential ugliness. Some saw it as a signal to the world that his legendary friendship with Gates had cooled over the years.

French Gates has said publicly that she wanted the marriage to work. The two even went to marital counseling after an especially rough patch in the early- to mid-2000s around the time their youngest child, Phoebe, was born, according to a person who knew about the events. But Gates assumed that his behavior would have no consequences. In the spate of publicity following the announcement of their divorce and reports of Gates's extramarital affairs, French Gates shared some of the ugly aspects of her marriage. In media appearances, she was sometimes harsh toward her ex-husband while also displaying her own vulnerability. She told the CBS anchor Gayle King that it wasn't one thing, but rather many things that had led to the divorce. There came a point when there was "enough there" that it wasn't healthy. In the interview, she all but stated that there was a pattern of conduct from Gates that she tolerated for a long time until she decided she couldn't anymore. "I couldn't trust what we had anymore," she said, adding that there were nights when she found herself lying on the carpet, in tears, wondering how to move forward. "I was committed to this marriage. I gave everything to this marriage. So I don't question myself now." Asked by King about a report that said Gates had multiple affairs, she responded: "Those are questions Bill needs to answer." When journalists asked her why Gates continued to meet with Epstein, French Gates responded: "Those are questions for Bill to answer."

On several occasions, French Gates has said that her ex-husband's relationship with Epstein contributed to their divorce. She had met Epstein once, in 2013, around the time when Gates's staff had been running their campaign for a Nobel Peace Prize for the foundation's work on polio eradication. On September 20, a Friday, French Gates and Gates were in New York to receive the Lasker-Bloomberg award for public service, awarded to them for "advancing global health through enlightened philanthropy." That evening at 7:30 P.M., as the day's pleasant warmth gave way to the gentle chill of early fall, they arrived for dinner at Epstein's residence—a seven-story mansion on the Upper East Side of Manhattan, just off Central Park, that was built in the French neoclassical style with a limestone facade popular in that part of town. From the moment she walked in the door, French Gates was unsettled. The entryway and reception area took up two stories. One wall was lined with framed and signed photographs of famous men, including former president Bill Clinton. Female figurines, some of them suggestively dressed, sat by the marble staircase. A life-size female doll hung from a chandelier.[23] On the second floor, there was a mural of a prison scene, with Epstein portrayed in the center. His taste in art tended toward the bizarre. According to a 2003 profile in *Vanity Fair*, one wall of his mansion displayed rows upon rows of framed eyeballs, which Epstein told the reporter had been made for injured soldiers and imported from England.[24] French Gates sat uncomfortably throughout the dinner, and later told friends she was furious that her then husband would not cut off ties with him. Since the divorce, she has also spoken publicly about her disgust for the convicted sex offender, calling him "abhorrent" and evil personified.

In 2022, she spoke at an event at which she said she had taken the psychotherapist Esther Perel's masterclass on relational intelligence.[25] It taught her, she said, to think about power and collaboration within a relationship, and that the power dynamic isn't necessarily a given but something that is negotiated by two people who make space for each other, even if one person is the breadwinner. French Gates said it was a reminder to her about how to approach future romantic relationships she might have. "She's been exceptionally transparent about her marriage," said an acquaintance of French Gates with knowledge of her thinking. "Melinda does nothing that isn't intentional. It had been coming for a long time."

Not long after French Gates's interview with Gayle King, Gates did one of his own with Savannah Guthrie on NBC. He didn't admit clearly whether he had had an affair, but stuck firmly to his talking points, admitting that he had "made a mistake," but that it was not constructive to go into the details. When Guthrie asked Gates what he had learned about himself through the experience of his divorce, and what advice he might have for others in his situation, he said he was more knowledgeable about scientific research than personal relationships. "There's areas like climate or health where I have expertise, on personal matters like this, I don't think of myself as an expert. I should be very humble about success, you know, has a tricky aspect to it, so you know . . . I don't have great advice for other people." Elsewhere, Gates has insisted that it was a great marriage from his point of view, and that he wouldn't have chosen to marry anyone else.

The Next Chapter

French Gates, with an estimated net worth of $11 billion, wants to make money off American society's sidelined goals. At Pivotal Ventures, the investment and advocacy firm she founded in 2015, social good is not the only return she seeks for her dollars. Rather, the firm sees an opportunity to bet on start-ups working on issues that are almost entirely overlooked by the traditional venture capital business. Among the companies in Pivotal's portfolio are Tia, which offers birth control and sexual health advice; Penny Finance, which is building tools to offer women financial education; and Candoo, which essentially offers tech support for older adults, helping them learn how to use new software and devices such as iPhones and Amazon's Alexa.

These are small investments of no more than a few million dollars. Made mostly within the past few years, they are tentative steps by Pivotal to see if it can make venture capital–style returns while sticking with its broader mission to pursue gender equality and women's empowerment in the United States. The firm has also invested in some higher-profile private companies, including Ellevest, the personal finance site geared toward women that was founded by former Wall Street banker Sallie Krawcheck; and All Raise, which is dedicated to women in tech. A consultant who studied Pivotal's investment strategy said the firm, despite having virtually no track record, expects to have greater credibility and better investment opportunities come its way by promoting French Gates's name and close involvement to company founders. "Melinda's name being attached to it carries a cachet," the consultant said.[26]

Nestled in a Seattle suburb, Pivotal operates out of an airy office suffused with light, plush in the way modern workplaces are, with a lot of "collaborative" spaces, wood and fabric touches, and a swanky kitchen. The firm is structured as a limited liability company rather than a traditional charitable foundation. Where the latter are bound by laws on how much they need to give away annually to maintain their tax-free status, and cannot fund political campaigns or lobby, limited liability companies pay taxes, but have the flexibility to embrace multiple strategies to promote a founder's goals, whether through venture investing, political contributions, advocacy, or charitable giving. Pivotal can thus invest in companies, make grants, or support advocacy, or do all three, in pursuit of its goal to increase women's political power, and as of 2024 it had invested in 150 such groups. It even has a publishing arm called Moment of Lift books, an imprint of Macmillan's Flatiron Books, which was launched in 2021 to publish nonfiction that promotes equality for girls. Through the LLC structure, which has become increasingly popular with philanthropists, Pivotal has sought to be more experimental and innovative, while bringing the same analysis and rigor to projects as the Gates Foundation does, according to an outside consultant who has worked with the firm. Pivotal's main goals are getting more women into technology jobs and elected to public office, supporting women and girls of color, and advocating for paid family and medical leave and caregiving. (In 2021, Pivotal called upon the Biden White House to appoint a "caregiving czar," an effort to transform childcare.) French Gates wants Pivotal to work with a wide range of players, including activists, advocates, investors, and innovators, hoping to use her substantial influence to bring focus to these issues.

For years, Pivotal was little more than a landing page as people who worked for French Gates conducted research to try to figure out what the entity should be. At the foundation, much of her work had been tied to gender equality and women's empowerment, but within the realm of global development. She had long sought to involve the foundation in domestic issues like getting more women into the fields of technology and computer science and increasing their representation on boards and in public life, but those ideas didn't get much airtime, partly because of the foundation's narrow focus on education within the United States. That was at least partly the impetus for starting Pivotal. The core insight that drove her gender-focused work at the foundation also underpins her work at Pivotal: that funding women's causes helps general development, and the world is better off if all girls are educated. In a video on the website of Pivotal, she explains the need to accelerate the pace of change for women. "My hopes and dreams for my daughters are exactly the same as [for] my son, which is I hope that they can do whatever they choose to do with their talents out in the world. And definitely, it's sad to think about, hey, will my daughters run into barriers that my son won't, just because of their gender?" By 2018, a year before her memoir *The Moment of Lift* was published, Pivotal became much more active. The following year, French Gates said she would commit $1 billion to her firm over a 10-year period to focus on gender equality.

As a philanthropist, French Gates has long advocated for contraception and the reproductive rights of women, especially those from poor backgrounds, arguing that women should be able to choose whether and when to have children, and that unplanned and unwanted pregnancies not only are devastating to women, but also hurt economic productivity. She came to that conclusion after seeing firsthand the struggles of poor women who'd had their agency taken away from them in African and Indian villages. That position put her directly at odds with her Catholic faith, impelling her to approach her advocacy for family planning through the lens of the Church's teachings on helping the poor, but also inviting its criticism. She addresses the conflict in her book by quoting from the Gospel of Luke: "And you experts in the law, woe to you, because you load people down with burdens they can hardly carry, and you yourselves will not lift one finger to help them."[27]

After the Supreme Court overturned *Roe v. Wade* in 2022, French Gates came out strongly in favor of abortion rights, seeing the reversal through the lens of female agency and autonomy—when "decisions are made for women as opposed to by them."[28] In the fall of 2022, Pivotal, the Obama Foundation, and the Clooney Foundation for Justice announced a partnership to build women's empowerment—to support "female change makers and their empowerment." As part of that effort, French Gates, Michelle Obama, and

Amal Clooney, the international human rights lawyer and wife of Hollywood actor George Clooney, have spoken on panels and at public events. In November 2023, the trio visited Malawi and South Africa as part of a campaign to end child marriage.

French Gates and her handlers at Pivotal have focused on the same high-visibility media strategy that the Gates Foundation employed. As with many public figures, including her former husband, the shaping of her image is a combination of taking her elemental qualities and transforming them into a consistent message. For years, she had been crafting a public persona distinct from her husband's at the foundation. One example was the foundation's annual Goalkeepers report, an assessment of how world leaders are doing against the 17 Sustainable Development Goals adopted by the United Nations in 2015. In 2021, Gates and French Gates each said their piece in slickly produced videos, but they couldn't have been more different in attitude and content. Each is reflective of the personality of its creator—exactly what the world has come to expect. In a one-minute video, French Gates focused purely on the power of women and how they hold up the world, and how women of all races and backgrounds did so during the pandemic. Gates's video was five minutes of statistics, maps, and factoids about global health and the pandemic response. In Pivotal, she has created a firm very much in her own image, setting a tone that combines ambition with humility, and expressing empowerment by embracing vulnerability. She speaks the language of empathy, compassion, and human connection, calling for "empathic leadership" and a "values-based" approach to work and life. "Heartbreaking" is a word she uses often to describe the things she has seen in her travels. Despite her high visibility and frequent public appearances, French Gates told a BBC interviewer in February 2024 that she finds it all unappealing. "I don't think it will ever sit particularly well," she said, when asked about why she gives interviews. "I've gotten more comfortable saying my truth, and much more comfortable in voicing what I know and have seen in places all over the world, but you know, I'm not particularly excited about the idea of being a public figure."

Her fraying ties to the foundation and to Gates, and her emergence as an independent philanthropist, had been visible in other ways. In 2010, when the former couple, along with Warren Buffett, had announced the Giving Pledge campaign, she and Gates had written a letter jointly, pledging to give most of their shared fortune to the Gates Foundation. But after their divorce was finalized in the summer of 2021, each wrote fresh Giving Pledge letters, renewing their commitment to giving away most of their wealth. In her letter, French Gates emphasized the importance of ground-up rather than top-down philanthropy and the need for flexibility rather than ideology to drive decisions around giving and grant-making, displaying a sensitivity and awareness to criticisms of big philanthropy.

That fortune, estimated at $11 billion, came to her as part of that divorce settlement. Gates had begun transferring assets to her soon after their divorce announcement—mainly billions of dollars' worth of shares in companies like AutoNation, Deere, and Canadian National, according to regulatory filings reported by *Bloomberg*. Gates transferred $2.4 billion of Microsoft stock to her in 2022. As of that year, she had more than $1.4 billion worth of stock she had received in different companies. Cascade, the private investment firm that oversees both the Gates fortune and the foundation's endowment, no longer manages French Gates's personal money.

When the divorce was announced, the foundation had said that its two cochairs would continue to work together, with the understanding that if they couldn't get along within or after a two-year trial period, French Gates would leave, and her ex-husband would give her funds to pursue her own philanthropy. The former couple maintained a professional relationship, working together to guide the foundation, a person close to her said, but French Gates found it challenging at times. In 2024, when she cut ties with the foundation completely, Gates gave her $12.5 billion—an amount of money that would give her enormous heft in carrying out her mission. As of May 2024, there were discussions underway about how those billions would be used, and whether it would all be directed through Pivotal. French Gates also planned to update sections of her Giving Pledge letter to reflect the new reality.

Even though French Gates is building Pivotal with a specific focus on women, observers of philanthropy don't expect her to veer fundamentally away from Gates's worldview. People who have worked with the couple say that Gates and French Gates are united in how they see the role of philanthropy in the world. She has embraced the same market-based fundamentals that drove decision-making at the Gates Foundation, the people said. It's just that she wants to do more for gender equality and women's rights, the way Gates handles his climate and energy investing through Breakthrough Energy, and his technology investing through Gates Ventures.

Comparisons between French Gates and MacKenzie Scott are inevitable. Both women got divorced around the same time and emerged as independent billionaire philanthropists. But that's perhaps where the comparisons end. At the same time, Scott, who inherited about $38 billion as part of her divorce settlement, has been giving it away silently. She maintains a low public profile and gives no interviews. Her style of giving involves doing the research on a nonprofit and writing a check for the organization to use as it sees fit. In December 2022, Scott launched an organization called Yield Giving. The website has no frills or fanfare. It is heavy on text and low on visuals, evocative of the unfussy and self-effacing way in which Scott has gone about her business of giving money away. Scott typically puts her money into donor-advised funds and relies on advisors around the country to help her figure out how and where to donate the funds. Nonprofits can send proposals to Yield Giving, which has a committee to review them and help with grant-making.

"I would say that they are more similar than different," said Jeannie Infante Sager, the the former director of the Women's Philanthropy Institute at Indiana University's Lilly Family School of Philanthropy and a faculty member of its Fund Raising School. "There is a transparency to their giving that is inspiring," said Sager. The institute received grants from the Gates Foundation that Sager said were initially spurred by French Gates as she developed her philanthropic strategy. It has continued to work with Pivotal, and Sager has also helped Yield Giving carry out some of its work. She added that both have been thoughtful, rather than slapdash, about their approaches. The high profile of Pivotal has drawn attention to what Sager said has been a growing trend of giving in the past decade by women and for women's causes. Her research has found that women often approach philanthropy differently than men, preferring to give collectively and holistically. Empathy can drive their giving, as can rage. So-called rage giving to women's organizations spiked in 2016 after Donald Trump was elected president, Sager found. There was a similar spike after the Supreme Court overthrew the constitutional right to abortion in 2022.

Elizabeth Dale, the Seattle University professor who teaches nonprofit leadership, said that Pivotal's impact has been hard to assess. "Is Pivotal making a difference on the ground yet? It's been eight years," Dale said. The firm hasn't gotten the kind of attention one would expect given French Gates's star power, she said, partly because the giving has been relatively minimal. "Outside of the gender space, I don't think a lot of people have heard about it."

French Gates remains undeterred. She has harnessed the press and other online platforms to get her message out, from writing opinion articles to teaching a masterclass on "impactful giving," convinced that a steady drumbeat of publicity is essential to Pivotal's work. She considers herself a medium through which the experiences and realities of other women can be told, and a powerful voice that tells women they can do anything. It's the voice she used in 2018, when she penned a missive about the importance of computer science education for girls and women. The essay was titled: "The Next Bill Gates Won't Look Like the Last One."

Chapter 7

Global Savior, Big Philanthropist

The Vaccine Czar

The history of the world is heavy with tales of epidemics, disease, and death. Terrifying plagues, pestilences, and poxes have felled populations through the centuries. Fevers and humors, outbreaks and contagions have confounded generations of medical experts. But the history of virulent disease is also the story of human ingenuity. In May 1796, the British physician Edward Jenner inoculated a healthy eight-year-old boy with cowpox, a milder cousin of smallpox, the deadly virus. Two months later, after the boy had recovered, Jenner introduced matter from a smallpox lesion into him, and found that the boy did not develop the disease.[1] He named the process "vaccination," after "vacca," the Latin name for a cow, and in doing so, set humanity on the long course to modern vaccines.

Today, vaccines are a proven method of protecting against a host of illnesses. In many parts of the world, routine immunizations protect children against diseases such as polio, chickenpox, mumps, measles, tetanus, malaria, and diphtheria. On its website, the Centers for Disease Control and Prevention lists fourteen such diseases under the title "Diseases You Almost Forgot About (Thanks to Vaccines)." Yet, viruses by their very nature are a step ahead of the cure. Quick to figure out vulnerabilities in the human body, a virus can propel itself from person to person on little more than a gust of exhaled air or a casual touch, mutating even as it spreads and sickens.

Globalization is a virus's delight, making it easy to hitch a ride from country to country on the ever-thickening flows of trade, travel, and commerce.

Although public health professionals have long been concerned about pandemics, it is hard to sound the alarm on a hypothetical premise. Inevitably, the real work begins only when a deadly virus exits its stealth mode. That's exactly what happened on January 30, 2020, when the WHO declared a global health emergency. The novel coronavirus had been first detected in Wuhan, China, one month earlier. Within two weeks, it reared its head in Thailand, followed by Japan. By the third week, the first case was reported in the United States, and soon after, the virus began popping up around the world. Less than a month after the WHO declared Covid-19 a global pandemic in mid-March 2020, sending countries into lockdown mode, there were more than one million confirmed cases of the illness in April—a more than tenfold increase. In those first confusing months, the WHO launched a global campaign to find vaccines against the virus and develop diagnostic tests and therapeutic treatments. It urged its 193 member states and private donors to fund protective equipment for frontline health workers and held meetings with Silicon Valley companies to fight misinformation about the virus. It also created a strategy to develop vaccines in partnership with scientists and researchers, and to focus on treatments for those who had contracted the disease. Its donors pledged $675 million. The WHO's role in orchestrating a global response to the pandemic was unsurprising. Founded in 1948 as a unit of the United Nations, the organization has been the primary agency in charge of global public health since the end of the Second World War. According to the United Nations, the WHO is "responsible for providing leadership on global health matters, shaping the health research agenda, setting norms and standards, articulating evidence-based policy options, providing technical support to countries and monitoring and assessing health trends."

What was far more surprising, amid all the chaos and fear, was the presence of a single, high-profile actor: the Gates Foundation. In the decades since its inception, the foundation had become one of the top three donors to the WHO, along with the United States and Germany. It thrust itself into the global pandemic response, establishing itself as an authority alongside the WHO and other government agencies. Foundation experts worked closely with government officials to determine the best policy responses and identify the best vaccine candidates. Even the decision to use testing swabs that only required circling inside the nostril—making at-home diagnostic tests less uncomfortable and easier to use—was taken with the input of Gates Foundation researchers. Gates began to use his bullhorn to advocate for Covid-19 vaccines, often speaking alongside Dr. Anthony Fauci, then the director of the National Institute of Allergy and Infectious Diseases who became the most trusted face of the U.S. response. Gates held discussions with global leaders like Boris Johnson and Angela Merkel by videoconference. On social media and in interviews, he dwelled on the most promising vaccine candidates, weighed in on policy, laid out the best- and worst-case scenarios. The technology billionaire was no medical expert, but he had enough of an understanding of the vaccine science and enough star power that his opinion appeared to be accepted as fully as those of many professional scientists, especially with the world awash in uncertainty and fear, and thirsty for information. Although he was careful to stay out of political debates, Gates became an unusually vocal critic of then president Donald J. Trump's approach to the pandemic and his administration's initial unwillingness to embrace scientifically established methods for testing and setting up a system of disease surveillance. His sense of urgency about the pandemic and frustration with Trump administration officials was palpable; as someone accustomed to having presidents and top public officials take his counsel, his disbelief made him unusually vituperative. He told the medical news site *Stat* that the Trump administration was appointing people unqualified to run the pandemic response just because they agreed with the "crackpot theories."[2]

As of 2023, the foundation had committed more than $2 billion to various Covid-19 response efforts. It directed funds to implement testing and improve health infrastructure in some parts of the world and to conduct research into new treatments and vaccines, and it extended loans to support the development of vaccines in poor and middle-income countries. It guaranteed Abbott Laboratories, the giant pharmaceutical company, and SD Biosensor, a maker of diagnostic tests, that there would be $100 million worth of demand for low-cost rapid antigen tests in developing countries. It has struck similar deals with other companies to accelerate the production of vaccines. Among the other large philanthropic outfits, the Rockefeller Foundation stands out for its $1 billion commitment to the pandemic recovery, announced in October 2020, but those commitments were made with far less fanfare. The Gates Foundation's singular role in the pandemic response may have surprised some in the wider world, but public health experts, policymakers, and economists in the field of global development had long been aware of its heft in the world of vaccines and the quiet, careful ways in which it had deployed its dollars to build a tightly controlled network.

Vaccines are close to Gates's heart. They are scientific breakthroughs with measurable impacts, a combination that spoke to his rational mind: The more vaccines were developed and delivered, the more lives could be saved. "Vaccines work," is a mantra he has repeated often. In the 1990s, the billionaire had been jolted awake by the plight of the world's poorest, witnessing firsthand how people died of easily preventable diseases because their governments couldn't afford enough vaccines. At the same time, big drug companies had little financial incentive to pursue vaccine research for diseases that had been eradicated from the developed world. In that unmet need, Gates saw a role for his dollars. In 2000, soon after it launched, the Gates Foundation partnered with the WHO, UNICEF, and the World Bank to create the Global Alliance for Vaccines and Immunization. The alliance, known as GAVI, provides purchase guarantees to drug makers to encourage them to manufacture vaccines at a lower cost so that poorer nations can buy them. The alliance, which has received more than $4 billion from the Gates Foundation, built up enough market power that it could negotiate prices with big drug makers like Pfizer, Sanofi, and others, a strategy that has led it to immunize more than half of the world's children in the past two decades. GAVI also funds institutions to accelerate vaccine research. More than a decade ago, the alliance and the Gates Foundation also muscled their way into the Global Polio Eradication Initiative, which was created in

1988 by the WHO, UNICEF, the Centers for Disease Control and Prevention, and Rotary International, a community service organization. The Gates Foundation is also the primary partner of the Coalition for Epidemic Preparedness Innovations, or CEPI. Funded by the governments of several countries, including the United Kingdom, Belgium, and Ethiopia, as well as the Wellcome Trust, a U.K.-based healthcare philanthropy, CEPI makes grants to speed up development of vaccines during pandemics and outbreaks. In 2010, the Gates Foundation launched the "decade of vaccines" in partnership with governmental and multilateral organizations including the WHO. Its goal was to spur research and delivery of vaccines to the world's poorest countries, and to that end, it pledged $10 billion.

The foundation is the largest private donor to an international organization called the Global Fund to Fight AIDS, Tuberculosis and Malaria. The fund was born in 2002 under the auspices of the United Nations. As of 2022, the Gates Foundation had committed $3.6 billion to the fund's efforts to fight those diseases in more than 100 countries. It is an ally of the National Institutes of Health (NIH), the primary U.S. agency responsible for medical and public health research. The two entities have collaborated on several different projects; together, they fund 54 percent of global research and development into diseases prevalent in poorer countries. For more than a decade, Gates had been a regular speaker and guest at NIH events, discussing the zika virus, tuberculosis, and other topics of public health. During the pandemic, that network of alliances funded and nurtured by the Gates Foundation over the years gave it substantial influence in shaping the direction of vaccine research and delivery to low-income countries. The Gates-backed vaccine alliance GAVI jointly led another vaccine alliance called COVAX, which aimed to pool together demand for Covid-19 vaccines. The other co-leads were CEPI and WHO, along with UNICEF as the delivery partner. An investigation by *Politico* and *Welt* published in September 2022 found that GAVI, CEPI, the Gates Foundation, and the Wellcome Trust together have spent nearly $10 billion on the global Covid response since 2020.[3]

The COVAX partnership spearheaded the global Covid vaccination effort. By stepping in and negotiating pricing with individual pharmaceutical companies and guaranteeing them payments using donor funds—what is called "advance market commitment"—it created collective purchasing power and procured more than one billion doses for people in poor countries. Countries that committed to buying vaccines from COVAX's facility got them at a discounted rate, while those who opted for the "optional purchase" agreement paid a higher rate. Still, supply bottlenecks and other disruptions during the pandemic meant that vaccines didn't reach residents of poor countries swiftly. That led to calls from many public health experts to waive patent protections on the vaccines so that they could be manufactured locally by generic drug makers. But pharmaceutical companies were reluctant to give away their intellectual property for free, and COVAX agreed, saying that patent protection was critical for innovation, and that vaccine manufacture was a complicated process that local drug makers might struggle with.

As a firm believer in preserving intellectual property rights, Gates appeared to have his fingerprints all over the discussion. Rather than set aside his convictions in the face of a global health emergency, Gates used his foundation's power and influence to buy vaccines from the companies and deliver them to developing countries, acting as an intermediary to solve a problem. Critics accused him of "vaccine colonialism."[4] Eventually he agreed to a temporary waiver on IP for Covid vaccines. The foundation also played a big role in convincing Oxford University to sell the vaccine it had developed, with funding from the British government, to AstraZeneca rather than share the science with developing countries for free so that they could manufacture it locally. Later, French Gates explained the reasoning behind it. Oxford had the science but not the skill to bring a vaccine to market, which is why they encouraged the university to partner with the drug maker.[5]

A Data-Driven Approach

The WHO has a metric to calculate the years of life lost due to premature deaths and disabilities around the world because of the prevalence of certain illnesses within a population. Known as disability-adjusted life years, or DALYs, they are a helpful measure of the overall global burden of disease. One DALY is equivalent to one year of lost health, according to the WHO. Those numbers spoke to Gates in a way that personal experiences and reports could not, because they showed numerically how a child born in the Indian state of Uttar Pradesh had a far lower chance of survival than a child born in the United States. Trevor Neilson, the early Gates Foundation employee, recalled just how disturbed Gates was by the DALYs. "That is fucking insane," Gates would tell Neilson. "That's unfair." With his logical approach, Gates couldn't get past the irrationality of the "ovarian lottery," a term his close friend Warren Buffett coined to describe the divergent fortunes of children based on where they were born. "In Bill's brain, it made no sense to him, so there was this very quiet outrage."

Science and math have always been Gates's way of connecting with the world. He found comfort in the incontrovertible nature of facts. Numbers told the story every time. The moral compass that guided his philanthropy was underpinned by a faith in metrics, datasets, and evidence. Much as a cartographer puts a surveyor's data to work to build a map, Gates digested mountains of available data to understand the features of the global health landscape—the lush mountains of the rich Western world where healthcare was abundant, and the parched deserts of the poor where it was not. These neglected regions were the targets—or in capitalism speak, potential markets—for his philanthropy. In the crevasses between government ineptitude and corporate cupidity, Gates found the unmet demand that his billions could help fill. The "profit motive" was social good, and the return on invested dollars, in this case, would be measured in terms of lives saved and problems solved in the poorest countries. Gates called his approach "catalytic philanthropy," which simply meant finding causes where his money had the biggest potential to accelerate change, whether by funding innovative technology or making grants to nonprofits.[6] In a 2013 essay for *Wired*, Gates wrote that capitalism "is the best system ever devised to make self-interest the wider interest."[7] Or as the former journalist and Canadian politician Chrystia Freeland wrote in *Plutocrats*, her 2012 book about the rise of the new global super-rich, Gates became "an evangelist for the idea that capitalism must do good, and do-gooders must become more capitalist."[8]

To identify the biggest problems and determine where the foundation's money would make the biggest quantifiable difference, Gates relied mainly on scientists, researchers, economists, policymakers, and other experts trained in the West to help him build core areas of focus, namely health-care, agriculture, education, and financial services. The foundation attracted people with a technocratic bent, well versed in the argot of the development community. Global public health was the perfect starting point for the foun-dation and remains one of its biggest areas of focus to this day because both the causes and the fixes were evident in existing data and science and because governments routinely underinvested in it. The bias toward data sometimes had the opposite effect: Areas of public health that didn't already have data exhibiting an unmet need were less likely to get funded because it was harder to justify the need for dollars.

In the beginning, the foundation's priorities were broadly informed by the United Nations' Millennium Development Goals, a set of eight global health and development targets to meet by 2015, which the world missed. Since then, the foundation has taken its cues from the United Nations' Sus-tainable Development Goals, which were adopted in 2015 as a "universal call to action to end poverty, protect the planet, and ensure that by 2030 all people enjoy peace and prosperity." Currently, the Gates Foundation makes grants largely in five big areas: global health, gender equality, global devel-opment, global growth and opportunity, and global policy and advocacy. A sixth big grant-making unit focuses on the foundation's work in the United States. Each area of focus is headed by a president and staffed with academics and experts in the field. Under the areas lie different program strategies—41 at last count. Agricultural program strategies sit under "global growth." The programs for tuberculosis and vaccine development fall under "global health." Charter schools and "economic mobility and opportunity" are part of the U.S. focus. The teams have ambitious objectives. To meet them, they pick the nonprofits to give grants to and use internal metrics to track and as-sess the success of their grant-making. Typically, foundation representatives dole out the money in tranches, subject to the nonprofit meeting specific goals or implementation milestones. Individual programs may be shuttered, and funds redirected, if they don't meet the foundation's performance criteria. Program officers in various countries and regions act as intermediaries between the foundation and the grantees to make sure everything is working as intended. It is a highly structured organization, with more than 2,000 people and nine offices, including in India, China, and three African countries; multiple committees, advisors, planners, and operations managers; and hierarchies known only to those who sit in it. Projects often need the approval of as many as 10 people. On top of that, there is an extensive staff operation, where dozens of assistants and others work with executives to manage their schedules and arrange travel and security. "They are not people with a light footprint," said a former foundation employee.

The Good and the Bad

It can be difficult to fathom the extent of the Gates Foundation's influence around the world, especially in global health and development. The pandemic provided a glimpse into how deeply embedded the foundation is in public health networks and research efforts that most people assume are the preserve of a few big, multilateral organizations like the WHO and the United Nations. But because of the billions of dollars it has given away, the Gates Foundation often shows up alongside countries on lists of donors to these types of entities. In a 2018 study, the Brookings Institution found that the foundation was the seventeenth largest donor to 53 multilateral organizations. It was the only private actor; the rest were all countries.[9]

The foundation's annual budget alone is $8.3 billion, about the same as the annual gross domestic product of Monaco, or the 2023 net worth of Marc Benioff, the cofounder of technology giant Salesforce, philanthropist, and owner of *Time* magazine. That kind of money has given the foundation incredible heft and prominence, especially with the two cochairs being such forceful and visible advocates of their work. Since the Buffett money started coming in, the foundation has given money to an ever-growing pool of nonprofits, universities, media entities, research centers, and start-ups and other for-profit entities whose work fits into its mission. It has given away more than $70 billion since its founding, which works out to $3.5 billion a year on average. At the end of 2022, it had an endowment of $67 billion. There is no dearth of money to spend or trade-offs to make. This largesse has become increasingly troubling to critics because it allows the foundation to exert a level of influence that is often far larger than the money. Gates can easily get an audience with leaders of governments, businesses, and other organizations. The multiple relationships the foundation has built through formal alliances and informal networks given the revolving door between the foundation, policy experts, and employees of multilateral organizations—one high-profile example is Dr. Rajiv Shah who, before he became the president of the Rockefeller Foundation, was the USAID administrator appointed by President Obama, before which he held a number of government roles and played a crucial role in developing the vaccine industry for the Gates Foundation—allows for a tremendous amount of purchase that it can use to direct outcomes in line with its preferences. Together, the cash, the star power, and the leverage can and does skew the priorities of nonprofits, multilateral agencies like the WHO, research universities, and even governments, whether it's about how best to deliver vaccines or which tools to use to increase crop yield.

One study published in 2008 found that as early as 2003, the National Institutes of Health, which is funded by tax dollars and focuses primarily on biomedical research to address the health problems of Americans, allocated $1 billion to fund global health priorities during a period when its budget grew little. The researchers attributed it to an initiative called the Grand Challenges in Global Health led by the Gates Foundation.[10] By engaging the scientific community and drumming up positive coverage in the media, the foundation was able to direct the best researchers and funds to global health, one of its biggest priorities, the study concluded.

Bequests to universities are a big focus of grant-making. Since 2010, the Gates Foundation has given away at least $11.6 billion to 471 universities, according to one study, and the money was directed to fund research in three of its primary areas of interest: maternity and early childhood, agricultural research, and HIV/AIDS. Most of that money went to universities in the United States, but also the U.K. and Canada.[11] In 2017, the foundation gave $279 million to the Institute for Health Metrics and Evaluation at the University of Washington, the largest private donation in the university's history, on top of a $105 million grant it had given a decade earlier to help launch the institute. The massive amount of money enabled the independent institute to conduct research and build databases on the state of global health, including Covid, tuberculosis, malaria, and other diseases, and become the preeminent source of data cited by media and other public health organizations. To build more databases in priority areas such as financial inclusion, the foundation has also provided funding to organizations like the World Bank. Since 2011, the bank has published the *Global Findex Database* report every three years to track people's access to digital financial services such as payments around the world. Directing resources to overlooked problems such as patchy data can be a good thing. At the same time, critics have long chafed that the foundation decides to fund whatever it deems important without inviting input from the broader scientific and research community. The criticisms can tend toward the polemical and the hyperbolic, but they are essentially arguments about unchecked power and accountability.

Academics, policymakers, and journalists, particularly leftists and progressives, as well as rival foundations, nonprofits, and disillusioned former workers have attacked multiple aspects of the foundation's work and principles. Some take issue with the foundation's reliance on a market-based, technocratic, fix-it attitude that entrenches long-standing power dynamics between rich and poor countries, and between donors and recipients. Others point to the pitfalls of relying on a narrow, top-down, data-based and expertise-driven approach that ignores local and cultural realities. Yet others say such untrammeled private power without public accountability is antidemocratic. A fourth group of critics says that the rigorous reporting the foundation demands from its grant recipients and its bureaucratic approach place unnecessary burdens on the staff of nonprofits that might not be set up to meet those requirements. And although it is a low-level hum, the way the Gates Foundation casts its own work irks some critics. Often, the foundation will describe its work in terms of "lives saved" rather than "deaths prevented." The latter term, which is drier and more technical, is often used by multilateral agencies. It might be a matter of semantics, but the Gates Foundation's terminology plays into the notion that it has a superior mission, a loftier goal than others working in the field. When is a life saved, after all?

At the same time, defenders of the Gates Foundation point out that the data alone is evidence that its style of philanthropy works. The criticisms don't carry much meaning for the people on the ground who have seen their incomes rising, their access to basic necessities like food, water, and medicine improving along with their health, or the yield from their crops increasing. If the critics are idealists who attack the foundation's influence on normative grounds and question the underlying system that allows for one entity to have so much influence, the defenders are the beneficiaries and the realists who point to the fact that improving the quality of life for some within an unfair system is better than complete apathy.

Many observers and partners, however, take a nuanced view that acknowledges the successes on the ground while pointing out how the foundation sidesteps trickier questions about its size, influence, and lack of accountability. Manoj Mohanan, a public health expert who teaches at Duke University, said that the foundation could do a better job of disclosing how it makes decisions and assesses its success, inviting independent verification of the success or failure of a project they have undertaken. Mohanan, who has received grants from the foundation for his work, said that many other big grant-making bodies invite competitive proposals for grants and give out the funds. But with the Gates Foundation, academics and nonprofits searching for a grant often end up turning to their networks for introductions to foundation employees who might consider their project. Rather than making it about a bigger call for proposals, which would perhaps be more democratic, the foundation's mandate comes from the two cochairs sitting at the very top. The level of control is such that you might be sitting in a room discussing a grant and get an email from Gates asking for numbers about a specific disease. It suggests that the former couple want to keep the controls in their hands like it's a small organization, Mohanan surmised. "I hate to say it because I'm a beneficiary of the process, but networks become much more important in that setup than in a purely transparent process."

The world was largely uncritical of the foundation in the first decade of its existence.[12] If anything, much of the West was still on its free-market high at the beginning of the new millennium, and a business-focused approach to solving the problems of the world seemed to be a natural outgrowth of wealth creation. Two writers for *The Economist* even coined the term "philanthrocapitalism" to describe how individuals and corporations could apply market fundamentals for social returns.[13] At the World Economic Forum in Davos in 2008, Gates gave a much-lauded speech on "creative capitalism," arguing that businesses, nonprofits, and governments can collectively harness market forces so that people can work to reduce inequities without giving up profitability.

But talk of worsening inequality and rising billionaire influence in recent years has raised new questions about everything from political donations to philanthropy.[14] One of the earliest and fiercest critics of the Gates Foundation is Linsey McGoey, a Canadian-born sociologist who teaches at the University of Sussex in the United Kingdom. In her book *No Such Thing As a Free Gift*, McGoey takes aim at philanthrocapitalism and, in particular, Gates, for his role in "shifting the global discourse on philanthropy in recent decades." Through initiatives like the Giving Pledge, McGoey writes, Gates offers a "powerful antidote" to critics who point to the widening global wealth gap, because he and other billionaires can always say that they're giving their money away.[15]

In his book *Winners Take All*, the journalist Anand Giridharadas criticizes all big philanthropy, including the Gates Foundation, for trying to "solve for" individual, intractable issues via technology, rather than fighting for ground-up social and economic justice or change. Giridharadas and others point out the irony of big philanthropy, which seeks to address the problems created by extreme wealth generation while doing little to change the underlying system that caused the problems in the first place: Is it fair that the very billionaires who created or exacerbated some of the world's problems, or benefited from a lopsided system, be given the keys to act as agents of change with little or no oversight?[16]

Melissa Berman, formerly of Rockefeller Philanthropy Advisors, helped wealthy people and big foundations think about how to make their giving most effective. She is an ardent defender of the role philanthropy can play, but also sensitive to the criticisms. To Berman, the Gates Foundation, from which her former nonprofit has received a grant, is not unique. Rather, she says it is a creature of an existing system that imposes Western values on developing countries without taking ground-level feedback into account. To single it out is to ignore the systemic problems that it's not the foundation's responsibility to solve.

Other supporters of big philanthropy point out that private foundation money should be free to pursue innovation and underwrite experimental efforts that governments can't and businesses won't, with the expectation that public funding will follow a successful project. An entity like the Gates Foundation can take risks and accept the possibility of failure precisely because its money is not accountable to shareholders or governments. Supporters commend the Gates Foundation and other big philanthropists for their willingness to drop a project that isn't delivering results, because cutting it short and admitting failure is better than leaving money in something that isn't working.

Critics acknowledge that being able to try different things and take risks with philanthropic dollars is a boon. But they argue that limiting the costs of a mistake by dropping a program doesn't account for the havoc wreaked by the decision on end beneficiaries like nonprofits, which changed course in response to the flood of money and now have to reverse direction because a big philanthropist decided the metrics weren't meeting its goals.

The foundation's controversial work in U.S. education is an important example. Until Gates stepped up as a public advocate of Covid vaccines during the pandemic, the foundation's efforts in America primarily involved attempts at reforming education. Both Gates and French Gates held deep convictions that access to education was the best way to give every child an equal footing. Since its earliest days, the foundation made it a domestic priority to improve the quality of education by pushing for smaller classrooms, which were thought to reduce dropout rates. It directed more than $2 billion toward school districts that agreed to establish smaller high schools, according to one estimate.[17] As part of the effort, the foundation also earmarked funds for charter schools, which are privately run but publicly funded. A whole clutch of billionaires, including former New York mayor Michael Bloomberg, the hedge fund manager Bill Ackman, Netflix founder Reed Hastings, and Facebook's Zuckerberg, joined Gates in pouring money into such schools, assuming that they would provide a better alternative to traditional school systems. However, after two decades of the experiment, the data has been mixed, showing that students of charter schools perform, on average, no better than students who attend public school.

The foundation also spent hundreds of millions of dollars on a project tying teacher evaluation at least partly to student performance and test scores, with the participation of local governments. But the metrics eventually didn't appear promising enough and the foundation pulled its funding, leaving many school districts with the additional costs. Another effort involved directing hundreds of millions of dollars to promote common core standards, under which states adopt the same assessment metrics for subjects like English and math. However, teachers were not initially trained to teach the curriculum, and as children began failing, states pulled back from using common core standards. By the time the foundation recognized the importance of training and tailoring teaching to local realities, it was too late. It has since deemphasized the program, acknowledging that national standards didn't give individual schools enough adaptability.

Diane Ravitch, a former research professor of education at New York University and an outspoken critic of the Gates Foundation, once called the billionaire the nation's unelected school superintendent. On her blog, Ravitch pointed out that by 2022, no one had expected that charter schools, given all the money spent on them, wouldn't outperform public schools on average—and, in some cases, would actually do worse than public schools.[18] Aware of that data, both Gates and French Gates acknowledged in annual letters that their efforts to reform education didn't go quite as expected, but the foundation would continue funding innovative ideas. As of 2020, the foundation has turned its focus to math education in U.S. schools. On its website, there is no mention of its small school and common core efforts.

There are yet other critics—philosophers and political scientists—who argue that private philanthropy, which is subsidized by taxpayers because charitable deductions are essentially lost tax revenue, is antidemocratic because a massive entity like the Gates Foundation reports only to itself; with no voters or shareholders to hold it publicly accountable, it can ignore alternate points of view and direct outcomes in line with its preferences. In the book *Just Giving*, the Stanford political scientist Rob Reich makes the argument that large-scale philanthropy of the kind Gates engages in is fundamentally incompatible with democracy. It confers enormous power to its practitioners, allowing the wealthiest to have a say in the affairs of a country without being elected, and while gaining a virtuous image and points for civic gratitude.[19] The political scientist Emma Saunders-Hastings has also written about the need for political scientists to study philanthropy because "elite influence can be undemocratic even when public-spirited in its motivations and even when it bypasses formal political institutions."[20]

Melissa Berman refutes the notion that philanthropy is antidemocratic. Rather than attacking philanthropy, she said, society should lobby for changes in taxation policy. If taxation is more redistributive, people can have a say on what private money is best used for. "Philanthropy by definition is voluntary," Berman said. "If it's not then it's called a tax."

Joel L. Fleishman, the Duke University professor who has long set aside a part of his paycheck for charity, vigorously opposes any kind of mechanism that restricts individuals from doing what they want with their dollars. "One of my criticisms of the critics of philanthropy is that they don't like the idea of people with a lot of money giving it away to whatever they want to give it for," said Fleishman. "When people start substituting their own judgment or imposing it on the private money of others, it's a problem." He agrees with the critics that aspects of the underlying systems should be corrected, but "don't take out your frustrations on philanthropy. I think philanthropy is doing good."

The foundation itself is aware of the growing criticism and sensitive to it. In January 2023, it held a call with subscribers to its mailing list, and Mark Suzman, the foundation's chief executive, addressed the topic in his letter. "Does the foundation have too much influence?" read the title. Suzman didn't disagree that the foundation had a lot of influence, given that it had more funds at its disposal than any other philanthropy. "It's true that between our dollars, voice, and convening power, we have access and influence that many others do not," Suzman wrote.

He redirected the question to one of how and why the foundation uses its influence. Its very heft can bring attention to otherwise neglected or overlooked problems, according to Suzman, and its megaphone can be used for good. He insisted that the foundation doesn't set the agenda but is merely carrying out the Sustainable Development Goals set by the United Nations in 2015. The question of whether the very act of directing billions of dollars toward causes they believe in can effectively shape a policy or disrupt existing methods of doing things, irrespective of the foundation's intention, was addressed obliquely. Even if the absolute amounts appear large, the foundation's contributions are a drop in the bucket compared to the budget of big governments. On separate occasions, foundation executives have acknowledged the entity's influence but also minimized it by comparing it to the total spend of the U.S. government on social programs and pointing out that millions of lives still remain untouched.

More than once, the foundation has been accused of "neocolonialism," an ism that is generally defined as the use of economic, social, and cultural power to maintain a grip and control or direct outcomes in other countries, especially those that were former colonies. The term has long been used to critique postwar multilateral agencies like the International Monetary Fund and the World Bank, whose efforts to "solve" poverty with Western expertise either backfired or produced mixed results at best. It doesn't help that the Gates Foundation seems to borrow freely and extensively from those approaches to global development, where words like "partnerships," "stakeholders," "progress," "prosperity," "equity," "transformation," "solutions," and "sustainability" convey a collaborative tilt and lofty aims, and where acronyms are intended to be phonetically viable, like ACT, REACT, and AGRA. It also doesn't help that there are revolving doors between the foundation and the agencies.

The Gates Foundation also caught the eye of Vandana Shiva, an Indian environmental activist who has made it her life's work to protect biodiversity, indigenous knowledge, and the livelihood of small farmers. Shiva has her share of critics—in a 2014 profile of her in *The New Yorker* magazine, Mark Lynas, an environmental expert, told the writer that Shiva was "blinded by her ideology and her political beliefs," making her both "so effective and so dangerous"—but she has developed a strong following among radical leftists in Europe and elsewhere.[21] Roughly a decade ago, she began targeting Gates and the foundation, lambasting it for its dogmatic, play-God approach. She is among those who say that the foundation replicates the power dynamics of colonialism by imposing its agricultural and health preferences on developing countries without considering local knowledge and customs. "Gates has created global alliances to impose top-down analysis and prescriptions for health problems," Shiva wrote in her book *Oneness vs the 1%: Shattering Illusions, Seeding Freedom.* "He gives money to define the problems, and then he uses his influence and money to impose the solutions."[22]

In 2013, Peter Buffett, a music composer, philanthropist, and a son of Buffett, made a similar point. In a *New York Times* opinion piece, Buffett called out the emerging industry of "philanthropic colonialism," where acts of giving by the wealthy in the name of upliftment and improvement in the quality of life only perpetuate the existence of an inherently unequal system. Rather than push for systemic change, Buffett wrote, causes like microlending and financial literacy only bring people into a cycle of debt, interest, and repayment.[23] In later discussions, including with the philosopher-rabbi of the "effective altruism" movement, William MacAskill, Buffett appeared to be directly critiquing the "data-driven" approach that was au courant in philanthropy, arguing for an approach that was based more on intuition than simply data.

Additionally, the Gates Foundation has come in for criticism for its unquestioned belief in the power of technology to solve problems. Tied to its technological bias, critics say, is the foundation's dependence on experts to determine courses of action even when their training, typically acquired in the West, is not necessarily directly applicable or viable in the developing world. Those who have worked with the foundation reflected on what one Harvard-trained academic who studies public health called "a cult of authority," relying on experts within a very narrow circle of top universities, and on global advisors who "speak in a voice that shows a lack of hesitation."

Some of the harshest criticism in that vein comes from agricultural and development economists and other philanthropists who have followed the Gates Foundation's work in Africa. In 2006, the foundation unveiled a program called Alliance for a Green Revolution in Africa, or AGRA. Modeled on India's Green Revolution in the 1960s, which used scientific innovation to improve crop yields and made the country self-sufficient in food, AGRA is criticized because of its Western, scientific approach that focuses single-mindedly on increasing crop yield as the way to lift millions out of poverty. Although the goal is admirable, it is incomplete, they say. Critics point to the Indian experience—which ultimately wasn't a cure-all given that it reduced biodiversity and high rates of poverty remained—as an example of why local input is necessary; but so far, the foundation appears to have ignored calls to incorporate local knowledge into its work in African countries.

Unlike many other private foundations, which nonprofits can seek grants from, or MacKenzie Scott's approach, which is to find nonprofits and give them the money to use as they see fit, the Gates Foundation is scriptwriter, director, and producer. It develops ideas and strategies about how to enact change, and then finds partners to implement them. If foundation executives determine that telemedicine is the best solution to build a public health system in a poor country, their next step is to search for partners who can help carry out that plan. Being an active participant also means that the foundation partners up with nonprofits, governments, multilateral agencies, and top researchers to think through the right approaches to tackle a problem. The collaborative approach has allowed the foundation to piggyback on the knowledge of others while providing financial support and minimizing the risk that something they backed would fail completely.

However, the foundation's approach to making grants and keeping tabs on how those funds are being used and how successful a program is, can be intimidating to nonprofits. Grants for specific projects are typically tied to milestones and quantifiable metrics to assess progress. The goals must be agreed upon with partners so that both sides know beforehand what will be deemed a successful outcome. In exchange for funds, foundation executives demand a level of reporting, documentation, and individual treatment that can be burdensome for small nonprofits, which might not have the most sophisticated systems to provide that feedback.

Gates and French Gates long held the reins despite the foundation's size and constantly expanding influence. Major decisions needed their approval. Until 2021, when the couple split up, they were two of only three trustees—the third being Buffett—who sat atop the foundation. The three met in their official roles about once a year, every May, to approve budgets and long-term plans. Its unusual board structure often drew criticism from philanthropy experts who said that the concentration of power was troubling at such a massive and influential foundation and highlighted the need for governance changes.

By comparison, foundations of comparable size and influence have a much more professional structure. The Wellcome Trust, a U.K. based foundation founded in 1936 that focuses on healthcare, with an endowment and employee count comparable to that of the Gates Foundation, has ten board members. The Rockefeller and Ford foundations too have far larger boards. Of course, the founders of those entities have long since died, allowing their successors to build institutions run entirely by professionals.

"As living donors, Bill and Melinda Gates make all of the foundation's critical strategic decisions, and the organization's impact depends as much on its cochairs' reputations and moral authority as it does on their money," wrote Alex Friedman and Julie Sunderland in an opinion piece for *Project Syndicate* in 2021. Both Friedman and Sunderland are former senior foundation executives. Friedman is a former chief financial officer for the Gates Foundation, hired in 2007 to help the entity grow and manage its finances better after the Buffett gift. Sunderland led the foundation's investment partnerships with the private sector until 2016. "This conflation of the personal and the institutional is a serious problem for all private foundations with living donors," the authors wrote, before going on to propose reforms that would rectify the top-down nature of the foundation.[24] The authors called for stronger governance mechanisms and more transparency in their filings.

Amid calls to professionalize its governing structure, especially after the couple's divorce, the foundation created a more formal board of trustees. Suzman, the foundation's chief executive, took the seat occupied by Buffett, who stepped down in 2021. In January 2022, it added Strive Masiyiwa, a London-based Zimbabwean billionaire businessman and philanthropist; Minouche Shafik, an international development expert and president of Columbia University; and Tom Tierney, a cofounder of the philanthropic consulting firm Bridgespan Group, to the board. That summer, it added two more board members: Ashish Dhawan, a former private equity investor with an India-focused incubator for nonprofits, and Dr. Helene D. Gayle, the president of Spelman College. Suzman acknowledged that the foundation had long had an unusual structure, and addressed fresh criticism that its new trustees didn't truly represent diverse perspectives because they came from the same academic and professional backgrounds as the majority of the foundation's staff. The new trustees, Suzman said, possessed "amazing expertise and background that could really add value to helping us make better strategic decisions." However, Suzman was very clear that the Gates Foundation was "unequivocally" a family foundation that wasn't about to change its mission and priorities.[25] In the summer of 2021, the foundation had said that if, after two years, either Gates or French Gates decided that they couldn't work together as cochairs, French Gates would step down but receive personal funds from Gates to pursue her own work. She remained in her role until mid-2024 and left with $12.5 billion. In a note to employees, Suzman said that the foundation would change its name to "the Gates Foundation to honor Bill Sr.'s legacy and Melinda's contributions, and Bill will become the sole Chair of the foundation." Gates's father had been instrumental in shaping his son's philanthropic efforts, and he was the third cochair of the foundation until his death in 2020 of Alzheimer's disease. For all the criticisms, though, the foundation is undeterred. Paul Schervish, a professor emeritus at Boston College who has long studied philanthropic models, likened the Gates Foundation to an elephant, and the critics to mosquitoes. "The mosquitoes won't bring down the elephant and you may not hear the elephants doing much except swishing their tails."

India: A Nuanced Portrait

In 2017, two years after the United Nations announced the 17 Sustainable Development Goals agreed to by its member states that the world should try to meet by 2030, the Gates Foundation put together its own initiative called Goalkeepers. It brought together what it called "a global collective of collaborative and diverse changemakers," a jumble of public sector officials and private sector innovators whose mission was to accelerate progress toward the U.N. goals. Since then, the foundation has handed out annual Goalkeepers Global Goals awards to recognize the work of "remarkable individuals taking action to help achieve the Global Goals by 2030."

In 2019, one of the recipients was Narendra Modi, the prime minister of India, for his work on improving sanitation in the country. With more than 1.4 billion people, nearly two-thirds of whom live in rural areas, open defecation, good hygiene, and safe handling of fecal matter are among the country's toughest challenges. Millions of people defecate in fields, open pits, side streets, and rivers. Hindu belief holds that a dip in the Ganges River washes away all sins; yet, Hinduism's most sacred river remains a toxic spew of human and animal excrement, sewage, plastic debris, and industrial effluents. Despite decades of efforts to clean it up and some success under the Modi government, it is one of the world's most polluted rivers. When Modi took office, improving sanitation was among his priorities. In 2014, his government launched the Swachh Bharat Abhiyan (Clean India Mission). By 2019, the government claimed to have built more than 100 million toilets. That year, the Gates Foundation, which works closely with the Indian government, presented its award to Modi at the U.N. General Assembly in New York.

The move attracted a lot of opprobrium from academics, civil rights leaders, and even Nobel laureates for its tone-deafness, given the controversial nature of Modi's rule. Since coming to power, Modi has conducted an exclusionary politics, according to his critics, and he stands accused of cracking down on dissenters, oppressing minorities, and emboldening groups tied to his political party to pursue their goal of turning India into a Hindu majoritarian state. (At the same time, Modi is worshipped by millions of Indians who laud his efforts to promote economic growth and lead India onto the global stage.) Several critics pointed out the irony of presenting an award to a leader whose anti–human rights record went against the very ethos of the foundation: that all lives have equal value. At least one India-based employee resigned from the foundation, registering her protest in an op-ed column.[26] The former employee, Sabah Hamid, wrote that she had not been consulted until much later, by which time, executives in Seattle had already made up their minds. "That this endorsement of Mr. Modi would not do the Gates Foundation any good did not seem to be up for discussion," Hamid wrote. In response to the controversy, the foundation said that the award was narrowly focused on Modi's record in improving sanitation. However, it did not share the process by which it had arrived at its decision or whether it had tested the Indian government's claims.

The criticism notwithstanding, Gates is a hero in India, twice over. There are so many software developers of Indian descent at Microsoft's U.S. offices that "Indian" no longer meets the software giant's diversity criteria for some managers. Satya Nadella, the chief executive of Microsoft, under whose leadership the company touched a market valuation of $3 trillion, hails from India. Microsoft's largest data center outside the United States is in the Indian city of Hyderabad. The IT campuses it has built in the South Asian country employ around 20,000 people. Gates, who has visited India dozens of times over the decades, has often said that the quality of engineering talent in the country has been great for Microsoft. On one of his earliest trips to India for Microsoft, Gates remarked to a colleague how surprised he was that so many people in the country spoke English, apparently unaware of its legacy of British colonialism.

Ingrid Srinath, who formerly led the Centre for Social Impact and Philanthropy at Ashoka University, a privately funded institution on the outskirts of Delhi, agreed that Gates is very much a hero because of Microsoft and the country's general technology bias, but also because the Gates Foundation's presence is so significant, even if its hands are tied in what it can do because of the Indian government's restrictions on foreign funding for domestic nonprofits. Gates is also a role model for India's emerging billionaire class, whose wealth has spurred their philanthropic ambitions. Indian billionaires like Nandan Nilekani, a cofounder of the IT giant Infosys who helped the government build a biometric ID system called Aadhaar, have signed the Giving Pledge. With private philanthropy slowly becoming a more professional undertaking, criticisms of the big philanthropy of Gates haven't yet reached the country, Srinath said. In India, "philanthropy is an unadulterated good."

During Microsoft's bruising antitrust battle with the U.S. government in the late 1990s, the company's public relations team regularly ran opinion polls to monitor Gates's image around the world. But in any global poll, they had to interpret the results after discounting the data from India, because Gates was so admired that the feedback from Indian poll respondents would skew the results. As he moved away from his Microsoft duties to philanthropy, Gates's engagement with India only deepened. In the fall of 2000, Gates visited a maternal and child health clinic in New Delhi, where he administered polio drops to children. Soon after, he announced a $25 million donation to polio eradication efforts. The Gates Foundation's first foreign outpost was India, where it set up an office in 2003. It is also the foundation's largest operation outside of the United States. With roughly 80 employees, the foundation has its India headquarters in a lush, green area of New Delhi. India, with its massive population, has long attracted the attention of the global development community, acting as a crucible for innovation in global public health and agriculture. For decades, especially after India won its independence in 1947, large multilateral agencies such as UNICEF and the World Bank were involved in providing aid and support to the South Asian country, but more recently, the focus of Western experts has moved to sub-Saharan Africa.

The Gates Foundation's early interest in India was therefore no surprise. The country is attractive to Gates because it presents the challenges in global health and development that are closest to his heart: vaccines, public health, child nutrition, sanitation, and agricultural productivity. India has been the second-largest recipient of Gates Foundation grants after the United States. Between 2015 and 2018, the Gates Foundation was the top private source of funding in India, at $1.1 billion—twice as much as the next biggest donor, Infosys.[27] At least as of 2018, India was the foundation's largest focus; second was Nigeria. As of that year, the bulk of its funds earmarked for gender equity issues went to India, in particular reproductive health and family planning.

The foundation's work in the country started in 2003 with a program to combat HIV/AIDS called Avahan, a Hindi word that roughly translates to "challenge." The virus disproportionately affected sex workers, truckers, and men having sex with men in a few southern Indian states, and drug injectors in the northeastern part of the country. Assuming that the virus was spreading because people didn't have access to condoms and didn't know how it spread, the foundation began distributing free condoms to female sex workers and set up clinics. But former foundation workers and those who studied the program said it was a modest success at best, partly because staffers failed to anticipate how cultural beliefs and gender norms—such as a female sex worker having no agency if a male client refused to use a condom—would impede their efforts. By 2009, the foundation had poured $338 million into the initiative. By its own assessment, the impact of the program was unclear, but it said there were encouraging signs based on data they collected using their own paradigm. Ultimately, its model wasn't sustainable or transferable to other regions, including to the Indian northeast, where the mode of transmission was through shared needle use. In some African countries, the youth population was far more affected by HIV/AIDS than were sex workers, and the sources of infection and the modes of transmission, such as neonatally, were different, which meant the foundation had to develop different strategies. The foundation also participated in the Indian government's campaign to eradicate polio, a feat of coordination between volunteers and community health workers, some sponsored by the Seattle organization, going to the deepest corners of rural India to administer oral polio vaccines. India was declared free of the wild polio virus in 2014.

The Gates Foundation has maintained a high profile in India and a constant presence at the side of the Indian government, even as other foundations including the Ford and Rockefeller foundations, which have long histories in India, have practically folded their operations. Over the years, Gates's visits have been highly publicized, and he has been received much as a rockstar would be. Heads of industry, state chief ministers, and top government officials routinely line up to meet him. In media interviews with India's top journalists, he is careful to be diplomatic and deferential, and to underscore that the foundation only works alongside the Indian government, not independent of it. In 2023, he wrote on his blog of a successful sit-down with Modi. In March 2024, just weeks before India's general election, the Indian prime minister sat down with Gates for a fireside chat about technology and artificial intelligence, during which the philanthropist talked about the foundation's work in India and how impressed he was with the Modi government's digital infrastructure plans, and Modi invited Gates to try out his free "NaMo" app, through which users can get information about the Indian government's initiatives.[28] Long aware of the government's close watch on which domestic nonprofits get foreign funding, the billionaire has routinely said that its decisions and priorities are set by the government, but that his philanthropic dollars and private-sector participation can fund innovation and research in those areas.

The Modi government can be didactic. In 2018, it launched the National Nutrition Mission because one of the chronic problems India faces is malnourishment, which has long-term implications for the workforce, including productivity and mortality. The Gates Foundation and other agencies partnered with the government to carry out its mission. However, the visuals they created of nutritional and balanced diets contained images of eggs—a cheap and plentiful source of protein. The government directed the foundation and others to remove the eggs from those images, which have become a flashpoint in the country, especially in states led by Modi's political party, the Bharatiya Janata Party, because many Hindus consider them animal products. It had to comply by redoing the posters.

At the same time, the close association with Gates has acted as a legitimizing force for Modi, who has an ambitious agenda to move India up the ladder to the status of a middle-income country. To do so, it needs to improve the lot of its poorest citizens, bringing healthcare services, eliminating diseases, improving sanitation, providing vaccines, increasing access to digital financial services, harnessing new technology to improve education, all while trying to do so in a sustainable manner given climate change. By bringing its scientific thinking and technological expertise, the foundation can help the government achieve those goals.

Manjari Mahajan, who studies public health, philanthrocapitalism, and digital governance at the New School for Social Research, has followed the foundation's work closely in India. To Mahajan, the Modi government and the Gates Foundation each understands its role in a delicate dance. In 2015, Gates and French Gates were among four foreigners to receive one of India's highest civilian honors, the Padma Bhushan, for their work in health and development. Mahajan has suggested that there were far bigger reasons for the award than the foundation's work on HIV/AIDS and health. In her view, the Indian government was cementing its ties to Gates as much for its health efforts as for the recognition that the Microsoft cofounder stood for much more: "Here philanthropy for global health was tacitly, if not explicitly, understood as being part of a larger global assemblage that included not only viruses, vaccines and well-meaning foundations but also multinational technology corporations, H1B visas, and software engineers," she wrote in a 2017 paper. "The Padma Bhushan was to them less a sign of the government being beholden to the foundation or Microsoft, and more an indicator of a pragmatic appreciation of the [Gateses]." At the same time, Mahajan wrote, the foundation saw the Indian government as less a "weak victim and more a player in its own right within global exchanges."[29]

The same narrow, vertical thinking that the foundation used to defend the Goalkeepers award it presented to Modi has led to other challenges in India. One example is the foundation's telehealth program in the Indian state of Bihar. In 2010, it signed an agreement with Bihar's chief minister, Nitish Kumar, to launch a telemedicine health program that would address some of the state's most pressing diseases and conditions, including tuberculosis, leishmaniasis, diarrhea, and malaria, by using a combination of telemedicine and local franchises. By harnessing the power of modern technology and introducing "social franchising"—a concept popular in the global development community that is similar to the McDonald's franchisee model, except that the product being delivered is healthcare, not burgers—the goal was to transform the way healthcare is delivered in the state, especially to its rural residents. The foundation committed more than $23 million to the project, which may have been doomed from the start. Gates Foundation staffers, sitting in Seattle, had mapped out how it would all work and recruited a nonprofit to administer the telehealth program. But several studies later found that assumptions made about the demand for diagnoses made over shaky internet connections, and the number of franchisees available to participate in the project and their incentives, hobbled the experiment.[30]

The program also sputtered because of its focus on treating individual diseases rather than addressing public health as a whole, said Manoj Mohanan, the public health expert. Each of the foundation's teams that focused on these diseases was supposed to work with the others on the telemedicine project. But the TB team decided to pull out halfway through the implementation after realizing that the model wouldn't work for them since TB was more prevalent in urban locations. "You can't have broad efforts to change the system when the foundation has targeted verticals" in terms of their disease focus, said Mohanan, who was part of a team of independent experts that the foundation commissioned to review the program in Bihar that, after three years, didn't produce the impact it had been hoping for.[31]

The foundation's focus on certain geographies in India also tends to create imbalances because health challenges aren't confined within borders. Salaries, resources, and opportunities in the states they focus on go up, meaning that neighboring states can see an outflow of talent. More broadly—and this experience is not unique to India—the foundation's priorities and funds can determine which nonprofits get that money. An organization attempting to address malaria, a focus of the foundation, might get more funding than one that is focused on other mosquito-borne diseases or on diarrhea. A public health professional in Vietnam who has worked with the Gates Foundation dubbed it the "Gates effect."

Imprint

Billionaires have long endowed university chairs, funded hospitals, given support to religious or humanitarian causes, or written checks for restoring museums and monuments. Often, such occasions are splashy affairs written up by the press. The University of Chicago renamed its famous economics department after Ken Griffin, after the hedge fund manager donated $125 million in 2017. The following year, Michael Bloomberg, the cofounder of financial information giant Bloomberg LP and former mayor of New York City, gave $1.8 billion to Johns Hopkins, his alma mater, to be used for financial aid. As of 2023, it remained the largest single gift to a college or university, according to *Forbes*. There are low-key donors as well, such as Charles Feeney, who made his fortune running duty-free shops and founded the Atlantic Philanthropies, popularizing the concept of "giving while living."

But Gates was among the first, or at least the most high-profile, billionaires to approach philanthropy as a professional enterprise, tilting the entire field toward the idea of strategic giving, and bringing a business-capitalist and technological mindset to determine where one dollar "invested" would produce the greatest social return. Philanthropy thus became an accessible and deployable tool for many billionaires who are fluent in the language of returns, markets, and capitalism. His focus on the idea that issues like poverty can be "solved" resonated with technology billionaires. Gates tapped into the general feeling among billionaires that governments are inefficient, and that philanthropy can be nimble where the public sector is lumbering. By creating the Giving Pledge with Buffett, Gates also gave the extremely wealthy an opportunity to make public and moral commitments about giving away their fortunes—without any real accountability—in an age when rising inequality has raised numerous questions about the fairness of the system.

"What is the social return on a dollar has become a major paradigm," said Amir Pasic, dean of the Lilly Family School of Philanthropy at Indiana University, which launched in 2013 and bills itself as the first institution dedicated to the study and teaching of philanthropy. Pasic said that the Gates Foundation made an impact quickly, because of both its size and its style of giving. Its endowment dwarfed those of the Rockefeller and Ford foundations, which had been preeminent in global philanthropy for decades and had long set the agenda.

Michael Kurdziel, who works with family offices, as the private firms that invest the money of billionaires are known, said that the Gates Foundation had a big impact on how the wealthy think about philanthropy. "The notion of, 'I've acquired the wealth and now I wanna sort of work toward donating that wealth and having the influence through those donations'— that definitely comes through, especially in the U.S.," in his conversations with billionaires, Kurdziel said. By contrast, he said, the wealthy don't draw the same kind of inspiration from philanthropic organizations with more of a political bent, such as Open Society Foundations, founded by the billionaire investor George Soros in 1993. Even Bloomberg Philanthropies, the grant-making entity for Bloomberg, which contributes to a variety of causes from education to the fight against climate change, is perceived as a politically focused entity designed to support his causes.[32] That's not surprising given Michael Bloomberg's presidential run in 2020 on the Democratic ticket—even though he is one of the most active philanthropists around, having given away more than $17 billion.

Trevor Neilson, one of the early employees of the Gates Foundation, built an entire business around philanthropic strategy. He created the Global Philanthropy Group, which worked with 40 or so philanthropists to build out their strategy. "I was going around to philanthropists saying I did this for Bill Gates, I could do this for you," Neilson said. He and his partners at the firm marketed themselves as consultants who could get top-notch professionals to work at philanthropic foundations. They would first create a strategic plan for the philanthropist that often predated the buildout of the foundation. Next, they would do the research and identify potential philanthropy partners, build advisory boards, hire people, and get the outfit up and running. Neilson used his brief but formative experience at the Gates Foundation to tell others: "Gates is the model to emulate if you're trying to build a strategy for philanthropy."

In Silicon Valley, where wealth creation has exploded—in 2021, there were 85 billionaires in the Bay Area and more than 163,000 millionaire households—the number of private foundations and the variety of philanthropic approaches have also expanded. According to a 2016 study, the number of foundations in the region with more than $10 million in assets has doubled since 2000, with 28 percent of them founded in the last 10 years.[33] The push in the Valley is to find "disruptive" solutions that have the most impact, the study said. But while the names of philanthropic endeavors run the gamut from venture philanthropy to effective altruism, the conceptual underpinnings don't stray too far from the return-on-investment philosophy that has defined Gates's approach.

Traditionally, philanthropists set up foundations to handle their charitable contributions, which allows them to maintain a tax-free status as long as they donate 5 percent of their endowment to charity every year. But many billionaires in Silicon Valley are doing things differently, mingling their for-profit and nonprofit investments through the creation of limited liability companies. Such entities don't get the full tax benefits of philanthropic foundations but allow the owners more flexibility to determine where and how their fortunes should be directed, including to political campaigns or lobbying activities. There are also fewer reporting requirements than traditional foundations.

A prominent example is the Chan Zuckerberg Initiative. Although the couple consulted with Gates and sought his advice when deciding what form their philanthropy should take, they were among the early adopters of the LLC model. Founded in 2015, the entity describes itself as a new kind of philanthropic organization whose mission is "engineering change at scale." In 2023, the entity laid off dozens of people after deciding that its approach to education-related causes wasn't working, and that its strategy needed a refresh and clarity.[34]

In 2021, during the throes of the pandemic, Jack Dorsey, a founder of Twitter and Square, the payments app, announced that he would be earmarking $1 billion for Covid relief through an LLC called #startsmall. The organization has since made donations to nonprofits working on girls' health and education, and Dorsey has also directed tens of millions of dollars to charitable outfits run by Hollywood celebrities including Rihanna and Sean Penn, a friend.[35] In the interest of transparency, he created a public Google document to track his donations that anyone could look up. Pierre Omidyar, the founder of eBay, also combined for-profit and nonprofit investments through one firm, the Omidyar Network, after deciding that a business-based model was the best way to carry out his philanthropic objective of "making the world a better place."[36] Among the entity's priorities: reimagining capitalism. In a 2011 article for *Harvard Business Review*, Omidyar argued that the LLC structure allowed for more risk-taking than a traditional foundation and compared it to the venture capital business.

Emerson Collective, the LLC organization founded by Laurene Powell Jobs, the widow of Steve Jobs, blends philanthropic grant-making, venture capital investing, and even art to make an impact in its chosen areas, including immigration, health, education, journalism, and the environment. Powell Jobs, with an estimated net worth of $12 billion, took the name for her organization from Ralph Waldo Emerson, drawing from the core message of the Transcendentalist movement led by the nineteenth-century essayist and philosopher—that the individual could move beyond physical limitations to find oneness with God. French Gates's firm Pivotal Ventures and Yield Giving, the primary philanthropic entity for MacKenzie Scott, are also LLCs. The latter entity, however, is mainly focused on grant-making to nonprofits.

The funds earmarked for charity can sit in endowments or in donor-advised funds, which have become extremely popular among the wealthy in the Valley. In 2014, after the action camera manufacturer GoPro went public, the company's founder and chief executive, Nicholas Woodman, along with his wife Jill Woodman, gave $500 million to a donor-advised fund overseen by a nonprofit called the Silicon Valley Community Foundation. The move was seen by many as a cynical ploy to save on taxes Woodman would have incurred from his IPO riches.[37]

Some of the other approaches to philanthropy include the venture capital–based model espoused by Reid Hoffman, the LinkedIn founder. "What pattern shapes these philanthropic investments? The venture investing model: a selected and unique entrepreneur, a bold plan frequently with intelligent risk, the potential assets and skills to execute the plan, and favorable market conditions," Hoffman and his wife wrote in their Giving Pledge letter. (Eli Broad, who made his fortune as a home builder, also called his model "venture philanthropy" in his 2010 Giving Pledge letter.) Jeff T. Green, who made his fortune in digital advertising and has an estimated net worth of more than $4 billion, calls his approach to giving "Dataphilanthropy," seeking to fund and assess programs, the success of which can be verified by data.

One of the biggest philanthropic ideas to take hold in the Valley in recent years, especially among younger billionaires, is "effective altruism," which uses metrics and evidence to determine where a dollar will do the maximum good. Before his downfall, Sam Bankman-Fried, the founder of cryptocurrency exchange FTX, was one of the more high-profile so-called effective altruists, talking about his philosophy often in public and using his philanthropic activities to build FTX's reputation. The movement, which owes its origin to the philosopher Peter Singer, takes an unsentimental, utilitarian approach to charitable giving—essentially applying quantitative standards to subjective goals. Those ideas have been updated by William MacAskill, a thirtysomething Oxford-educated philosopher, who has become a rabbi to the tech crowd.

Once again, the concepts aren't that different substantively from what has driven Gates and his foundation. Neither is the lofty nature of ambition.

Among the most high-profile practitioners of effective altruism are Dustin Moskovitz, a cofounder of Facebook and Asana, which builds task management software, and his wife, Cari Tuna, a former reporter at *The Wall Street Journal*. The mission of their organization, a limited liability entity called Good Ventures, is to "help humanity thrive."

Chapter 8

The Gates Keepers

Good Steward

It is a Thursday evening in Tampa, the April air muggy and leaden. There is a modest buzz of activity along the city's downtown waterfront. Diners, suntanned and relaxed, mill about, the men in cargo shorts, the women in sleeveless dresses, sipping beers against the backdrop of a falling sun. A few determined runners weave their way among groups of tourists idling along a two-mile path that hugs the water. The Amalie Arena, home to the Tampa Bay Lightning ice hockey team, is steps away, and the GO BOLTS signs are unmissable. The slogan is painted upon the path and on flags that flutter behind low-flying helicopters. It's hard not to note the irony of having an ice hockey stadium in a hot, swampy city. Perhaps that's where Tampa residents go to cool off.

A few yards inland, there are about a dozen newly built high-rise buildings, their sides gleaming. Restaurants, upscale in their decor, are ready for the evening, their maître d's waiting, expectant smiles on their faces. Tampa's first five-star hotel, the Edition, signals its presence with the familiar waft of its signature scent, a blend of tea and bergamot that suffuses the lobby of every hotel in the chain. All around are mixed-use complexes—residences, offices, hotels, bars, restaurants, gyms—designed in an aesthetic best described as global anodyne luxe that is increasingly popular in cities from Manhattan's new Hudson Yards development to high-rises in Tokyo to the suburbs of New Delhi. This sixteen-block area around the city's downtown waterfront is Tampa's biggest real estate development in recent years. Called

Water Street Tampa, it is scheduled for completion in 2027, a decade after construction started. The bet is that Tampa will become a destination for tech companies, and young, urban workers will follow, bringing business and hipness to central Florida's often overlooked city.

"Tampa had long been a donor city of our intellectual capital to other cities in America," said Bob Buckhorn, the former two-time mayor of Tampa. Buckhorn, a Democrat who was in the seat from 2011 to 2019, was speaking by phone from his law offices in one of the new buildings, the view a daily reminder of what he considers among his biggest accomplishments. Buckhorn ran on the campaign platform: "I'm not gonna lose my kids to Charlotte, North Carolina."

Not long before Buckhorn became mayor in 2011, Jeffrey Vinik, a former hedge fund manager and former minority owner of the Red Sox, had decided to buy the Tampa Bay Lightning, almost on a whim, and move to the city of about 390,000 people. There, Vinik, with an estimated net worth of roughly half a billion dollars, began buying up vacant parcels of land— parking lots that had fallen into disuse, abandoned buildings—around the hockey arena, which already came with two plots, figuring they would be a good investment in Tampa's future. He found a willing partner in Buckhorn, but they needed a big investor.

Tod Leiweke, a friend of Vinik's, whom the hedge fund investor had hired as chief executive of the Lightning's parent company, had an idea. For years, Leiweke had been telling Michael Larson, a powerful money manager who ran a little-known investment firm called Cascade Asset Management, about the potential of Tampa. With Vinik's interest and the city's support, might Larson be interested in teaming up?

Buckhorn pitched the project as an "opportunity to create a walkable, livable, workable investable district that was different than what we had seen in Tampa but transportable to other cities." Cascade bit, he said, "partly because they saw the Tampa project as a test run to see whether this concept could work and could be replicated in other jurisdictions."

In 2016, Cascade and Vinik started a real estate joint venture called Strategic Property Partners to invest $3 billion in Water Street Tampa. Vinik was the face of the development until 2023, when he sold his interest to Cascade, which had provided most of the funds. The first phase, which took $2 billion to build, wrapped up in 2022. Including the Edison, there are three hotels, 1,300 apartments, and an assortment of restaurants and amenities. By the time the project is done, the total cost is likely to be $4 billion. An independent report released in May 2023 said that Water Street Tampa has so far created nearly 6,000 jobs and its economic impact amounts to $520 million.

So it came to be that Bill Gates is bankrolling Tampa's biggest redevelopment project. Cascade is a 30-year-old investment firm owned by Gates, with two goals: to oversee his vast fortune and carefully invest the money that sits in the endowment of the Gates Foundation. At last count, Gates had a net worth of about $124 billion—an amount that rivals the assets managed by many Wall Street firms—and the foundation had an endowment of about $70 billion. And Larson is the man entrusted with running it all.

The Tampa project is the latest outpost of Gates's ever-expanding, but mostly under-the-radar, investment empire. Over the decades, Larson diversified Gates's wealth away from Microsoft and put it into stocks, bonds, hotels, farmland, private equity, real estate, and other assets—all while keeping his boss's name largely out of the headlines, although the firm has had to give up much of its anonymity in recent years as Gates's ballooning wealth leaves it in search of bigger and bigger investments. As of 2023, Gates owned about 1.4 percent of Microsoft, worth about $20 billion.

"Melinda and I are free to pursue our vision of a healthier and better-educated world because of what Michael has done," Gates once told guests at a dinner in 2014 to celebrate two decades of Larson's service. He had special lighting installed in the living room of his mansion so that the lights glowed pink—Larson's favorite color. He added that he had "complete trust and faith" in his money manager.[1]

Gates had hired Larson, only a few years younger than him, in 1994 when he was working as a bond fund manager at Putnam Investments. The son of an engineer, Larson grew up in North Dakota and graduated from high school at the age of 16. He attended Claremont McKenna, a liberal arts school in Claremont, California, graduating with a degree in economics. By

21, he had obtained an MBA degree from the University of Chicago. After an initial stint as a mergers and acquisitions banker, Larson joined Putnam. Bert Early, a former executive director of the American Bar Association who ran an executive search firm, put the two in touch.

Larson wasn't Gates's first money manager. Not long after he had become a billionaire after Microsoft went public in 1986, Gates had hired a close friend, Andy Evans, and his wife, Ann Llewellyn, to invest some of his money for him. The couple had founded a brokerage firm called Evans Llewellyn Securities in 1980 that bought and sold mostly high-tech stocks. In 1993, *The Wall Street Journal* reported that the couple were convicted felons who had served time in prison for committing bank fraud.[2] The article described how Evans got into a scrap with regulators for alleged securities violations. Having pleaded guilty, they had been sentenced to prison for six months. Gates even visited his friends in prison, according to the *Journal* story. After the rash of bad publicity forced Evans to quit as Gates's money manager, the Microsoft cofounder apparently decided that his financial affairs should be conducted in near total secrecy. He needed someone who could invest his swelling fortune for him, and also manage the assets of the foundation, without bringing attention to any of the deals or tainting his reputation.

From the start, Larson understood the nature of his job. He even picked the name "Cascade" because it was the most generic name he could find in the Pacific Northwest, he told *Fortune* magazine in a rare interview in 1999.[3] A big part of Larson's mandate was to invest in a way that kept the spotlight on Gates's philanthropy rather than his investments, according to people who have worked at Cascade. Larson avoided splashy moves. He pursued opportunities with the utmost discretion, often creating shell companies to hold Cascade's investments. "Avoid all headlines, that was the driving culture there," said one former employee who worked at Cascade for more than a decade.

Based out of a nondescript office building in Kirkland, Washington, about 10 miles east of the Seattle headquarters of the Gates Foundation, Cascade employs around 150 people who work on various investment strategies set by Larson. The culture of secrecy at Cascade was emphasized by the fact that Gates's name wasn't on any employee's business cards or the office. When meeting with prospective investment partners or sellers, employees were in-structed to say that they worked for a small money manager based in Kirkland. The vagueness was also necessary so that a seller wouldn't try to charge a pre-mium for an asset because Gates was the buyer. The commitment to secrecy was so high that even though Cascade had hired the small business group at Microsoft to handle its technology, most people in that division didn't know the owner of the entity whose technology they were servicing. Employees and others who worked with Cascade were required to sign nondisclosure agree-ments, which were often strict and expansive. "Most of the people hired were young people, just out of college, so the fear was there, that Bill is going to sue you if you talk about any of this," the former employee said.

Occasionally, glimpses of the vast nature of Gates's holdings would slip into wider view in unexpected ways. In 2015, an onion grower at Stanley Farms in Georgia got into trouble after rival farmers accused it of passing off regular yellow onions as Vidalias, which are a unique type of the allium that can only be grown in a certain part of the state. The farm, which sat on land owned by Gates, was put on probation after the alleged fraud came to light, and although it didn't pay a fine, it lost $100,000 in spoilage during a probe by the state, according to *Bloomberg*.[4]

When Larson joined in 1994, he created Cascade to manage the former couple's personal fortune. In 2000, after Gates stepped down as the chief executive of Microsoft, the two foundations that he had created in the 1990s merged to form the Bill and Melinda Gates Foundation, and he began di-recting billions of dollars' worth of his shares into it. The entity that oversaw Cascade and the foundation's assets came to be called Bill Gates Invest-ments, updated in 2015 to Bill and Melinda Gates Investments to reflect her growing role. In June 2021, after Gates and French Gates got divorced, the BMGI name was retired, and the umbrella entity is now called Cascade Asset Management—the overseer of both Gates's money and the endowment funds. By many accounts, Larson has been a successful steward of Gates's for-tune. It is difficult to assess how his portfolio has performed, given the dearth of publicly available data. However, the performance of the foundation's en-dowment provides some clues because the stock portfolio Larson manages for it doesn't differ too widely from the stocks he invests in with Gates's personal fortune. Charles V. Zehren, a spokesman for Larson, said the Gates Foundation endowment has outperformed the S&P 500 stock index.

Cascade is a type of firm that has become popular in the past couple of decades among wealthy individuals. Called family offices, such firms are unregulated entities that invest the fortunes of billionaires. Traditionally, many wealthy people used external wealth managers at banks and other firms to run their money for them. But as wealth has grown, and new fortunes have been made, many billionaires have sought to create family offices to run their investments, and sometimes their philanthropy. Depending on the owner's wealth and ambition, a family office can be a small affair with a handful of employees. Or it can be like Cascade, which essentially operates like a sophisticated Wall Street firm, using hedging techniques to protect investments, combining short- and long-term strategies across multiple classes of assets, making direct investments, or coinvesting with others. Larson started with around $11 billion to manage. Adding up Gates's personal fortune and the foundation's endowment, Larson today directs close to $200 billion in investments. Although it is small compared to giant asset managers like BlackRock and State Street, which manage trillions of dollars, Cascade would be on any list of the industry's top 100 firms given its size.

Larson adopted a more conservative investment strategy popular with family offices, where the preservation of capital was paramount. Families don't often want to take too many risks with their money, so they are willing to settle for steady returns. Larson embraced Warren Buffett's style of investing, an approach known as value investing. Value investors buy stocks that are underpriced relative to their intrinsic worth and hold them for the long run. He bought stocks of the kind of unfashionable but sturdy companies—from trash haulers to railways to makers of agricultural equipment—that Buffett has long championed. Cascade holds large positions in brick-and-mortar companies like the railway Canadian National, the trash hauling service Republic Services, and equipment maker Deere. There is a clutch of other investments, including small energy holdings, such as an unregulated Texas power company and Otter Tail Power, a Minnesota-based coal-burning power plant. In

2021, it teamed up with Blackstone and Global Infrastructure Partners to buy Signature Aviation, a company that provides aircraft maintenance and hangar services, for $4.7 billion. Cascade had first invested in Signature in 2009 and controlled 20 percent of the company at the time of the deal. As it has grown larger, Cascade has had to look for bigger opportunities to put Gates's money to work, signing up for deals like the Tampa real estate complex, but more than half of Gates's personal investments remain in stock. After the divorce, Cascade transferred billions of dollars' worth of shares in companies like Coca-Cola Femsa, Grupo Televisa, and Canadian National to French Gates, who now has other investors managing her wealth. Cascade isn't a big investor in private equity, which is generally considered a risky category where the pay-offs can be huge, but investors could be stuck with big losses or poor returns. However, the firm has invested alongside Silver Lake because Roger McNamee, a founder of the technology investment firm, knew Gates. In the past, McNamee has referred to Larson as the "Gateskeeper."

One of Cascade's oldest and highest-profile investments is its 75 percent ownership of the operating company behind Four Seasons, the hotel brand synonymous with luxury. The hotel company, founded by Isadore Sharp, opened its first Four Seasons in downtown Toronto in 1961 and followed an innovative business model. While the hotels could be owned by individuals or companies, Four Seasons would operate and manage them based on their stringent standards, offering travelers a consistent and luxurious experience at Four Seasons hotels around the world. Cascade had first invested in Four Seasons in 1997 when it was a public company. A decade later, Cascade teamed up with Kingdom Holding Company, the investment firm of Saudi prince Alwaleed bin Talal, which also owned a substantial chunk of Four Seasons, to buy the bulk of the hotel operator for $3.8 billion. Sharp retained a 5 percent stake. Soon after, the stock market tanked as the financial crisis of 2007–9 led to a recession that crimped spending on luxury hotels. The partnership, though equal, was rocky in the beginning as the co-owners quibbled over strategy.[5] Cascade wanted to strip costs to increase profitability, taking measures like not stripping sheets every day, but Sharp thought it would dilute the brand. Eventually, they settled on a compromise: guests could place a pinecone on their beds to indicate that they didn't want their sheets washed every day. Cascade and Kingdom also tussled over who should lead Four Seasons after Sharp stepped down as chief executive in 2010.

Gates doesn't typically get involved in negotiations involving his money, but he made an exception for Kingdom, sitting down for a meeting with his fellow billionaire Alwaleed in 2013 to resolve a dispute between the two sides about the direction of Four Seasons' growth, and the two have partnered on philanthropic projects. But Four Seasons eventually recovered. In 2021, Cascade said it would take control of the operating company by buying half of Kingdom's 47.5 percent stake at a valuation of $10 billion. It now owns more than 70 percent; Sharp continues to own 5 percent. Because of Gates's ownership stake in Four Seasons, employees of the Gates Foundation are typically not allowed to stay at any of their hotels to avoid any appearance of impropriety.

In 2021, *The Land Report* tallied up all the land owned by Gates and determined that he is the nation's largest private owner of farmland. The report, by the publication that calls itself the "Magazine of the American Landowner," startled people because the news was so unexpected. The article, titled "Farmer Bill," counted roughly 270,000 acres of farmland that the technology billionaire had amassed.[6] Those close to Cascade have defended the land ownership by pointing out that the land Gates owns is a small slice of the 900 million acres of total farmland in America. There are other private owners of farmland with larger holdings than Cascade, including the Mormon church. (Also, Gates is not the only billionaire who sees land as a valuable investment. John Malone, the media mogul, is the nation's largest private landowner, with 2.2 million acres, which include ranchland. More than a dozen other billionaires and their families also own ranchland and farms.)[7] Gates has made it clear that the farmland investments are not part of his work on climate change but rather, a decision made by his investment team. Larson saw farmland as a valuable but limited resource that offers investors a way to hedge against stock-market volatility and inflation (Cascade is also a big buyer of Treasury Inflation-Protected Securities, or TIPS). The firm began buying up parcels of land in the early 2000s and owns those assets through layers of subsidiaries and shell companies. The ownership is structured rather like Russian nesting dolls, not only to maintain secrecy but also to shield Gates from direct ownership, one person with knowledge of the arrangements said. Since farmers get large subsidies from the federal government, Larson was careful to structure the purchases so that it didn't appear as though Gates was benefiting from government subsidies, the person said, underscoring that Gates himself did not receive or benefit from such subsidiaries. Typically, Cascade would buy both the land and the lease from a farmer and lease the land back. That way, the government subsidies went to the leaseholder, but the revenues were shared with the owner.

Cascade's agricultural team sometimes bought farmland portfolios from other big investors. The firm also purchased farms directly from farmers, especially those in need of upgrades and new equipment such as tractors, and worked with them to improve techniques, introduce sustainable farming measures, and increase productivity, the person said. The land that Gates owns cultivates a range of crops, including soybeans, carrots, corn, and even the potatoes used in McDonald's French fries.[8]

As part of his investment strategy, Larson has cultivated a network of money managers and other investors to source new opportunities and stay looped into the financial world. He organizes conferences, and a lot of people stop by to meet him at Cascade. From time to time, Gates himself brings Larson investment ideas since he is constantly in touch with people from a range of backgrounds, from electric vehicles to farming techniques.

The two meet at least once every month or two to discuss the state of Cascade's portfolio, but the larger investment group gets to meet with Gates—and while they were married, French Gates—once a year at an all-day meeting. Employees present investment updates and highlight the mix of assets in the portfolio. Sometimes, big Wall Street investors stop by. David Bonderman, the private equity investor, and Bill Miller, the asset manager, have been past guests.

Bad Boss

For seven years, Bob Sydow had managed about $1.6 billion for his asset management firm's only client: the Gates Foundation. His firm, Grandview

Capital, invested a small portion of the foundation's endowment in the high-yield bond market. But one day in February 2006, Sydow was abruptly dismissed. His firm's relationship with the foundation had been terminated overnight. As he struggled to find new clients, Sydow found that he had become a pariah in the asset management industry. People refused to work with him unless they understood why the Gates Foundation had kicked him out. And when there was no explanation forthcoming, the possibility that Grandview had done something criminal made potential clients wary. It was impossible for him to start a new business. Sydow had become "untouchable," they said.

Sydow described his ordeal to Gates and French Gates in a six-page letter dated November 3, 2006, having spent most of the year trying to drum up new business and salvage his reputation without making any headway. His goal was to alert them to the behavior of Larson. "I really do believe you have an agent there with the potential to greatly embarrass both you and the Foundation," Sydow wrote. Although the letter was addressed to both, it was sent to separate addresses—Microsoft headquarters for Gates, and Watermark Estate Management Services, the entity that handled the couple's family matters, for French Gates. Sydow believed that Larson had cut him off out of spite. The two had been close friends for 24 years, he wrote, and he had even been godfather to Larson's firstborn child. Yet after Sydow told Larson that he needed to stop using his power to hurt people, Larson decided to stop using Grandview's services. Zehren, Larson's spokesman, said it was within Larson's right to terminate the services of external money managers based on their performance, or because he wanted to change the mix of investments. Larson also said, through Zehren, that Sydow is not godfather to any of his children.

To some who worked for Larson, the Sydow incident was no surprise. A heavyset man who liked to dress in pink shirts and once sported a hairstyle that channeled the bangs of Johnny Depp, Larson largely ran Cascade as he saw fit for years, with complete control and few procedures in place. He often recruited young employees straight out of college, including from his alma mater, Claremont McKenna, and didn't see the need for human resources staff. He would sometimes reward people with new job titles before

handful of people. But as he began to diversify Gates's fortune away from Microsoft, the firm had to hire more people—lawyers, tax and regulatory experts, investment analysts, IT specialists and others—to carry out its work, like any sophisticated investment firm. At the same time, there was little initial thought given to building the supporting infrastructure common to professionally run entities, such as staff to hire and recruit people, help employees plan careers, and provide feedback and monitor their well-being.

Larson's personality, which friends and foes alike have described as brusque and direct to the point of rudeness, and his lack of sensitivity and tact, were thus on full display, especially because he insisted on a largely flat organizational structure. Kalbfleisch, the early employee and a personal friend of Larson's, described him as the kind of boss who would think nothing of berating someone in front of others. Once, he hit "Reply All" to tell her she was not qualified to address a tax matter, she recalled, prompting her to go into his office and tell him never to do that again. At the same time, Kalbfleisch found him considerate and compassionate. Larson was someone who "cared about things like benefits and compensation, and if an employee had personal challenges, he would get involved, and if someone left, he would also help people get jobs."

At some point, because of various complaints about his style of communication and unpredictable behavior toward staffers, the question came of what to do. One decision was to introduce physical distance between Larson's office and the rest of the employees by moving some of them to a different floor, but that "didn't change his behavior, it just changed the location of where the behavior happened," a former longtime employee said. "It happened through emails." Some employees took to calling those emails "Larson bombs." Kalbfleisch remembered them as "e-bombs," and added that as far as she knew, the office spaces were reorganized to accommodate hires. He had some fans, including one who joined Cascade in 2016, worked there for three years, and thrived in its "no-wuss culture," which she said was very different from the general "please-and-thank-you culture" of Seattle workplaces. Larson acknowledged, via email, that he had once been abrupt and demanding, but said it had never been personal. "Years ago, in my career, I used harsh language that I would not use today," he wrote, adding that he had since done "a lot of work to change."

In 2021, *The New York Times* reported that there were at least six complaints against Larson about his behavior, including four from Cascade employees; at the time, another spokesman for Larson said there were "fewer than five complaints" over the years. Zehren reiterated that reports of complaints were "flatly untrue."[10] Settlement payments were made to half a dozen employees, who were forbidden from speaking about their time at the firm, *The Times* reported. Such nondisclosure agreements are not unique to Cascade, and many complainants who settle with their companies behind closed doors sign them in exchange for a payment. But many who did sign Cascade NDAs said they were so expansive as to prohibit employees and external managers from talking about their employer, Larson, Gates, French Gates, and even the Gates Foundation. Similar NDAs were also required of senior executives elsewhere in the Gates universe. Lawyers for Cascade have sometimes called people who they thought had broken their NDA and threatened to sue. On their way out, many former employees told Gates and French Gates about the culture that Larson had created. Even though Gates was aware of Larson's conduct, he often seemed to approach complaints with a "get rid of it" stance rather than try to change the culture at Cascade or issue a severe reprimand his money manager, according to several former employees. The takeaway for some employees was that as long as Larson was preserving the fortune, doing a good job managing the foundation's money, and avoiding bad press, he was free to do as he pleased. About fifteen years ago, Cascade began introducing more traditional HR training programs, including "processes, policies, procedures," performance reviews, and even an anonymous reporting hotline, Larson's spokesman said. Kalbfleisch said that over the years, Cascade also brought in many consultants to conduct internal surveys, "but you wouldn't get the feedback, you wouldn't be hearing the things you needed to hear about the culture and environment. People weren't necessarily honest with what they thought, so that didn't help."

Zehren, the spokesman, who did most of the talking for Larson, denied that Larson built Cascade as anything but a welcoming, open, and considerate place where people were encouraged to speak up. Larson has built a "world-class organization with strong governance for the past three decades" with the help of talented managers and HR professionals, he said, and credited Cascade's flat organizational structure, free of rigid hierarchies, for the firm's successful track record. "Cascade is an organization where anyone, no matter their professional position, feels free to present ideas that make the group and its investing performance better," Zehren said. Larson also vehemently disagreed with the portrayal of him as rude and domineering. Through Zehren, he provided the names of several people who could provide another perspective, including two whom he had nominated to the board of Republic Services, one of the country's biggest waste disposal companies. Cascade owns more than a third of Republic Services and is its largest shareholder, and Larson is also on the board.

Tomago Collins, one of those directors and a longtime friend of Larson's, said he was wowed by the breadth and depth of his friend's relationships with everyone, from managers of sports teams to fellow investors. Collins was also struck by the genuine interest Larson took in young people's careers, whether they were holders of MBAs from Ivy League universities or restaurant servers, offering them advice if he thought he could be helpful. "I'm not used to people that successful giving advice to other people," said Collins, who sees Larson about half a dozen times a year. He added that he has never seen Larson do "anything hurtful or harmful," either in social or professional settings. Collins, an executive in the sports and entertainment industry, is also on the board of Four Seasons as a representative of Cascade, which is the luxury hotel company's largest shareholder.

"He's different, he's a savant, wicked smart, he's taught me a ton," said Jennifer M. Kirk, another director of Republic Services whom Larson brought on when he was looking to diversify the board by gender, color, and thinking. Kirk, a senior executive at Medtronic, the medical device company, called Larson a "mentor of sorts." Kirk, who's in her forties, found that he grasped how younger generations think about companies beyond profits, and he peppered her with questions about her young children: "What do your kids drink, Jenn? Do they like those energy drinks, do they drink soda?" In her interactions with him, which were mostly professional, Kirk found him direct but never disrespectful. "He's not a long-winded guy," she said, adding that one-word emails from Larson were more about efficiency than rudeness. Kirk mused that in general, the directness that was off-putting to many was almost a cultural aspect of certain industries like banking, of people who are "smarter than the average person" and expect them to keep up. Kalbfleisch agreed; she found Larson bright but "lacking people skills, like a lot of investment people. He just didn't think about it."

To people like Collins, Kirk, and others, especially those outside Cascade, Larson can be personable—someone whose directness is part of the persona, as is his capacious mind, which they said harbors information as wide-ranging as the mechanics of wine production and the performance statistics of sports teams. "He's his own walking Wikipedia and LinkedIn," said Mike Jackson, the former chief executive of AutoNation, the automotive retailer, and a longtime friend of Larson's. "He travels incessantly, he works like crazy and then at the end of the day he's highly principled. You want to talk sports, he can do sports, you want to talk farming, he can do farming, or exchange rates," Jackson said in an interview conducted for a profile of Cascade that ran in *The Wall Street Journal* in 2014. "About the only thing he stays away from is technology. He says, 'It's Bill's.' I cannot tell you how curious this man is about anything and everything, all day long."

The Broader Gates Universe

It takes a village to raise a child. It also takes a village to support a billionaire's interests and activities. More than 2,000 people depend—directly or indirectly—on the Gates fortune for their careers and livelihoods. Most are at the Gates Foundation, whose salaries and benefits are paid for by Gates money that has been earmarked for charity (and cannot be claimed back by the billionaire under tax laws). In 2019, the foundation spent around $300 million on salaries and benefits for its employees. Some 200 people manage his family's homes, horse farms, meals, security, jets, travel, and lifestyle through a company called the Gates Family Office, formerly known as Watermark. Another 150 or so people are employed by Cascade. Gates Ventures, the billionaire's private office and investment firm, has at least 80 people. There are yet others who work at Breakthrough Energy, also a venture capital firm founded by Gates that focuses on sustainable energy solutions.

Many of the people who work in the Gates orbit circulate between the various entities the billionaire is associated with. The foundation's first two chief executives came from Microsoft; Jeffrey Raikes, who held the chief executive's job from 2008 to 2014, is also a close friend of Gates. Larry Cohen, the chief executive of Gates Ventures, is a former Microsoft executive. Nathan Myhrvold, Microsoft's first chief technology officer, is a longtime friend and ally in whose patent firm, Intellectual Ventures, Gates has invested. It's hardly unique for the world's uber wealthy to have armies of people around them. From philanthropy advisors to personal chefs, entire industries exist to channel the largesse and serve the whims of the rich. Gates's activities continue to expand steadily, as a universe does, requiring more staff and holding companies. Although Cascade remains at the heart of the Gates financial engine, the billionaire has for years made personal investments through Gates Ventures. It was essentially a vehicle through which Gates indulged his passion for new, experimental technologies, making small, venture capital–style investments in things like synthetic meat and Alzheimer's research. Through Gates Ventures, he provided seed money to Ambri, a liquid battery metals manufacturer cofounded by an MIT professor whose online curriculum Gates had followed. It houses Gates's stake in Myhrvold's firm, and has a line into Breakthrough Energy, which held his energy-related investments but was spun off into a separate firm that also invests the money of other wealthy individuals with an interest in the field. Gates also directs some personal gifts through the outfit. A gift of $2 million that he made to the Massachusetts Institute of Technology's Media Lab came from bgC3, the predecessor to Gates Ventures. The gift became known during investigations into Epstein's death.

Gates is also an investor in patent licensing firms, sometimes called "patent trolls." His deeply held belief that intellectual property must be protected and paid for—the same belief that led him to charge for software and license Microsoft Windows to hardware makers, and the same belief that made him an arch defender of vaccine patents during the coronavirus pandemic—led him to back Pendrell, a company that typically buys intellectual property and collects royalties by licensing that patented knowledge. Such firms by nature tend to be litigious, and in recent years, Pendrell has sued companies like Apple for patent infringement. Intellectual Ventures, cofounded in 2000 by Myhrvold, a longtime friend of Gates who is also a scientist, cookbook author, and dinosaur researcher, has an innovative business model. Essentially, the firm buys patents and generates revenue by licensing the intellectual property and sharing the profits with inventors of those patents. It also acts as an incubator for inventors. Its portfolio of more than 35,000 intellectual property assets has generated more than $2 billion in licensing revenue, including $400 million for inventors. Myhrvold alone holds 900 patents and some of his technologies have been spun out of Intellectual Ventures into independent companies, some of which Gates has invested in. As of 2022, the firm had spun off 15 companies including TerraPower, a nuclear technology company. Intellectual Ventures also ran a fund called Global Good, created by Gates and Myhrvold to focus on developing technologies to solve "some of humanity's most daunting problems." The fund works with commercial, research, and government partners to bring new technologies to market.

Breakthrough, the energy firm "dedicated to helping humanity avoid a climate disaster" that Gates founded in 2015, invests in companies that are working toward clean technologies with the goal of reducing greenhouse gases and getting to net zero emissions. Since 2017, the firm has invested in more than 100 companies. Breakthrough has raised at least two funds, which collectively hold more than $2 billion. There is also a smaller, Europe-focused fund. Gates is by far the largest investor in Breakthrough, but there are more than three dozen other investors, mainly businessmen and -women from all over the world, including those that many Americans likely haven't heard of, such as Patrice Motsepe, a South African mining billionaire. One had to be a billionaire to invest in a Breakthrough fund; they were not intended for less wealthy people who might seek returns on investment and other specific performance-based targets, said one person with insight into the funds' setup. It was yet another example of the billionaire using his star power and influence to push toward things he thinks are for the general and societal good.

Then, there is the sprawl of the Gates family life, and the range of services and the efforts that go into lifestyle upkeep. Like many in the billionaire class, Gates owns multiple homes around the United States. Those alone add up to about $300 million. During their 27-year marriage, the primary home of the former couple, the place where they raised their children, Jennifer, Rory, and Phoebe, was the high-tech mansion, nicknamed Xanadu 2.0, located on the shores of Lake Washington in Medina. Originally intended as a high-tech pad for Gates before he married, the home took six years to build and was last valued at $130 million. Gates kept the mansion as part of the divorce settlement. Other homes the ex-couple own or have owned include a beachfront mansion in Del Mar, California, just north of San Diego, worth at least $40 million; a six-bedroom home in the Vintage Club in Indian Wells, California, assessed at $12.5 million, and a horse farm on 5.5 acres in Wellington, Florida, a popular spot for the horse-riding set, that sold for $26 million in 2022.[11] There is also a Gates family vacation compound with multiple houses in the Hood Canal area of Washington State.

Gates is famous for his love of fast cars, having gotten a speeding ticket in 1977. Over the years, he has indulged in luxury wheels, from Porsche Taycan 911s to Ferraris and Mercedes Benzes to a Tesla. He owns at least two customized planes, including a Gulfstream, which are known to cost at least a couple of hundred million dollars. There are helicopters and sea planes for short distances. The $30.8 million that Gates paid for his Leonardo da Vinci Codex in 1994 remained the highest price for a document bought at auction until 2021, when the hedge fund billionaire Ken Griffin purchased a rare early print of the U.S. Constitution for $43.2 million.[12] Gates's art collection includes works by American artists, among them an 1885 oil painting by Winslow Homer that Gates bought for a reported $30 million.

Watermark—now renamed the Gates Family Office—which for years managed the Gateses' personal assets, has had on its payroll, at various points, project managers, financial planners, a coordinator for "gifting," a recruiter, as well as real estate managers and travel and logistics experts, among other professionals. There is a chief of "protective operations" with a background in counterintelligence and special investigations; not only do security personnel constantly tail Gates family members, but they are also required for the protection of dignitaries who visit the Gates mansion. An event planner, an "interiors" specialist, a horticulture program manager, stylists, personal shoppers, audio and video specialists, and even a professional to train people in business etiquette are or have been on staff. As of fall 2022, the family office also employed a professionally trained private chef with experience working on yachts, islands, and estates, practiced at all styles of cuisine and dietary preferences.

Although the Gates Family Office no longer handles French Gates's personal affairs, it was once in charge of managing her wardrobe, makeup, and hair, and styling her. The office staff also has included an expert in rare books to catalog their collection, experts in "chemical-free" housekeeping, tennis, golf, boating, massage, yoga, meditation retreats, and riding golf. The family office is also the primary entity through which Gates holds interests in equestrian properties for Jennifer, who is a professional show jumper and doctor. The portfolio also includes ranches and horse barns, including its remaining properties in Wellington, Florida—known as horse country for its miles of bridle paths—not far from Equestrian Village, site of the U.S. Dressage Festival for many years, and the equestrian grounds for Palm Beach. At one point, entities tied to Gates through the family office bought up properties on an entire street in Wellington totaling 16.5 acres to ensure privacy and security.[13]

Kalbfleisch, who worked with the estate manager of the Gates household, lending her accounting expertise to do the budgets in addition to her duties at Cascade, remarked dryly that the more the uber wealthy acquire, the more they need. "First there is one residence, and then you buy a second home and multiple homes, and then you want to make sure that you replicate all the things you need in every home, and that requires budgets and staff," she said, speaking generally. "Then your kids are born, and you need additional staff. And in the beginning, there was one plane, one pilot and one backup pilot, but there came a second plane. You need someone on staff to walk the dogs, handle the personal affairs, like property taxes, charitable donations, and then the family protection and security, and making sure everything worked smoothly."

Chapter 9

Cancel Bill

The Toxicity of Epstein

When Warren Buffett, Bill Gates, and Melinda French Gates announced the Giving Pledge in June 2010, publicly committing to giving at least half their wealth back to society during their lifetimes or in their wills and urging other billionaires to do the same, Jeffrey Epstein saw a way to make money. Two years earlier, the registered sex offender had pleaded guilty to soliciting prostitution, including from an underage girl, following his 2006 arrest. After serving a light, work-release sentence in a Florida jail, he resumed what he had done for more than a decade: cultivating a network of scientists, musicians, bankers, Nobel laureates, politicians, billionaire businessmen, academics, filmmakers—just about anyone with influence who could give him a sheen of legitimacy by association, a valuable introduction, a piece of information he could keep in his back pocket to be wielded in exchange for a favor. Tucked in between haircut appointments at the upscale Frédéric Fekkai salon and massage appointments were endless meetings, video calls, private jet trips, dinners, and cocktails.

An egregious name-dropper, Epstein was fully aware that the more names he dangled and the more connected he was to people, the more accepted he would be in those rarefied circles, where the best vetting mechanism was a friend-of-a-friend introduction. Out of his multiple residences, including in New York and Palm Beach and on Little St. James, his private island in the U.S. Virgin Islands, Epstein conducted his business and was welcomed by those he courted, his sordid background reduced to a footnote.

The Giving Pledge had created an enormous splash. The star power of two of the richest and weightiest billionaires made the effort hard to ignore. Buffett's commitment to give the bulk of his fortune away during his lifetime to the Gates Foundation, through which Gates and French Gates were tackling some of humanity's most intractable problems, gave them the moral authority to ask other billionaires to step up. By August 2010, 40 billionaires and billionaire couples had signed the pledge. By year's end, 17 more had joined the group. At the same time, some who had taken the pledge began to wonder: How to disburse that money? Many billionaires had private foundations, but they often were modest, family affairs. Building a foundation to hand out big sums of money is a significant undertaking akin to launching a new business. Some billionaires thus turned to Gates, the one person who already had a massive operation going, wondering if they could partner up with his foundation in some way, or have it direct their money. Connected as he was to scientists, billionaires, and Gates's trusted lieutenants, Epstein heard about the unanticipated outcome of the pledge for the foundation and began to tunnel a way into the philanthropist's orbit.

In 1992, he had met a young woman named Melanie Walker after he walked up to her at New York's Plaza Hotel and suggested that she could be a model. Walker demurred but they kept in touch. By 2010, she was a neurological surgeon married to Steven Sinofsky, a senior Microsoft executive and ally of Gates, and was working at the Gates Foundation. Boris Nikolic, the former chief advisor on science and technology to Gates, and Nathan Myhrvold, the scientist and one of Gates's closest advisors, had also known Epstein. Myhrvold knew Epstein because the two often ran into each other at TED conferences, and because Epstein donated to scientific research. Assured by the connections that some of his trusted allies had to Epstein, Gates decided to meet with the disgraced financier, despite the consternation of some foundation employees. One evening in January 2011, not long after a blizzard had menaced the city of New York, Epstein hosted a dinner at his Upper East Side townhouse for Gates, pitching the evening to some invitees as a relaxed gathering with a group of influential people. It was the kind of gathering Epstein excelled at—entertaining and stimulating, a setting where social chatter mixed seamlessly with business talk. Gates appeared to find it an enjoyable evening. That May, Epstein hosted another meeting for the philanthropist. Among the guests were Larry Summers, the former U.S. Secretary of the Treasury and president emeritus of Harvard University; James E. Staley, a former senior executive of JPMorgan Chase; and Nikolic. At some point in the evening, the five men posed for a picture, which would later accompany a 2019 *New York Times* article. Epstein used the opportunity to present an idea to Gates, and even included slides: Could some of the billionaire philanthropic dollars being pledged be pooled into a charitable fund created for the Gates Foundation? Such donor-advised funds are vehicles created by banks and other big asset managers into which wealthy individuals can deposit money that they eventually plan to give to charity. Donors get to decide the causes they want to direct their philanthropic funds to, but until they do, the money managers oversee the funds for a fee.

Gates was receptive to the idea, emboldening Epstein to begin pushing his proposal more steadily. He roped in JPMorgan, the nation's largest bank where he was a client, to set up a donor-advised fund for the Gates Foundation, which would "enhance the current giving" by the outfit. Bank executives were already in touch with foundation staffers about a separate project, which led to the creation of a healthcare fund in 2013. Epstein had long been friends with Staley, who goes by Jes, at the time a top lieutenant of JPMorgan's chief executive Jamie Dimon. Over hundreds of emails studded with typographical errors sent to JPMorgan executives including Mary Callahan Erdoes, who led the bank's private wealth and asset management business, Epstein laid out his ambitions for the donor-advised fund. It would be a "very high profile" club with an entry donation of $100 million. Like other donor-advised funds, this one too would provide donors the tax benefits up front. The proposed structure would involve silos—areas that the Gates Foundation focused on, such as polio, maternal health, vaccines, and agriculture—that donors wanted to direct their money into. Membership to this donor club would be known, but donors could choose to remain anonymous about how they directed their money. This was because, Epstein wrote to Erdoes and Staley, many potential donors who had spoken to Gates about giving money did not want to do so publicly. JPMorgan would run the donor-advised fund. Epstein suggested that the bank collect all the audit, investment management, trustee, and related fees from the fund and act as its fiduciary; he would take a cut of those fees amounting to millions of dollars. If done right, he promised the JPMorgan bankers, the fund would grow from billions of dollars to tens of billions of dollars by its fourth year of operation. Nikolic, the Gates advisor, was copied on some of the email exchanges between Epstein, Erdoes, and Staley.

"In essence this DAF will allow Bill to have access to higher quality people , investment , allocation , governance without upsetting either his marriage or the sensitvites of the current foundation employees," Epstein wrote, in one of the badly punctuated and typo-riddled emails. He repeatedly warned the bankers not to engage with too many "low level" foundation employees, who he claimed were confused and without direction. The emails don't explain why the donor-advised fund would upset Gates's marriage. The fund would be marketed to billionaires as a hassle-free way to engage in philanthropy. When Erdoes asked if the foundation could be convinced to actively participate in marketing the fund to potential donors, Epstein replied that it would be easy as long as the foundation were given "emotional credit" where it was due. "They are a very very sensitve bunch that has spent billions,, seperate from polio. there is little that can be held up as a great success and even polio is not yet finished," Epstein continued, unburdened by the rules of spelling, grammar, and punctuation. At the time, the Gates Foundation was in the midst of a high-publicity campaign around polio eradication. It had become a personal mission for Gates; the foundation had already directed hundreds of millions to the effort, and he expected that other billionaires too would see the urgency. Gates was "terribly frustrated," Epstein wrote, and would like to focus on the foundation's successes rather than on the failures. Thus, he added, it was necessary to showcase in the proposal materials that a donor-advised fund would bring additional money for vaccines by highlighting efforts that had worked.

As of October 2011, Erdoes and Epstein were still going back and forth on the terms, with Epstein getting increasingly frustrated about the slow pace of the deal and pushing the bankers to finish the proposal. He insisted that the proposal be tailored only to Gates, and that it be negotiated directly between Staley and the billionaire to avoid internal politicking at the foundation. By January 2012 they were still trying to get the project off the ground, and the effort eventually sputtered. "The incentives were misaligned," said a person involved in the discussions. "JPMorgan was looking to run the fund, Bill wanted the money [for vaccines], and Epstein wanted the connections." It died down, this person added, "because there was no money, there were no pots of money looking for a place to go. Once it became clear that there was nothing to what he was offering, the conversations stopped."

Epstein appeared to be in contact with Gates in early 2014. A January 12 entry in Epstein's schedule mentions him ordering sweatshirts for Gates and four others, including "Boris and Joi" (presumably Boris Nikolic and Joichi Ito, then the director of the MIT Media Lab, a research unit of the university to which Gates had donated). Epstein was also supposed to participate in a Skype call with Gates on January 28 arranged by Larry Cohen, the billionaire's longtime right-hand man and chief executive of Gates Ventures. On September 8, 2014, Epstein arranged a day of meetings between Gates and other billionaires. By the end of that year, Gates had stopped talking to him, Epstein told an associate.

Perhaps none of this would have spilled out into public view had Epstein not been found dead at 6:30 A.M. on August 10, 2019, of an apparent suicide in his jail cell at the Metropolitan Correctional Center, a squat, Brutalist structure the color of cardboard in lower Manhattan. Just one month earlier, he had been arrested in New York on federal sex trafficking charges, after the *Miami Herald* published a series of stories questioning the lenient plea deal Epstein had struck in 2008 when Alexander Acosta, who was serving as former president Trump's labor secretary, had been the U.S. attorney in Miami. (Acosta stepped down from his cabinet post less than a week after Epstein's July 2019 arrest.) Reporters, sensing the beginnings of a hot story, began digging. Over the next two years, they would unearth the deep network Epstein had built of high-profile and influential men. What could have drawn so many luminaries into the realm of a convicted sex offender? As the skeletons kept tumbling out, they ravaged the reputations of powerful men. One of the first to go was the billionaire Leslie Wexner, then the chief executive of L Brands, the parent company of Victoria's Secret, and one of Epstein's oldest connections who had given to Epstein as a gift the Manhattan townhouse he lived in. Britain's Prince Andrew, whose friendship with Epstein had been tabloid fodder for decades, was stripped of his royal privileges. The billionaire private equity investor Leon Black was so backed into a corner after it emerged that he had paid $158 million in fees to Epstein for tax advice that he retired from Apollo Global Management, the firm he had cofounded in 1990. Black, a serious art collector, with a collection that some have estimated is worth $1 billion, was also forced to step down as the chairman of the Museum of Modern Art and retreat from New York's charity and social circuit due to his association with Epstein. In 2023, four years after his ties to Epstein were revealed, Black continued to fight allegations of rape from women who had also been involved with Epstein. Staley, the JPMorgan banker who had become the chief executive of Barclays, lost millions of dollars in bonuses, and eventually his job at the British bank. His long-standing ties to Epstein and alleged participation in some of his activities, and JPMorgan's financial involvement with the sexual predator, would eventually result in multiple lawsuits.

Lawyers for Prince Andrew, who has denied any wrongdoing, have said the royal regrets his association with Epstein. Black has said he did not know of or participate in the sexual activities of Epstein. Staley, who once described his friendship with Epstein as "profound," has repeatedly said he knew little about the allegations against his friend and denied any wrongdoing. Wexner has said he knew nothing of Epstein's activities, and he cut off ties with Epstein in 2007. This symphony of innocence, ignorance, and regret has only highlighted the fact that some of the world's smartest, savviest, and wealthiest men appear to have had the exact same failure of judgment about the exact same man, who is no longer around to present his side.

And then there was Gates. Nikolic, who is widely reported to have introduced Gates to Epstein, told this reporter that he had not done so. He added that he met Epstein in 2009 through Walker, whom the disgraced financier had once appointed his science advisor. "I remember this day—and I greatly regret that day," Nikolic said. Walker had a different recollection of events from Nikolic, according to someone briefed on her version of events. In September 2019, a month after Epstein died, *The New Yorker* magazine published an article by Ronan Farrow detailing the close fund-raising relationship that the MIT Media Lab had shared with Epstein. A research unit within the Massachusetts Institute of Technology, the Media Lab studies the intersection of art, science, design, and media. Farrow reported that Ito, the lab's director, accepted gifts from Epstein even though he was listed as a "disqualified" donor in the university's database, and went to great lengths to conceal Epstein's identity. After some MIT staffers said they were uncomfortable with Epstein's visits because he brought along "assistants" who were in their twenties, Ito began to meet Epstein off campus.[1] John Tye, a lawyer and the founder of Whistleblower Aid, who helped former MIT coordinator Signe Swenson go public with her allegations against Epstein and MIT Media Lab, told Farrow that this was a way for Epstein to launder his reputation through philanthropy. Additionally, Farrow reported, Epstein also "directed" gifts from others, including Gates, who had made a $2 million donation to the lab. Within the university, the gift was only listed as a contribution from Gates at the request of a friend. It was not included in any public material because Gates wished to remain anonymous to the outside world. Not long after, *The New York Times* reported that Gates had met Epstein mulitple times between 2011 and 2014, following up on a CNBC report from August 2019 that said the two men had met to discuss ways to "increase philanthropic funding."[2] The stories noted that the interactions between the two men had started three years after Epstein had been convicted of sex crimes and served time in jail.

The news reports in 2019 triggered an MIT inquiry into whether its professors had engaged in misconduct, and its executive committee hired two law firms to investigate the university's ties with Epstein. Board members were especially worried that their association with Epstein via MIT could tarnish their professional image, so the review was largely limited to screening for the university's exposure. Gates refused to be interviewed for the investigation, but his counsel said the philanthropist often donated anonymously and the $2 million donation to MIT had nothing to do with Epstein.[3] The gift came not from his foundation, but from Gates Ventures. Although the donation may or may not have been at Epstein's recommendation, Ito used it to seek other donations, telling potential donors that if Gates was donating at Epstein's behest, it was legitimate. "It was left at he said, she said," one person familiar with the law firm's investigation said.

But Gates was often mentioned in the thousands of emails that lawyers reviewed between Epstein and MIT employees, two people familiar with the investigation said. There were references to Gates visiting Epstein's residences, and Epstein arranging for "Big Macs," which one of the people said referred to Epstein's interest in young women—and also the food he was sometimes known to serve to guests at his Manhattan townhouse, on silver platters. Although Gates visited Epstein in Florida, he did not visit the sex offender's private island. Gates also flew on one of Epstein's private planes when he had at least two of his own; a former acquaintance of Gates found it curious, remembering the billionaire once declaring that he would never fly on another person's jet. Gates had been unaware that it was Epstein's plane, a representative said at the time.

When news of Gates's ties to Epstein first came tumbling out in 2019, Gates's media team did what spinmeisters do—they employed a high-visibility strategy that included multiple television appearances, harnessing the press, just as they had after the Microsoft trial. Gates has always maintained that he met with Epstein because he was told that the financier could connect him with a lot of rich donors who could help raise more money for philanthropic causes. "I had several dinners with him hoping that what he said about getting billions of philanthropy for global health through contacts that he had might emerge, and when it looked like it wasn't a real thing that relationship ended," Gates told CNN's Anderson Cooper in an interview. "It was a huge mistake to spend time with him, to give him the credibility of being there." His discomfort at being asked about Epstein is obvious. Every time he was asked about it in a public setting, Gates offered nothing but regrets and apologies, calling it a mistake and blaming it on poor judgment. In a televised interview in 2021 with Judy Woodruff, then anchor of *PBS NewsHour*, Gates got visibly shifty and nervous, stammering and fidgeting without providing an iota of information beyond stating his regret and poor judgment, lines that he had delivered repeatedly. When the talk turned to philanthropy, he became much more at ease. In more recent media appearances, Gates has also displayed exasperation about the continual Epstein questions.

But instead of providing a detailed, honest accounting by the billionaire's representatives, explaining how and why Gates met a convicted sex offender repeatedly, the number of meetings, the subject of those meetings, and why those meetings ended, the Gates media machine put out strongly worded statements designed to obfuscate. The initial strategy, according to two people who were involved in the deliberations, was to shut down the stories rather than giving them air by engaging with reporters. The approach partly came from Gates; one person described it as typical of the billionaire's evidence-driven mentality where, if a reporter sends a query without supporting evidence, his tendency is to deny. As stories about the extent and nature of Gates's relationship with Epstein continued to emerge—with supporting evidence—Gates's team was forced to backtrack and acknowledge some of the events, which only served to increase the persistent speculation and raise more questions about what else Gates had to hide. In 2023, *The Wall Street Journal* reported that Epstein tried to blackmail Gates about the billionaire's 2010 affair with Mila Antonova, the bridge player. One of several young women who occasionally stayed at Epstein's Manhattan mansion, Antonova had been introduced to Epstein by Nikolic, Gates's advisor. Just before he died, Epstein updated his will to list Nikolic as the executor of his estate should the two named executors be unable to do so, which the latter said came as a surprise to him.

Why Gates hung around with Epstein may remain a head scratcher forever. By many accounts, Epstein and his larger-than-life behavior was an adventure for Gates, who observed to colleagues that Epstein had an unusual lifestyle, but added that it was not for him. More than once, long before Epstein's sexual depravations became widely known, the tabloid press had compared Epstein to Jay Gatsby—one of Gates's favorite fictional characters. In Fitzgerald's book, Gatsby is an enigmatic character, a social climber with a multimillion-dollar fortune of unclear provenance, who throws lavish parties in his grand mansion on Long Island.

To give Gates the benefit of the doubt, one might assume that employees and longtime associates like Walker and Nikolic told him Epstein was someone worth knowing, especially given his mission to induce more philanthropic giving among the rich. Still, the failure of judgment on Gates's part is surprising, given that he continued to see Epstein over a four-year timespan despite his former wife's warning, and because the allegations against Epstein were widely known by the time the two of them were introduced. It's even more surprising given the media battalions at the Gates Foundation and Gates Ventures, who are paid to maintain the philanthropist's upstanding public profile and brief him on the backgrounds and expertise of the people he meets. Some senior foundation executives were aware of the interactions between Gates and Epstein and knew that their boss met the disgraced financier at his house several times, but they were not privy to the subject of those visits. Others visited Epstein's townhouse to discuss the potential donor-advised fund at Gates's behest, including for lunch. Gates referred to Epstein in at least one instance as a "buddy," said a person who met Epstein once at "Bill's behest." The potential liabilities of dealing with Epstein were flagged to Gates by some employees of Gates Ventures, but the billionaire either chose not to listen, or made the trade-off that Epstein could offer him something that was worth putting aside the image risk. Those employees were also fully aware of the meetings since some were listed on Gates's schedules, prompting questions about why they were doing business with Epstein. In 2019, when the first stories about Gates's ties to Epstein emerged in the press, along with the photograph, Cohen, who has a full view into his boss's calendar and communications, emailed his colleagues to say that associating with the convicted sex offender was "a significant lapse in judgment." Later, at a meeting to address employee concerns, Cohen seemed to "choke up" as he spoke, one person recalled.

Even a cursory search of Epstein in any database of archived news—or a simple Google search—would reveal enough stories about his questionable behavior and habits to raise red flags. In a 2003 profile of Epstein in *Vanity Fair* magazine, the journalist Vicky Ward wrote: "His advantage is that no one really seems to know him or his history completely or what his arsenal actually consists of. He has carefully engineered it so that he remains one of the few truly baffling mysteries among New York's moneyed world. People know snippets, but few know the whole." The profile mentions that he left Bear Stearns, the investment bank where he got his start, under a cloud. But Ward also reported that billionaires like Tom Pritzker, the chairman of Hyatt Hotels; the real estate mogul Mort Zuckerman; the businessman Ron Perelman; and Black would often stop by his house for dinner.

Epstein appeared occasionally in gossip pages and was routinely referred to as a billionaire (even though he was not), a connoisseur of women, a financier with a small roster of billionaire clients, a property developer, or an employee of Wexner. There were always gossipy tales of multiple young women, particularly from Eastern Europe, in his life. By the mid-2000s, Epstein was making news for his lifestyle and his failed bids to buy media properties. In a 2005 article about executive assistants on Wall Street, *The New York Times* described him as someone who maintained an office in New York but lived and worked on a private island in the U.S. Virgin Islands, with a "three-women executive team, which manages his hectic life for globetrotting and hobnobbing with the likes of former President [Bill] Clinton." That year, he made news for teaming up with Zuckerman to buy *Radar*, a magazine founded in 2003 that fizzled for lack of funding, was brought back to life in 2005, but folded once again after only three issues before eventually relaunching under new ownership as an exclusively digital property. Epstein was also mentioned as one among a consortium of buyers for IMG with Teddy Forstmann, and of *New York* magazine with Zuckerman, Harvey Weinstein, and others. By then, well-known names like Summers and Alan Dershowitz were in his orbit; he got written up for pledging money to Harvard University to launch a program in "evolutionary dynamics" when Summers was the university's president. Harvard shut down the program in 2020 and revised its donor policies after an internal review.[4]

At the same time, there were lawsuits against him, including one with Citibank, which said he had defaulted on $20 million of loans from their private bank. When he was arrested in Florida in 2006, after multiple underage girls accused him of sexual assault, major media organizations like the Associated Press, *The New York Times*, *The Guardian*, and various Florida newspapers ran stories. And there was yet another flood of coverage when he pleaded guilty to charges of soliciting prostitution and soliciting prostitution from a minor in 2008.

Even when the revelations around Epstein brutalized the reputations of once-powerful men, sending them scurrying to private shelter, Gates, although tainted, somehow managed to remain standing. He had transformed very publicly from an arrogant bully when he stepped away from Microsoft into a sort of patron saint of global public health, and a savior of the developing world. Thus, the two-year stretch that began in the summer of 2019 with news reports about his multiple meetings with Epstein and ended with his 2021 divorce, followed shortly after by accounts of his personal conduct and infidelities, was all the more shocking because of the high moral ground he occupied. Upon hearing the news, one former Microsoft employee said it felt like God had fallen to earth. Gates was suddenly both philanthropist and philanderer, and a womanizer whose foundation worked for women's rights.

The Gates Foundation, already sensitive to the criticisms about its top-down structure and size, used the opportunity to make changes in its governing structure. In January 2022, it announced a newly created board of trustees, specifying that these trustees were outside of the Gates and Buffett families, to provide input, guidance, and fiduciary oversight to the foundation. It was signaling to the world that it was an institution with clear governance, diverse viewpoints, and credibility. The thinking, according to a person advising on those efforts, was that it was vital for the foundation to manage its institutional reputation, and having it controlled too closely by Gates could become a liability in its work in the nonprofit world—echoing Gates's move away from Microsoft two decades earlier.

A Reckoning at Microsoft

In 2015, Katie Moussouris filed a lawsuit against Microsoft alleging gender-based pay discrimination, describing in detail a sexist culture inside the software giant, where women were openly propositioned. Documents produced in 2018 as part of the suit revealed that there had been at least 238 complaints by women about the internal culture at Microsoft, where women were sexually harassed, passed over for promotions, or paid less than their male counterparts. The suit said that there were systemic problems with the way Microsoft paid and promoted women, and that it discriminated against women based on gender. It also claimed that Microsoft fostered a "boys' club" atmosphere rife with harassment and discrimination, where female employees returning from maternity leave were asked, "How was your vacation?" It described an environment where male employees would grope and harass their female colleagues at work functions, and complaints to HR went unheeded. Moussouris and her lawyers sought to turn it into a class-action lawsuit, but they dropped the case in 2019 after a judge denied the move. At the time, Microsoft said it did not discriminate on pay based on gender.[5] In 2019, the news website *Quartz* reported about an email chain between female Microsoft employees complaining about sexual harassment and discrimination.[6] Women felt systematically undervalued and underpaid, according to the emails. Two years later, after the divorce, news reports about Gates's behavior when he was at Microsoft—including at least one affair with an employee—added to questions about the company's culture and values.

Natasha Lamb, a founding partner at an impact investment firm called Arjuna Capital, had been paying attention to the accusations of sexual harassment and gender and pay discrimination at Microsoft. Arjuna, which takes its name from the warrior-hero in the *Mahabharata*, invests in companies with an eye to their performance on environmental, social, and governance (ESG) issues. With its motto of "enlightened investing" and about $300 million in assets under management, Arjuna Capital is a minnow in the world of giant asset managers. Its shareholder proposals—investors present these at annual meetings to push a company or its directors to act on an issue—often tried to hold companies accountable on gender and pay equity but got little traction. Big shareholders like BlackRock and Vanguard, with trillions of dollars they manage on behalf of pension funds and others, typically vote with management.

Arjuna Capital had met with some success in getting companies to disclose their median gender and racial pay gap ratios. In 2018, some of the biggest Wall Street banks agreed to publicly share the progress they had made to close the gender pay gap, largely due to the efforts of Lamb. But her firm would get stonewalled just as often. Also that year, it had filed a shareholder proposal to get Comcast to conduct an independent board investigation into allegations of workplace sexual harassment, but the company had refused, and other shareholders had not sided with the firm. Arjuna had also teamed up with Time's Up in 2019 to push Microsoft for a fuller disclosure of racial and gender pay gap disparities, but the not-for-profit, which focuses on creating a safer and more equitable workplace for women, secured a grant from Pivotal Ventures, the firm run by French Gates, around the same time and dropped out of the campaign.

When the reports about Gates's inappropriate behavior emerged in 2021, including that he had made sexual advances toward Microsoft employees, and that his decision to step down from the board of the company he co-founded had been at least partly driven by a board committee's investigation into sexual harassment claims against him, Lamb saw a fresh opportunity to push Microsoft.[7] That November, during the company's annual meeting of shareholders, held via teleconference because of the pandemic, Lamb filed a proposal asking Microsoft to "transparently address sexual harassment claims through independent investigations and reporting." Microsoft had been under intense public scrutiny because of sexual harassment allegations and complaints that the company failed to address them adequately, she said, reading out her statement. The Gates news, she said, added to concerns that the company had a "culture of systemic sexual harassment." Lamb called for an independent investigation, citing a Harvard study about how a poor workplace culture could be detrimental to investor returns. She also asked for the results of the investigation to be shared publicly in the interest of transparency.

Microsoft dismissed the proposal and asked other investors to do the same. The proposal then went to a vote. When the results came in, Lamb, whose firm owned only about $20 million of Microsoft shares, was both shocked and ecstatic. More than three-quarters of Microsoft's shareholders, including some of the world's largest asset managers who collectively held nearly $2 trillion of the company's stock, had voted in favor of her proposal. Lamb, an ESG investor for two decades, had benefited from the societal vibe shift sparked by the #MeToo movement in 2017, around the time news reports surfaced about how the movie producer Harvey Weinstein sexually abused women. The wider culture had begun reckoning with the impunity of powerful men and in the months following the Weinstein revelations, there was a relentless flood of accusations of sexual abuse and harassment by women against dozens of celebrities, politicians, businessmen, media executives, sportsmen, performers, and others. The lack of accountability inside institutions, many of them with toothless HR departments, also came under scrutiny as people contended with the wide chasm in pay based on gender and color, the systemic racism underpinning public life, and the lackadaisical attitude toward climate change. As social issues began to drive consumer decisions, forcing corporate America to brush up on the language of diversity and inclusion, and burnish their earth-friendly credentials, big investors were suddenly paying attention. Investing with an eye to ESG was becoming popular, and Lamb found herself becoming an "influencer." The overwhelming support from shareholders for her proposal forced Microsoft to agree to an independent investigation, and to do more to reduce racial and gender pay gaps. The law firm that conducted the investigation recommended that Microsoft strengthen its sexual harassment and gender discrimination policies. Microsoft said it would strengthen its policies, including making executives undergo training and promoting more women to senior roles.

"What galvanized the support from investors was that there was this a-ha moment, not only about Epstein but also Gates's employee relationships and whether there was more, and questions around how the board addressed these allegations and whether his departure was on a voluntary basis," Lamb reflected. "It was a combination of the high-profile allegations against Gates and the track record of unresolved sexual harassment issues around the company which had been going around for years" that led to the support. One way of interpreting Gates's behavior is to look at it through the lens of the work environment he grew up in, according to people who have observed him from up close. The early culture of tech companies consisted of a largely male workforce, and the gender segregation was clear. Female employees were noticeable more for their absence. When they existed, many were in positions as handlers to male executives or in supporting functions. Coders and engineers, who were mostly male, didn't necessarily get reprimanded for lewd or sexist behavior. After bouts of programming and meeting deadlines, largely male workforces often let off steam at bars and strip joints. In the 1980s and 1990s, Microsoft was well known for hiring skimpily dressed performers and escorts to weave their way through the guests at company parties or industry events. Gates was often on the dance floor shimmying with women late into the night. Even as recently as March 2016, Microsoft's Xbox unit hired go-go dancers to perform on the podium on the same day that the unit hosted a "women in gaming" lunch at a game developers' conference. The head of the unit apologized the following day.

Maria Klawe first met Gates in 1987 at an industry conference and got to know him better when she joined Microsoft's board in 2008. In her seventies, Klawe is the former president of Harvey Mudd, a small college in Claremont, California, that focuses on science and engineering. A computer scientist with a doctoral degree in mathematics and honorary doctorate degrees from about 20 universities in Canada, where she is from, Klawe is one of the few high-profile women in a field dominated by men. She has long made it a priority to advocate for more women in the fields of science, technology, math, and engineering (STEM). When the topic of succession planning at Microsoft came up at a board meeting not long after she joined, Klawe asked why the list of 50 or so people included no women.

"Are you fucking trying to destroy the company?" Gates shot back, in Klawe's telling. She recalled being stunned at the response. "This is my belief about Bill," said Klawe, who has since become openly critical of Gates. "One of the consequences of having been so successful in building Microsoft is that he truly believes that he is the smartest person in the world. That for an academic computer scientist to ask [the question of women successors] just meant I had no idea what it took to be successful at Microsoft." Klawe said that during her time on the board of Microsoft, there were no mentions of Epstein since his contact with Gates was tied to the foundation's work, and that she never heard any discussion of allegations of sexual harassment. But there were complaints about "Bill yelling and screaming at employees," she said. In 2014, Microsoft appointed Satya Nadella as its chief executive officer. Nadella, only the third chief executive of the nearly 40-year-old company, was more attuned to the changing mores around him than his predecessors. He promised a kinder and gentler Microsoft. Still, early on in Nadella's tenure, Klawe asked him at a public event she was moderating what women should do to get paid more in their professions. Nadella responded by saying that women should trust the system and that they would be rewarded for their labor. The gaffe was a public relations disaster for Nadella, who subsequently apologized for his comments to Microsoft employees, and said he would work to address the challenges women faced inside the company. The board asked for Klawe's resignation several months later. She said she was hurt by the move, and it took her a while to get to a point where she could talk about it publicly. "I felt horrible and if I talked about it, I would never get on a public company board again," she said. "And that turned out to be true."

Bill Kills?

Travis Chapman doesn't consider himself a conspiracy theorist. He describes himself as a dad and a normal guy who runs his own roofing company in Spokane, Washington. Some years ago, he became obsessed with painting, and turned to *The Joy of Painting* on PBS to learn techniques from Bob Ross, America's beloved painting instructor who taught via television. In his soothing, dulcet tones, Ross, with his fuzzy globe of a perm, dabbing a little ochre here, using his spatula to create some texture there, shows Americans how easy it is to paint. Chapman leaned toward satirical art and began putting his paintings up for sale on Etsy. A local restaurant or two commissioned his work. Finding a small measure of success, he began to spend more time in his studio, and eventually turned to art full-time.

Gates was not someone Chapman thought about much. "He was just kind of a famous guy, a go-to guy if you were gonna make a billionaire joke, super nerdy." But suddenly, during the Covid pandemic, Gates was unmissable, talking about vaccines and public health. "I'm not a conspiracy theorist or an anti-vaxxer," Chapman said. But something about Gates's omnipresence put him off, striking him as some sort of pandemic performance. What were his motives? Why was he pushing vaccines at a time when there were questions about their efficacy and side effects? "If I'm going to listen to someone about Covid, it would be a doctor or an epidemiologist," Chapman said. "Why is the Microsoft guy talking?" His friends, including one he described as a full-blown conspiracy theorist, shared the same unease. As Chapman began scrutinizing Gates closely, he was convinced that the philanthropist, with his V-necked sweaters and collared shirts, was channeling Mister Rogers in a very deliberate way. "He would never be in a ten-thousand-dollar suit that he could easily afford," Chapman said. "He always dressed down to be relatable. It felt like a costume that he was wearing." Why?

"It's totally Mister Rogers. He is universally loved and it's almost like Bill Gates was trying to be Mister Rogers but Gates had a nefarious purpose," Chapman ventured. If Gates had once existed as an easy shorthand for a billionaire joke among friends, his vaccine activism made Chapman wonder why Gates was so insistent. "I don't believe anything about you," he said of Gates. "You're putting out this image that I don't trust." He decided to turn his suspicions into art. In his painting, an acrylic on canvas measuring 16 inches by 20 inches, Chapman depicts Gates dressed in a red sweater with all the accoutrements of Mister Rogers. There is a syringe in the upper right corner. Gates is painted in the style of a comic strip, almost, his head large in proportion to the rest of his body. Chapman put it up on his Etsy page for $800. As of spring 2024, it hadn't found any takers yet. "I guess no one wants to look at it everyday, lol," Chapman said. The art itself is one thing. But the thinking that provoked Chapman's painting is indicative of how Gates's image evolved—not only in the mainstream of society but also in its rivulets, where it floats amid the flotsam of half-truths, mistrust, and disinformation.

Conspiracy theories—defined loosely as beliefs that elites and institutions, including the media, governments, and powerful individuals, collectively wield their power to achieve malevolent outcomes—have a long and robust history. They are similar to myths in that they provide an explanation for the inexplicable. But unlike myths, which exist in plain view and feed into the bigger storyline of humankind, conspiracy theories often are narratives involving an "us" and a "them," employing fabulism to sow distrust of power and authority. They have immense staying power, especially in societies deeply cleaved by political polarization, inequality, and racial and religious divides, filling the informational void created by a rapidly unspooling crisis or by a slowly widening chasm caused by a breakdown of trust between social and political groups.

Marita Sturken, a professor of visual arts at New York University who has studied the culture of paranoia that often drives conspiracy theories, said that they can provide a way for people to make sense of random events. "It's very hard to make our peace with the fact that life is arbitrary, and that things often happen in life that have no reasons other than say, bad luck or tragedy," Sturken said. Conspiracy theories are therefore comforting to people and can make them feel grounded. In particular, for disaffected groups, it is often easier to accept the idea that an anonymous power is orchestrating events—a dark state with an agenda, a cabal of billionaires pulling the strings—than settling for the reality of chaotic societies, tectonic shifts in work culture, and messy governments.[8]

One study of letters published in *The New York Times* and *The Chicago Tribune* between 1890 and 2010 found that conspiracy theories were prevalent, but that they increased during periods of rising inequality and diminishing trust in institutions.[9] There were a multitude of conspiracy theories in circulation in the early twentieth century, a time of great inequality spurred by the Industrial Revolution. The study found that conspiracy theories also rose in the period immediately following the Second World War. McCarthyism, the name given to Wisconsin senator Joseph McCarthy's years-long witch hunt for alleged communists in American institutions during the Cold War era, was one of the most popular. Conspiracy theorists were behind the rumor that John F. Kennedy was killed by the Central Intelligence Agency. In 1995, the Oklahoma City bombing lit up the internet with conspiracies, as some outlandish theories took hold, including that Timothy McVeigh, one of the suspects, was a "zombie" controlled by the government.

Conspiracy theorists whipped up false narratives about former president Bill Clinton and his wife, Hillary Rodham Clinton, in the 1990s. They villainized the left-wing billionaire George Soros and the right-wing Koch brothers. More recently, the falsehood circulated that former president Barack Obama had been elected in 2008 because of the efforts of a group of Democratic bankers.[10] Both during his presidential runs and his two terms in the White House, Obama was also dogged by conspiracies about his religion and birthplace that secured a lot of airtime, because Donald Trump, Obama's successor, constantly brought up those theories on his social media feeds and in public appearances. Conspiracy theories promoted by alt-right extremists became far more mainstream in the four years that Trump occupied the White House. The rise of the internet and social media has given conspiracy theorists a vast landscape upon which to plant the seeds of misinformation. Right-wing extremists like Alex Jones, the founder of Infowars, have built multimillion-dollar businesses peddling misinformation, disinformation, and wild antigovernment theories. In late 2022, Jones was ordered to pay $1.4 billion to the families of those who were killed at Sandy Hook Elementary School in Newtown, Connecticut, in 2012. For years, Jones had called the mass shooting a hoax. Jones also encouraged supporters of Trump to storm the U.S. Capitol on January 6, 2021.

One of the most potent internet-centric conspiracy theory communities is QAnon. Its origins unknown, QAnon has become a receptacle for all kinds of conspiracy myths in recent years, a lumbering, mutating monster of falsehoods that attracts a diverse group of followers, including yoga moms, right-wing extremists, and Wall Street executives. However, at its heart is the core belief that a pedophile ring runs the world, controlling the media and institutions. In an Ipsos poll conducted for NPR in December 2020, only 47 percent of the respondents believed that the following statement is untrue: "A group of Satan-worshiping elites who run a child sex ring are trying to control our politics and media." More than one-third responded that they were unsure, and 17 percent said it was true. The coronavirus pandemic, which seemed to come out of nowhere and spread with such speed and fury that it caught governments, doctors, and public health experts off guard, provided the perfect raw material for conspiracy theorists, on both the right and left. Gates, with his high visibility during the pandemic, was an easy target. As a philanthropist, Gates had long put himself out there as an advocate for global public health. In 2015, he gave an eight-minute TED talk in Vancouver entitled, "The Next Outbreak? We're Not Ready." Tanned and dressed in a pink sweater, he pushed a barrel onstage, the kind he said they had at home when he was a kid, because the biggest threat then was a nuclear war. If that happened, they were supposed to go to the basement and live off the supplies stored in that barrel. Fast forward 50 years and the biggest threat, Gates said, was not missiles but microbes. He told the rapt audience that the world was unprepared for a global pandemic, which he expected to be the biggest threat to humanity. A prophet of doom, Gates advocated for a military-style response to a potential pandemic.[11] Five years later, as the world reeled from the pandemic, the video became a viral sensation, viewed more than 37 million times. Gates became an oracle, but to a group of people, like Chapman, the Etsy painter, he also represented something far more sinister. How had Gates known it was coming?

An ardent supporter of vaccines given his foundation's work, Gates talked nonstop about the effectiveness of coronavirus shots at a time when the world was rife with misinformation about them. Gates was essentially in a public service announcement role for governments everywhere. He penned articles and went on popular shows hosted by Stephen Colbert and Ellen DeGeneres. He even wrote an essay for *The New England Journal of Medicine*—which typically publishes medical research—about how to coordinate a pandemic response. At the same time, the Gates Foundation was working closely with pharmaceutical companies and governments on vaccines. His public presence was so widespread that people like Chapman, who only had a passing acquaintance with Gates as a philanthropist and the cofounder of Microsoft, began questioning his motives.

One persistent conspiracy theory is that Gates engineered the coronavirus and was leveraging it for profit and population control. The evidence: the video of his prescient TED talk in 2015. Another theory held that Gates was pushing for vaccines so that he could implant microchips into people to surveil them. The germ of that theory was that the Gates Foundation and MIT had conducted a study about the feasibility of storing vaccine information in a microchip implanted under a patient's skin, akin to a digital certificate.[12] The conspiracy theories about vaccines and microchips, vaccines and depopulation, and vaccines and death by the thousands were picked up by anti-vaccinators on the left and right, including Robert F. Kennedy Jr., Roger Stone, and Laura Ingraham. As they gained steam, Fox News carried stories about the conspiracy theories, which in turn conferred upon them more legitimacy. Concerted efforts by the Russian government to sow disinformation on social media sites added to the general noise. Anthony

Fauci, the director of the National Institute of Allergy and Infectious Diseases during the pandemic, who often appeared with Gates in public, was also the target of conspiracy theories. Kennedy authored a book called *The Real Anthony Fauci* that purported to uncover a scheme between Fauci and Gates; the claims made in his book are unproven. Yet, Fauci didn't get the kind of raucous attention from conspiracy theorists that Gates did—perhaps because, as Chapman the artist said, Gates's advocacy in a field that he didn't belong to seemed suspicious, or perhaps because of his immense wealth, which conferred upon one individual a nearly unrivaled power. It didn't help that Gates had been critical of Trump's statements about the virus, including its cure, citing studies that undermined his claims.[13] The conspiracy theories were so rampant during the pandemic that more than a quarter of Americans believed that Gates wanted to implant microchips through vaccines, according to a 2020 poll by YouGov, a British market research firm that works with government clients but often conducts paid online surveys on a variety of themes. Also that year, another YouGov poll found that Gates was no longer the world's most admired man—a title he held from 2014 to 2019. In explaining the fall, the pollsters said it was potentially because of the rumors "that he is in some way involved in the spread of Covid-19."[14]

Gates was keenly aware that with his lack of professional expertise, he might be perceived in a negative light as he shared the pulpit with Fauci and other public health experts, telling people to get vaccinated and wear masks. In a discussion on the platform formerly known as Twitter with Devi Sridhar, an expert on global public health, Gates tried to combat the misinformation. The Gates Foundation posted an FAQ on its website to explain its role in vaccines and to rebut rumors about microchips. It addressed questions such as "Did Bill Gates know the pandemic was coming?" and "Why are vaccine trials being conducted in Africa?" Gates couldn't help but seem bewildered, even personally wounded, by the misinformation and conspiracy theories that singled him out, calling them stupid and strange and almost too ridiculous to address. "I'm experiencing the greatest pushback ever in my life, and [am] somewhat unsure how to deal with that," he told *The Washington Post*.[15]

Chapter 10

Why We Hate Billionaires

Disbelief and Distrust

"How do you become a billionaire in 2021?" Kathryn Kvas and Vignesh Seshadri had some ideas. Eleven, to be specific. Suggestion number three: "Be one of Elon Musk's sons. Turn eighteen. Take ten billion dollars out of your trust fund. Lose ninety per cent of said funds on careless investments. You are now a self-made billionaire! Congratulations." Suggestion number six: "Stop buying overpriced lattes. Become a billionaire overnight."

Kvas and Seshadri are a husband-and-wife duo who sometimes write comedy together. Kvas, who is originally from Canada, met Seshadri, who is of Indian origin, at advertising school in Miami. They were drawn to each other by their shared sense of humor—she leans satirical, and he leans dark. As visitors to a country that they hoped to call their own one day, Kvas and Seshadri were determined to make a go of it in America. Tired of being cooped up in their cramped Brooklyn apartment during the pandemic, the couple moved to Los Angeles. America's pitch as the "best place to go for opportunity and money" was a compelling one, Seshadri said. Kvas, with dark brown hair grazing her shoulders, and Seshadri, sporting a full black beard, both speak thoughtfully about the work they do and what they see around them. To two millennials, the belief that if only people saved and budgeted and worked hard, they too could become extremely rich, was incongruous. Kvas and Seshadri are on a relatively secure financial footing. Neither carries student debt; they have health insurance. "We've gotten to a place where we are pretty successful in our careers," Kvas said in a video conversation. "There is definitely opportunity here to be your own successful person. It's not a complete lie." Yet, the remarkable wealth accumulation by the top tier of the population and the impossibility for most people to get there, struck a nerve. Everywhere around them was googly-eyed talk about billionaires. In particular, the unqualified adulation and worship of billionaires, and the propaganda that goes into amplifying their image—something they saw up close in the advertising industry—sickened them. "It feels medieval in so many ways," Kvas said. "They are kings and overlords."

The enormity of inequality struck Kvas when she happened to come across an online post charting the wealth of top billionaires. "It literally takes you twenty minutes to visualize [the wealth of] Bezos," she said. "It's scary to think about the amount of lifetimes it would take to spend that kind of wealth." Kvas was particularly taken aback by the meme stock mania of 2021. That year, millions of small traders, stuck at home during the pandemic, launched an online campaign to buy the stock of GameStop, a video-game retailer that had been a mall mainstay in the 1990s. A big Wall Street hedge fund bet that GameStop shares would fall because of the company's dying business model; the "Redditors," as they came to be called because they co-ordinated via messages on the social media platform Reddit, decided to stick it to the fund manager by buying up the company's shares instead. It was an odd expression of wanting to take down a symbol of wealth—the hedge fund—by banding together, desperate to claim some of that wealth for their own wallets. The idea that "if you bet ten dollars on the stock of GameStop, you too had a chance of making it big" confounded her.

They turned their observations into a satirical piece for *The New Yorker* magazine, listing the ways one could become a billionaire.[1] (Suggestion number eight: "Buy four truckloads of water. Realize that this isn't what they meant when they said, "Keep your assets liquid." The next day, the world runs out of water. You are now the only source of water within a two-thousand-mile radius. Elon finds out, tweets about it. You accidentally become the next messiah. Make billions.") Their contribution to the "Daily Shouts" blog, an offshoot of the magazine's regular "Shouts and Murmurs" column, was a way to make fun of the idea that people could become su-premely wealthy if they got lucky, or if, as they wrote, people stopped "buy-ing overpriced lattes" or "paying for extra guac." The humor was deliberately absurdist, to underscore just how off-base the constant messaging about the American dream had become.

Americans appear to be growing increasingly uneasy about billionaires. While most people don't think that accumulating billion-dollar fortunes is a bad thing, many polls in recent years show that there is a heightened awareness about the excessive wealth accumulation by those at the very top, and the ways in which that wealth allows them to wield influence. A 2021 study by the Pew Research Center, an independent nonprofit, concluded that Americans have viewed billionaires in a somewhat more negative light since the pandemic, when a rising stock market lifted already enormous fortunes by billions of dollars. Roughly three out of 10 Americans agreed in July 2021 that having billionaires was a bad thing, an increase from about a quarter in January 2020, the poll found. It also found that adults younger than 30 were more likely than other age groups to look at billionaires more critically. There were differences in attitudes based on the political leanings of the respondents—liberal Democrats are more likely than moderate Dem-ocrats to find that billionaires are bad for the country—but both Democrats and Republicans have soured on the impact of billionaires on the economy, the study found. One poll found that 46 percent of American voters con-sidered billionaires a threat to democracy, although those who identified themselves as Republican saw them as less of a threat than Democrats did. Polls have also found widespread support among Americans for higher taxes on the mega rich. In 2021, a survey by Data for Progress, a progressive think tank and polling firm, found that more than two-thirds of likely voters, in-cluding 53 percent of Republicans, thought billionaires should pay more in taxes. A majority of Americans, by a 3-to-1 margin, or 66 percent, thought that billionaires shouldn't have the ability to contribute unlimited amounts of money to politics, while 23 percent said it was okay, and the rest were undecided, according to a June 2022 poll by RealClear Opinion Research.[2] "This isn't to say that Americans don't respect or admire the super-wealthy,"

John Della Volpe, who ran the poll, explained in an accompanying article. "They just don't believe that billionaires should be able to exert outsized influence or have the ability to corrupt a political system that needs to work for everyone." The preponderance of such polls itself suggests that billionaires loom large in the sociocultural and economic milieu.

Jesse Walker, an assistant professor of marketing at Ohio State University's Fisher College of Business, decided to study the apparent contradiction between people's love of individual billionaires and their dislike of the billionaire class. As a doctoral student, he and his thesis advisor, both lifelong tennis fans, got to talking about Roger Federer and how "it seemed weird that people don't get tired of seeing him win," and how that was different from what you see in team sports, where people get tired of seeing the same teams win. After Walker and his advisor, Thomas Gilovich, turned those observations into a paper, Walker decided to test his hunch that people seemed to be more tolerant of inequality when it was expressed in terms of individual success, than when it was described in groups. Walker, along with Gilovich and another academic colleague, found what appears to be a central contradiction about American life: People react positively to individual success stories, but success appears rigged when successful people are clustered together. "We really love individual success stories," Walker said. "It's easier to attribute the success of individuals to their person, because they're talented or hard-working or have some quality that made them succeed." But when groups or teams win, people put it down to benefits they have had as a group. Similarly, Walker found, when you lump people into a class, such as a billionaire class, people are more likely to believe that there is something wrong with the system that allows so much wealth accumulation for a few.[3] Their study concluded that people are unlikely to support high inheritance or wealth taxes if they're thinking of an individual billionaire's success, but they are much more likely to support higher taxes on the same for the wealthy as a group. That, Walker said, is an important policy takeaway for any politician advocating for higher taxes.[4]

People's growing distrust of the billionaire class comes from two interrelated occurrences: Not only has their wealth ballooned in the past decade, but it has increased at a rate well beyond what seems fair or equitable to many, especially on the left. In 2010, after the financial crisis, America had 404 billionaires whose combined fortunes stood at $1.4 trillion, according to estimates by *Forbes*. A decade later, the number of billionaires had risen to 614, and their collective net worth had more than doubled to $2.9 trillion. Although it's hard to make direct comparisons between estimated fortunes and income data, it's still helpful to look at the median income of American households between 2010 and 2020 for context. Adjusted for inflation, that number rose from $58,627 to $67,521, or about 15 percent, according to data from the Federal Reserve.[5] In 2017, Bezos became the first billionaire to cross the $100 billion mark since Gates, who had crossed it once in 1999. Billionaire fortunes only increased during the pandemic, as financial markets rallied after an initial dip. Globally, the wealth of billionaires grew by $2.7 billion a day from March 2020 to November 2022, according to calculations by Oxfam International.[6] The U.K.-based charitable organization, which works to fight poverty and inequality around the world, also estimated that $26 trillion of the $42 trillion in wealth gained since the pandemic had gone to the richest one percent.

More than a decade of mounting frustration at the ever-widening chasm between rich and poor has contributed significantly to the fracture of American society that will not mend, as people—fed on misinformation, exploited by politicians, searching for villains—become more and more polarized, the fora for civil debate disappear, and the opportunity for a meeting of minds narrows drastically. It is a diffuse but festering anger—of nativists who see immigrants as stealing jobs and changing the racial makeup of America, of the left at the right and the right at the left, of women toward men in power, of individuals against institutions—spreading across a rapidly altering landscape where people no longer know if they are failing or the opportunities for success are shrinking. There are signs of sociocultural reckoning and myth busting, and more trenchant demands for action, especially as the new generation of Americans, Gen Z, finds its political voice. Billionaires have become the target of ridicule and loathing from some quarters of society, especially given their soaring wealth and growing influence during this time of widening inequality. Efforts to create more welcoming environments for women and people of color in STEM show less tolerance for the brilliant nerd myth. A push to rein in unbridled profit-seeking by including ESG, goals indicates the demand for a more inclusive corporate sector. There is disgust about the behavior of powerful men toward women. Individuals and institutions are increasingly calling out systemic racism. The war ignited by the Hamas attack on Israel on October 7, 2023, has resurfaced painful historical conversations involving religion, colonization, and the pointlessness and inescapability of war. At the same time, there is more concern about the harmful effects of technology, a more urgent call to action on climate change, a recognition that decades of economic inequality have fed polarization with devastating consequences, and more scrutiny of the influence of billionaires on politics and how tax policies have helped the wealthy. In July 2022, YouGov polled Americans about whether the American dream still exists. Of the 1,000 adults surveyed, 65 percent of Democrats and independents responded either that the dream doesn't exist or that they're no longer sure if it does. The number was lower among those who identified as Republicans, but still 38 percent of the pool. Perhaps the late comedian George Carlin summed it up best: "The reason they call it the American dream is because you have to be asleep to believe it."

The Politics of Inequality

The global financial crisis of 2008 plunged the U.S. economy into the deepest recession since the Second World War.[7] For four straight years, median household incomes tumbled faster than rocks tumbling downhill.[8] As the rate of unemployment rose from under 5 percent to more than 10 percent, people were seething at Wall Street. Banks and other financial firms were directly responsible for the crisis; they had recklessly lent money to borrowers who could not afford to repay their mortgages. The banks had then packaged those subprime mortgages into securities and sold them to investors. When housing prices peaked and then went into free fall, the banks that had created the securities teetered and financial markets swooned. In 2008, the federal government was forced to rescue some banks and extend credit to others to avoid a potential collapse of the entire financial system. As people reeled from the impact, the anger directed at the so-called one percent was palpable.

In July 2011, inspired by the protests in Cairo's Tahrir Square where a popular uprising had overthrown Egypt's leader, Hosni Mubarak, just months earlier, *Adbusters*, a small, independent magazine in Vancouver, British Columbia, in Canada emailed subscribers urging them to "deploy this emerging stratagem against the greatest corrupter of our democracy: Wall Street, the financial Gomorrah of America." They set a date—September 17, 2011—and asked that 20,000 people gather in lower Manhattan to demand that President Barack Obama set up a commission tasked with "ending the influence that money has over our representatives in Washington." To go with the protests, it created a hashtag: #occupywallstreet. For a two-month period beginning in September 2011, people from different backgrounds—academics, intellectuals, students, left-wing radicals, activists—landed in Zuccotti Park, in Manhattan's financial district, to begin their protest. "Occupy Wall Street" became a catchall slogan for the outpouring of resentment, and a cry against injustice by thousands of protesters calling themselves the "99 percent."

The punch of the movement eventually fizzled out as activists hived off and people went back to their daily lives. But it was a tipping point, an inchoate expression of the frustration that many Americans were beginning to feel about a system that protected the wealthy at the expense of the rest. In the decade since, some of the early frustrations have only become more entrenched, as the conversation about income and wealth inequality has become mainstream. Those factors have driven the search for explanations, as academics, politicians, pollsters, journalists, and activists seek to understand the ways in which the structures and systems upon which our economy rests have tilted toward the wealthiest. There is argument among economists, the public, and even billionaires themselves about the degree to which they have harnessed favorable tax policies and market forces, including the imbalance of power between corporations and labor created by offshoring, along with their social, cultural, and racial advantages, enroute to their financial success.

The growing conversation about inequality is perhaps why *Capital in the Twenty-First Century*, the academic tome by French economist Thomas Piketty, resonated so widely when it landed on U.S. shores. The sweeping analysis of inequality had been translated into English for an American audience and published in 2014. Packed with charts and figures, *Capital in the Twenty-First Century*, which came in at around 700 pages, was hardly expected to become a popular hit. Yet, there it was, climbing up *The New York Times* bestseller list. For a time, it was the top-selling book on Amazon.com. Summaries and cheat sheets abounded. It has since sold some two million copies in multiple languages. Much to the surprise and delight of executives at Harvard University Press, the publisher, *Capital in the Twenty-First Century* became its best-selling book ever. In 2020, Netflix produced a feature documentary based on Piketty's core arguments.

Piketty makes the point that over time, the return on invested capital will outpace the growth in income, creating the conditions for dynastic wealth. He put the weight of an entire history of capitalism, with its propensity to make the rich richer, on a simple equation: $r>g$. The "r" stood for the rate of return on private capital while the "g" stood for the rate of economic growth. Redistributive policies, which taxed capital on a progressive basis, were the only solution for reducing wealth inequality, he argued. Specifically, Piketty called for a global tax on wealth. Piketty's argument resonated with many, especially those on the left. Writing in *The New York Times*, Justin Wolfers pointed out that based on Google data, searches for "Piketty" came largely from coastal, liberal states.[9] In other words, the book was a hit in places where you'd expect it to be a hit. It's easy to see that Democratic lawmakers and liberal elites embraced the book because it placed inequality within an easily graspable analytic framework. The book's message also resonated with the wider public by articulating a feeling among many Americans that the country was no longer a pure meritocracy. Instead, with every massive CEO pay package and every new billionaire, it seemed to be moving to a plutocracy, where the gains from wealth accrued to a small class of people at the top, while incomes stagnated for those in the middle and lower rungs. In comparing *Capital in the Twenty-First Century* to Piketty's 2019 book, *Capital and Ideology*, one reviewer pointed out that *Capital in the Twenty-First Century* struck a nerve because it "perfectly fit the post–Occupy Wall Street ethos, providing empirical rigor for the upswell in anger."[10]

But perhaps it is the work of two liberal economists on inequality in America, and their proposals for a wealth tax, that has captured the attention of Democrats in recent years as the conversation around billionaires became more pointed. So much so, that the idea of a wealth tax became a central talking point in the Democratic presidential primary in 2020. The previous year, the economists Emmanuel Saez and Gabriel Zucman had published *The Triumph of Injustice*, a historical study of the American tax system that highlighted how taxes for the wealthiest have fallen, while middle-income and lower-income groups have been forced to pay more. The duo, professors at the University of California at Berkeley, estimated that as of 2018, fewer than 250,000 adults at the very top of the income ladder held almost one-fifth of all wealth. That share had steadily increased over the decades. The professors, who have collaborated with Piketty on other studies, also called for a wealth tax. Their findings led to a raucous debate among economists— insofar as economists are raucous—on Twitter and in the opinion pages.

Nearly a decade earlier, Saez and Zucman had published research that showed how vastly inequality had risen since the 1970s.[11] "Wealth inequality, it turns out, has followed a spectacular U-shape evolution over the past 100 years. From the Great Depression in the 1930s through the late 1970s there was a substantial democratization of wealth. The trend then inverted, with the share of total household wealth owned by the top 0.1 percent increasing to 22 percent in 2012 from 7 percent in the late 1970s. The top 0.1 percent includes 160,000 families with total net assets of more than $20 million in 2012," the authors wrote. They updated their study once again in 2020.[12]

The simmering public resentment of billionaires has provided progressive politicians with the opportunity to bring the conversation about inequality center stage—and burnish their populist credentials. For much of his long career in politics, Bernie Sanders, the independent U.S. senator from Vermont, had been urging for redistributive policies as a way to reduce income equality. But it is only in the past decade that his message has resonated, particularly with young voters disillusioned by politics as usual and worried about inheriting a future with nary a social safety net, stagnating incomes, and a worsening climate, even as the top one percent continues to accumulate wealth. Sanders, with his white hair and fiery delivery, has become an unlikely hero for them. Other politicians on the left have also promoted several plans to tax the wealthy, encouraged in their stridency by the current political moment, which shows that their positions have a measure of public support that was difficult to imagine a few decades ago. Alexandria Ocasio-Cortez, a Democratic politician, activist, and the U.S. representative from New York's Fourteenth District, has been an outspoken critic, inserting a moral gravity into politics by arguing that a few people shouldn't accumulate so much wealth when so many parts of society are poor. Her former policy advisor Dan Riffle coined the phrase: "Every billionaire is a policy failure." Never one to shy away from a message—especially one fashionable to progressives—Ocasio-Cortez wore a gown to the 2021 Met Gala emblazoned with the words "Tax the Rich." Ironically, the move led people to accuse her of being a "sellout."

In her run for president, Elizabeth Warren, a Democratic U.S. senator from Massachusetts, not only proposed a wealth tax for those with assets over $50 million, but also picked public fights with billionaires. Following her central message as she ran for the Democratic candidacy for president, *Politico* and Morning Consult conducted a poll in 2019 among registered voters about whether the wealthy should pay more in taxes. The poll found that more than three out of every four voters said yes.[13] Other Democrats too have put forth proposals to increase taxes, but they have met with little success. During the negotiations over President Biden's infrastructure bill, which passed in 2022, U.S. Senator Ron Wyden, who chairs the Senate Finance Committee, specifically pushed for a billionaire income tax, which proposed to treat billionaire wealth as income. "Two tax codes allow billionaires to use largely untaxed income from wealth to build more wealth, while working families struggle to balance the mortgage against groceries, and utilities against saving for the future," Wyden said in his proposal. The money raised would help pay for the infrastructure bill. Wyden's proposal for taxing so-called unrealized capital gains had significant support from likely voters, according to the 2021 Data for Progress poll. President Biden also proposed a billionaire minimum income tax in 2022, which would impose a tax of at least 20 percent on all income on all households worth more than $100 million, including unrealized gains that are currently untaxed. How such proposals would work is a matter of debate. Aside from the politics of levying higher taxes on the wealthiest, a basic problem is that wealth is largely estimated, based on billionaire lists.

On the right, the defense of billionaires has largely been crafted around the idea that their numbers reflect a flourishing society, and that they deserve their wealth because their companies have created jobs, improved lives, spurred economic growth, and made America the world's envy. Their wealth reflects the value they brought to society, so the higher their value creation—providing jobs, increasing innovation, and improving society—the greater their fortunes. Taxes would destroy incentives, the reasoning on the right goes, sending taxes to the government would be inefficient, and philanthropy is a better way of doing the government's job.[14] Innovation and incentives for that innovation are necessary so that social wealth and value can be created—and personal wealth is the by-product of that.

A lot of billionaires have expressed support for higher taxes or acknowledged that such extreme wealth should not exist. Some, such as Warren Buffett, have agreed that the system is indeed unfair and that he shouldn't be paying taxes at a lower rate than his secretary. In an op-ed piece for *The New York Times* in 2011, the Omaha investor argued that a higher tax rate on investments wouldn't necessarily deter the mega rich from making investments, because they were likely to judge a deal on its merits rather than the tax rate.[15] More recently, Marc Benioff, the chairman of Salesforce, penned an op-ed for the same newspaper, calling for a fairer and more equitable capitalism that reduces inequality, equates doing well with doing good, and asks the wealthiest to pay more in taxes.[16]

Gates too has said he would pay more in taxes if the system were amended and has expressed support for estate taxes, which are levied upon death. Gates told the journalist and anchor Andrew Ross Sorkin in 2019 that he wouldn't mind paying $10 billion more in taxes. The wealthiest Americans have banded together through groups like the Patriotic Millionaires to call for more taxes. In 2019, Mark Zuckerberg, in response to a town hall question about Sanders and his attack on billionaires, said that the enormity of wealth that billionaires have accumulated is unreasonable. "I don't know if I have an exact threshold on what amount of money someone should have," he was quoted as having said, "but on some level no one deserves to have that much money."[17] For the most part, though, billionaires have remained silent on taxes, or quietly funded politicians sympathetic to their point of view. At least one billionaire stuck his neck out.

In October 2019, as Elizabeth Warren was stepping up her campaign, the hedge fund billionaire Leon Cooperman told *Politico* that there was nothing wrong with billionaires, and that one became a billionaire by making products and services that people paid for. Cooperman, a former Goldman Sachs executive who started Omega Advisors and had a net worth of $2 billion at the time, was one of the many people watching Warren's ascendance in the Democratic primaries warily. In the *Politico* interview, he said that he believed in a progressive tax system, but that Warren was "shitting on the American dream."[18] Cooperman is one of the few billionaires who has publicly expressed his surprise and bewilderment at the level of resentment against the ultra-wealthy. In 2022, he told *The Washington Post* that he couldn't understand why politicians like Sanders, Warren, and Ocasio-Cortez came after billionaires. After all, "he'd always imagined himself as the rags-to-riches hero, only to now find himself cast as the greedy villain in a story of economic inequality run amok."[19] Cooperman also cast his success as the result of his choices, comparing himself to his brother, who had the same opportunities but chose not to work 80-hour work weeks and died with only a modest amount of money to his name. "Different choices, different outcomes," he said in the *Post* article. "The world isn't meant to be totally even." Not one to back down, Warren responded on Twitter: "Leon, you were able to succeed because of the opportunities this country gave you. Now why don't you pitch in a bit more so everyone else has a chance at the American dream, too?"

The Myth of the Self-Made Billionaire

Did Gates reach the economic stratosphere solely on the jet fuel of his brilliance? His father wasn't so sure. Of course, his son was blessed with incredible talent and worked extremely hard, but Bill Gates Sr. often questioned whether Gates could have reached the levels of success and fortune he did had he been born without the privileges he had. His family could afford to send him to Lakeside, Seattle's most prestigious private school, where Gates was introduced to computers as a preteen, well before many children of his age or even their parents had seen one. He forged close bonds with his parents, who provided him and his siblings with a stable home atmosphere. Laurelhurst, the neighborhood where he grew up, was safe and family friendly. It was also a short walk from the 24-hour computer laboratory at the University of Washington, allowing the young prodigy to come and go as he pleased, and spend endless hours tinkering with the new machines.

Would a different child, with roughly the same raw material as Gates, be able to achieve the same level of success? Gates Sr., a prominent Seattle lawyer and civic leader who died in 2020, would often ponder these issues with Chuck Collins, an activist and author with whom he wrote a book about the dangers of repealing the estate tax.[20] Collins, a great-grandson of Oscar Mayer, the founder of the company best known for its hot dogs, gave up his inheritance at 26 to make fighting inequality his life's work. He is the director of the Program on Inequality and the Common Good at the Institute for Policy Studies, a progressive think tank, and coedits a blog on the topic.

"Gates Senior would debunk the great-man myth at every corner," Collins said, referring to the idea that great leaders are born, not made. He was "pretty tuned in to the web [and] matrix of multigenerational advantages that propel some people forward." Their book, published in 2003, argued in favor of reforming the estate tax rather than repealing it, because society played a far larger role in individual wealth creation than was acknowledged. In 2000, President Bill Clinton vetoed a bill sponsored by Republicans that would have repealed the estate tax, but George W. Bush, then the governor of Texas, made it the core of his presidential campaign. Between 2001 and 2003, Bush announced a package of tax cuts that included phasing out the estate tax. Collins and Gates Sr. launched a campaign arguing that removing the estate tax—also known as the death tax or inheritance tax—was harmful to society because it allowed wealth to be transferred from generation to generation without taxation, compounding economic inequality. Their plank was that wealth creation was a collaborative effort with society, and taxation was the right way to return some of that wealth to society. "'You earned it' is really a matter of 'you earned it with the indispensable help of your government,'" Gates Sr. told PBS. Gates has always acknowledged his father's point of view, but he chose philanthropy as the way to address it.

The idea of a "self-made" individual is a potent one, and foundational to America, a country formed by those who rejected aristocracy and beckoned all who wanted to build a fortune as opposed to merely inherit it. People came from nothing and made it in America. In their research, Walker, the Ohio State professor, and his colleagues found that people in more collectivist cultures, including China and other Asian countries, equate wealthy groups with the circumstances of their birth and existence. But because of the rugged individualism that has defined the country from the very beginning, Americans find it easier to believe that it is a person's talent that gets them where they are. In 2014, *Forbes* magazine began giving America's top 400 billionaires a "self-made" score, grading them from one to 10 depending on whether they had simply inherited their fortunes and done little to enhance it (a score of one), or had built their empires from scratch, overcoming economic and social adversity to do so (a score of 10). The magazine used as inputs such things as socioeconomic background and upbringing. Those in the middle of the pack were described as billionaires who "inherited a small- or medium-sized business and made it into a ten-digit fortune." Under its definitions, the magazine found that America's billionaires are overwhelmingly self-made. What's most interesting, though, is that of the 400, the largest group of "self-made" billionaires came from moneyed households or middle- and upper-middle-class backgrounds. In 2022, there were 184 of them, compared with 51 billionaires who came from working-class backgrounds and 28 who came from poverty. White men made up the largest group of billionaires. There were 56 women billionaires, few of them "self-made." Most of them inherited their wealth, like the Waltons, the Pritzkers, and the granddaughters of the Estée Lauder fortune. There are those who inherited their wealth from their spouses, like Laurene Powell Jobs, the widow of Steve Jobs. Divorcées like MacKenzie Scott and Melinda French Gates are recent additions. Oprah Winfrey, with a net worth of $2.5 billion, is one of the few self-made women who came from poverty. Only a handful of Black billionaires made the list, including Winfrey and Robert Smith of Vista Equity Partners, a private equity firm. To some extent, the racial makeup of billionaires mirrors the racial wealth gap between Black and white Americans. In 2019, the median net worth of Black Americans was $24,100. For white Americans, the number was $189,100.[21] *Forbes* also created a separate list of America's 100 richest self-made women, many of whom are not billionaires. In 2023, only 22 of them came from poor or working-class backgrounds. The rest were born into wealth, grew up middle class or upper middle class, or were highly trained professionals like Sheryl Sandberg.[22] The preponderance of individuals from favorable socioeconomic positions on the Forbes lists are an indicator that the circumstances of birth and upbringing can be important inputs in the creation of a self-made billionaire. Sometimes, children of affluent families also benefit from connections, such as when Gates's mother mentioned her son's name to an IBM executive who gave the young Microsoft a chance.

"A lot goes into the making of a success story, from the compounding of advantage over generations to socioeconomic privilege to stable homes [and] social safety nets," Collins said. "People retell their story through that meritocratic lens." He called for a more honest accounting from billionaires of their stories—the invisible forces that helped them along, such as "a stable home, debt-free college education, access to healthcare"—rather than reinforcing the self-made narrative. The circumstances of birth and upbringing also confer another significant advantage: the success of future generations, or what economists often call "mobility." There is plenty of research, including a landmark 1994 study, showing that children from stable homes with married parents had far better outcomes as adults than children born to single or unmarried parents.[23] They were at less risk of getting pregnant as teenagers, dropping out of high school, or being idle in adulthood. They had better chances of success. Moreover, the 1994 study found, the advantages of being white are closely tied to family structure and can disappear when parents get divorced. Research also suggests that the number of rungs up the economic ladder that children can climb depends on where they grow up. Intergenerational mobility is much higher in places with less inequality, better schools, less racial segregation, and more stable families.

The late labor economist Alan B. Krueger, a professor of political economy at Princeton who advised both President Clinton and President Obama during their terms in office, showed how the children of wealthier parents have more economic mobility than their parents, which leads to more inequality. "Children of wealthy parents already have much more access to opportunities to succeed than children of poor families, and this is likely to be increasingly the case in the future unless we take steps to ensure that all children have access to quality education, healthcare, a safe environment and other opportunities that are necessary to have a fair shot at economic success," Krueger once said in a speech. He termed it "the Great Gatsby inequality curve," which shows the relationship between the concentration of wealth in one generation and the ramifications of that in the next generation.[24] He identified the main causes of widening inequality as technology, globalization, and tax policy. Krueger, who died in 2019, also cited research showing that rising inequality has not been mirrored by rising consumption inequality—in other words, even if incomes are not growing at the same rate, spending has continued apace, which suggests that people are taking on more debt to maintain lifestyles. That of course has been encouraged and made easier by the financial industry, in terms of how easy it is to access credit.

Another cluster of economists led by Raj Chetty found that nine out of every 10 children born in 1940 were earning more than their parents, whereas that number had fallen to about half for children born around 1980, i.e., those entering the labor force in the decade preceding the study, which was published in 2017.[25] They also found that growth in the nation's gross domestic product alone wouldn't change that outcome. Rather, the economists concluded that the fruits of economic growth needed to be distributed more broadly to revert to the levels of "absolute income mobility" that people born in 1940 had enjoyed. The American dream "that hard work and opportunity would lead to a better life" was fading, the authors wrote in their 2017 study. A recent study of admissions into elite colleges led by Chetty showed that they are filled with children of the wealthiest families—not necessarily because they were brighter than the others, but because their resumes were more finely honed to the desires of those colleges.[26] That's an advantage that comes with economic class. Elite private institutions are the gateways to success, the authors argue. The paper argues that if some of America's most elite private colleges changed their admissions policies to give less weight to the children of alumni and those with extracurricular or sports skills that wealthy families are more easily able to afford, there could be more socioeconomic diversity rather than concentrating "privilege across generations." In addition to having a head start in life by dint of socioeconomic status, one of the more overlooked aspects of success is the lack of downside risk. A talented individual from a comfortable or wealthy background can pursue far bigger ambitions than they might otherwise want to, or be able to, because the cost of failure is minimized by economic security. Put another way, risk-taking is often easier when it is subsidized by economic security.

Michael Dell, the founder of Dell Computers, started his business in a college dorm with $1,000—meeting the requirement of a "self-made" billionaire. But as he describes in *Direct from Dell*, his autobiography, he was exposed both to computers and to the concept of commercial opportunities from early on. "The discussions at our dinner table in the 1970s were about what the chairman of the Federal Reserve was doing and how it affected the economy and the inflation rate; the oil crisis; which companies to invest in, and which stocks to sell and buy," Dell writes.[27] His math teacher in junior high installed a teletype terminal that students could play with after school.

His parents bought him a computer for his fifteenth birthday. "I had grown up with computers. Every paper I wrote in high school had been written on a computer. Computers were already well integrated into my life, and it seemed obvious to me that it was just a matter of time before every business, every school, and every individual started to rely on them."

Like Gates, Dell too famously dropped out of college to pursue his ambitions—Gates out of Harvard and Dell out of the University of Texas at Austin. When they started their companies as teenagers, both took big risks with their futures with the knowledge they could return to school, or their parents were in a position to help them financially. Had Gates failed to get Microsoft off the ground, he could simply have finished his college degree and twinned his talents with a Harvard education to lead a highly successful, if less famous, life. John Mackey, the famously outspoken, libertarian, antiunion founder of Whole Foods, grew up in a middle-class household with a professor father and a mother who gave up her job to rear her children. His father was also the chief executive of a healthcare company that sold for hundreds of millions of dollars. Mackey dropped out of college to start Whole Foods in 1978, raising $45,000 from family and friends. His father was his first investor.[28] While not a dropout, Sergey Brin, one of the founders of Google, also grew up in a university atmosphere; his father was a professor of mathematics at the University of Maryland, and his mother a research scientist.

Those from middle-class and affluent backgrounds have also been best placed to benefit from the tilt of the economy away from blue-collar and manufacturing jobs and toward intellectual labor. The overwhelming spread of technology and the growth of high finance has meant that the biggest gains are captured by people with technical knowledge and analytical skills, who are usually college-educated. Since the 1980s, when the current era of extreme wealth creation began, a key propellent of economic growth has been globalization, a catchall term for neoliberal policies that have reduced taxes, opened markets, supported international trade, and lowered barriers to entry. Essentially, companies have been able to go venue shopping around the world to locate parts of their operations in the cheapest locations. Although the relocation of jobs overseas has helped lift many lower-income countries out of poverty, technological innovation has meant that many of those jobs have not been replaced in the United States, especially those requiring lower skills. The resulting imbalance of power between companies and their blue-collar U.S.-based workers has allowed companies to gain more power to set wages, while reducing the ability of workers to form and sustain unions. As labor unions have weakened or disappeared entirely, workers have lost much of their bargaining power to seek higher wages, contributing to rising inequality, research has shown. Using micro-level data such as polls and household surveys, a 2018 study by economists from Princeton and Columbia found that strong union membership helped the lowest paid workers the most.[29] In recent years, efforts by workers at Starbucks stores and Amazon to unionize have been contentious. The relatively slow progress of wage growth, even for skilled labor, has come into even starker contrast because of median pay ratios that companies have begun to publish. The pay of the chief executive of an S&P 500 company compared to a median employee was roughly 300 to 1. Thus, what is marketed as an inexorable result of economic progress can be seen at least partly to be aided by government policies.

Billionaire Pursuits: Because We Can

Emily Bachel has lived for years on Highway 106, a 20-mile state route that hugs a natural waterway in Washington State called Hood Canal. About two hours west of Seattle, the canal carries water inland from the Puget Sound Basin. The area is fringed by lush forests of elegant Douglas firs, its eerie beauty familiar to fans of *Twin Peaks*, the David Lynch television drama series. Visitors can catch glimpses of the Olympic and Kitsap Mountains. About 70 miles in, the canal turns back toward Puget Sound; on a map, its 180-degree turn resembles a fishhook, or a bent elbow. Locals call it the Great Bend. For decades, some of Seattle's wealthiest families—the Nordstroms, the Gateses—have vacationed in Hood Canal, flying in on their seaplanes during the summer months. Gates grew up spending summers with his siblings and extended family at a family vacation compound with five cabins dubbed "Cheerio Camp."

A lifelong resident of the area, Bachel would often drive past a resort called Alderbrook on her way home. Originally built in 1913, Alderbrook, nestled in the crook of Hood Canal's elbow, is one of Washington's oldest resorts and had changed ownership many times. Its current owner, Jeff Raikes, a multimillionaire who was then a senior executive at Microsoft, had bought the building in 2001 from Crista Ministries, a nonprofit that used Alderbrook as a conference center for three years, with the goal of upgrading it into a luxury resort and spa. With interiors redesigned to look like a cozy chalet, the Alderbrook Resort and Spa opened in 2006. That fall, construction workers closed off a strip of the highway that ran in front of the resort, causing a daily nuisance for Bachel and other residents, but also feeding her curiosity. Wondering why a perfectly serviceable road was being dug up, Bachel, then in her mid-fifties, brought the construction to the attention of a reporter at the local newspaper.[30] "The rumors are that Bill Gates, who has property adjacent to the resort, is actually having a tunnel put under the road to simplify his access to the road," she wrote to the *Kitsap Sun*. "Could you verify this?" Bachel's information turned out to be mostly accurate. The Alderbrook property was right next to the vacation compound of Gates, one of Raikes's closest friends. In 1998, Gates and Raikes had tried to buy Alderbrook but were outbid by Crista Ministries, which paid about $6 million for the property.[31] Two years after the resort opened, Raikes became the chief executive of the Gates Foundation, a position he held until 2014.

Highway 106 cut through the Alderbrook property, putting its parking lot on the other side of the road. The problem could be solved by rerouting the highway to move the lot to the same side. But that meant the Gates vacation compound, which contained five homes, was going to be split into two. To fix the problem—and avoid the prying eyes of resort visitors curious about the billionaire next door—Gates reportedly paid the State of Washington more than $2 million to have a special tunnel built under the rerouted highway to connect the compound. The project took advantage of a state law that encouraged public-private partnerships, including to "facilitate the safe transport of people or goods via any mode of travel." It was managed by Watermark, the Gates entity that managed his personal affairs and real estate, and took about four years to complete. Although the state owns it, Watermark has exclusive use of the tunnel because an air space lease gives it right of way. Hidden by a thicket of vegetation, the tunnel is difficult to spot from the highway, but a paved, winding road hidden behind a discreet wrought-iron and wooden gate connects it to the highway. If guests of Alderbrook veer too close to the Gates property, the hotel's security guards speedily arrive on golf carts to shoo them away.

Bachel—who often saw the Gates children splashing about in the water from the Hood Canal side, while Gates sat in a chair and read, and armed security guards paraded up and down—said it was generally known in the area that Gates had the state highway moved for his convenience and privacy. "Bill was the instigator and he funded it," she said.

When Musk paid $44 billion for publicly traded Twitter in 2022 before renaming it X, it was one of the largest "take private" transactions in history, right up there with the $45 billion purchase in 2007 of a Texas utility called TXU, later renamed Energy Future Holdings, by KKR and a group of other private equity firms. Musk, ostensibly, had little reason to buy Twitter other than having decided that he could do a better job running the social media platform that he cherished as a way to communicate directly with his fans. He didn't like the way it clamped down on free speech, calling himself a "free speech absolutist," so he decided to buy it with his spare cash—plus a few more billions borrowed from banks—and seemingly without a plan. Thus, the company formerly known as Twitter is now a billionaire's plaything that responded to media inquiries with a poop emoji for a while.

Gates's $2 million tunnel and Musk's $44 billion purchase of Twitter are two examples of the ways in which billionaires often appear to be able to bend convention to fit their peculiar needs, feed their obsessions, act on their whims, and impose their preferences—in ways big and small, splashy and covert, dangerous and benign. Displays of wealth are not new among the wealthy. Before Henry Ford reimagined the automobile for the masses, they were leisure toys for the showy robber barons of the Gilded Age. In 1897, a hall of New York's famed Waldorf Astoria hotel was transformed into the facade of the Palace of Versailles for a ball hosted by the socialite

Cornelia Austin. Some of the world's most expensive art sits in the homes of billionaires—paintings that hang on walls of temperature-controlled, museum-like rooms, and sculptures that were hauled directly from an excavation site. In the fall of 2015, the hedge fund billionaire Ken Griffin paid half a billion dollars to a charitable foundation owned by a fellow billionaire, the entertainment executive David Geffen, for two masterpieces of Abstract Expressionism—a 1955 oil painting by Willem de Kooning and one of Jackson Pollock's drip paintings. Both paintings were on loan to the Art Institute of Chicago, where Griffin's firm Citadel was based, but the museum lost the paintings to the Norton Museum of Art, a museum in West Palm Beach, when Griffin moved to the Florida city during the pandemic. Griffin had earlier given the Norton $16 million to fund its expansion, the biggest donation in the museum's history and one that changed its entire trajectory; Griffin will have a building named after him.

Then, there are the private jets and yachts, de rigueur among the billionaire crowd. They aren't cheap. A customized Gulfstream G8 runs around $100 million, according to David Friedman, who cofounded a firm called Wealth-X in 2010 to provide wealth data to luxury companies, real estate companies, and others trying to sell products to high-net-worth individuals. An Airbus Corporate Jet (ACJ) can start at $100 million, and a Boeing business jet is similarly priced. Mega yachts can cost as much as $500 million. "It's a smaller group of people driving more influence through their purchasing power," he said. "A $100 million price tag means that most likely you will need to tackle someone with greater than a billion in net worth to have that amount of liquidity." Friedman also cofounded WealthQuotient, which aims to map out networks of the wealthy that can help firms pitching services to them to win referrals.

The frenzy of yacht and jet buying has made billionaires among the world's top polluters. The world's 20 top richest people in the world (most of them American) had an average carbon footprint of 8,190 tons per individual in 2018, according to one analysis.[32] The estimates included the residences of the billionaires as well as their yachts, planes, and helicopters. By comparison, Americans on average emitted 15 tons of carbon dioxide that year. The average around the world was even lower, at five tons or so per person. Even Gates has been called out for his hypocrisy. The philanthropist, a leading voice on climate change, owns at least two customized jets that fly him around the world, often to deliver lectures on how to combat global warming. Gates has said he buys carbon offsets from a company equal to his footprint.

Unlike private planes, which are often used for business travel, mega yachts—essentially floating mansions—appear to be little more than advertisements for billionaire profligacy. At more than 417 feet in length, *Koru*, the luxury schooner custom-made for Bezos, is like the average cruise ship you might see lazily skimming the surface of a river, dotted with dozens of tourists, rather than a private boat. It is so massive that a historic bridge in Rotterdam was almost dismantled to let it through, although local authorities decided against it at the last minute, deeming it too risky from the point of view of public opinion. And as if the skies and oceans weren't enough, billionaires are increasingly pursuing private efforts to explore and even colonize space and planets and push deep-sea exploration.

The past decade and a half has brought intense scrutiny on how big money is spent, and how the rise in extreme wealth allows billionaires to increasingly exert themselves in our society and polity, as well as in culture, media, and civic life. The wealthy have always tried to get their favored candidates elected by contributing to their campaigns. But billionaires appear to have essentially captured American politics. An analysis by the Brennan Center for Justice, a nonpartisan law and policy institute, found that billionaires accounted for 15 percent of contributions for the 2022 midterm elections. What's more, the 100 biggest donors in that cycle as a group spent 60 percent more than all contributions made by small donors, or those who gave $200 or less to a candidate.[33] Billionaires on both the right and left spend enormous amounts of cash on politics.

The billionaire brothers Charles Koch and his late brother David have funded a network of political campaigns, nonprofits, and other institutions to promote libertarian causes. One of the goals of their advocacy group, Americans for Prosperity, is to "empower every American to pursue their version of the American Dream." But the group is better known for its essential stranglehold on Republican politics. During the 2020 election cycle, the group poured $500 million into electing Republican candidates. For 2024, the network is putting money into making sure that former president Trump does not win the Republican nomination, *The New York Times* has reported.[34] In late 2023, the Koch network endorsed Nikki Haley, the former governor of South Carolina, for the Republican primary contest for president, although she ended her campaign in March 2024. The billionaire Peter Thiel, who made his money as an early investor in Facebook and is also a cofounder of PayPal, has spent tens of millions of dollars backing Republican candidates through whom he can reshape policies to fix America. An avowed libertarian with a penchant for launching vicious attacks on left-wing politics, Thiel bankrolled multiple Republican candidates during the 2022 midterm elections, including Blake Masters and J. D. Vance. He is also a backer of Strive Capital, the firm of investor Vivek Ramaswamy, who ran unsuccessfully for the Republican nomination for the 2024 presidential election on an "anti-woke" platform. On the side, Thiel has also pursued a Maltese citizenship and supported "seasteading," a movement that seeks to build colonies on international waters out of the bounds of national governments. Harlan Crow, the billionaire real estate developer, and his wife, Kathy Crow, have donated millions of dollars to right-wing groups and are said to focus on efforts to shape law and move the judiciary to the right. In recent years, their political contributions went almost entirely to Republican candidates, according to an analysis by OpenSecrets. The extent of their influence in political and judicial circles came to light in the spring of 2023 following a *ProPublica* report about how Supreme Court Justice Clarence Thomas took luxury vacations on Crow's dime and flew on his private jet without disclosing the largesse.[35]

On the left, George Soros is among the best-known political donors, who has contributed millions of dollars to the campaigns of Democratic candidates through his Open Society Foundations, and engaged in advocacy of left and liberal causes, in particular to sustain democracy, civic engagement, and voting rights. Another Democratic billionaire, John Arnold, has spent millions, some through philanthropy and others through advocacy, to promote liberal causes. The hedge fund billionaire Tom Steyer and Michael Bloomberg, the former billionaire mayor of New York, have donated hundreds of millions of dollars to Democratic candidates. The two men also spent around three-quarters of a billion dollars on their own presidential campaigns.

Increasingly, we have come to depend on billionaires to rescue our media organizations, our cities, and even our sports teams, making them seem indispensable to our cultural and civic lives. More than 40 billionaires on the Forbes 400 list own sports teams, including the hedge fund investor Steve Cohen, who owns the New York Mets baseball team, and Arthur Blank, a cofounder of Home Depot, who owns two Atlanta teams.[36]

In 2019, John Henry, the billionaire co-owner of the Boston Red Sox, asked the city to rename Yawkey Way, a short street leading to Fenway Park, the arena where the team plays. He did so to scrub the Red Sox of its association with Tom Yawkey, a wealthy industrialist under whose ownership the team was last to integrate Black players. Henry has also been a hometown hero in other ways. He paid $70 million in 2013 for *The Boston Globe*, the illustrious but ailing newspaper. He is also part owner of the Harvard Book Store, the centerpiece of Harvard Square in Cambridge. With his help, the 90-year-old store is undertaking an expansion. Other billionaires have swooped in to buy newspapers too, including Jeff Bezos, who paid $250 million for *The Washington Post* in 2013, and Patrick Soon-Shiong, who owns the *Los Angeles Times*.

One of the best examples of how a single billionaire can get deeply enmeshed in a city's affairs is Dan Gilbert, the cofounder of Rocket Mortgage, one of the nation's largest mortgage lenders, and a real estate developer. For years, Gilbert's relationship with Detroit, his hometown, has been one of reciprocity. Through his companies, Gilbert has invested hundreds of millions of dollars in Detroit and received handsome tax breaks. He has been called the "shadow mayor" of Detroit because of the influence he wields.[37] With an estimated net worth of more than $20 billion, Gilbert has almost single-handedly reshaped and revitalized Detroit's downtown neighborhoods through his Bedrock real estate company, earning the area the nickname Gilbertville because of the roughly 100 buildings it owns there. The restored and upgraded buildings have brought big tenants to the area, turning him into a crusader for Motor City and its biggest cheerleader.

Gilbert also cultivated close ties with the Trump administration. In 2019, *ProPublica* reported that one of the downtown areas where Gilbert owns properties was labeled an "opportunity zone" under a Trump-era program meant to jumpstart economic activity in poor neighborhoods by offering tax breaks, even though the area was too wealthy to be classified as such.[38] In 2022, the Detroit City Council approved a $60 billion tax abatement for one of Gilbert's skyscraper projects, after the billionaire's company said its building costs had increased. Bedrock made some concessions to obtain the abatement, but the approval came over objections from some residents and community groups who argued that taxpayers were forgoing money that could have been directed to more pressing city needs. Several Detroit news outlets, which follow Gilbert's entanglements with the city closely, reported that five city council officials to whose campaigns a Gilbert-affiliated political action committee donated to were among those who approved the generous tax break. At the same time, Gilbert, who also owns a majority stake in the Cleveland Cavaliers basketball team, donated $500 million through his family foundation to help erase property tax debt for distressed Detroiters that had led to thousands of foreclosures, working closely with Mayor Mike Duggan, a Democrat.

Inequality is inherent to the human experience, not least of all in market-based capitalism. But the more that billionaires make news for their outlandish purchases and ambitions, their rescues of flailing newspapers and spendthrift cities, their occasionally splashy philanthropy, their personal involvement in decisions of national and global importance, and the selfish hands with which they often direct politics and policy, the more numbed we become to their wealth, their numbers, and their behavior. The danger, then, is that vital socioeconomic and political questions are being effaced from the public forum, and there appears to be little need for debate on how much inequality should exist in a land of opportunity.

Conclusion

There is an aerial sculpture called the *Impatient Optimist* on the campus of the Gates Foundation. Built out of clear, lightweight fibers, it is strung between the foundation's two boomerang-shaped buildings like a net and hangs 55 feet above the ground. During the day, its gigantic folds sway as gently as a baby's cradle if the wind is mellow, and billow like curtains in a more insistent wind. The fibers capture the changing moods of Seattle's daylight. At night, the sculpture resembles an upturned, undulating jellyfish, almost bioluminescent from the LED lighting sequences that the artist, Janet Echelman, programmed so that they change color when the sun rises in the different countries where the foundation has global offices. Echelman, one of the country's most well-known visual artists, took the sky as her inspiration to communicate boundless optimism. Knots in the netting represent our interconnected world.

The phrase "impatient optimist" was dear to both Gates and French Gates; it's how they described themselves as philanthropists at the foundation. The term, which they began using regularly after the foundation's media team, back in 2009, found that it resonated with audiences, was meant to communicate their unshakeable belief that the goals they set for themselves were achievable, no matter the setbacks, and their impatience to get to a better world was what kept them going. Like the determinedly cheerful whistle of a military officer lifting his troops' morale, Gates strikes a note of optimism wherever he can—in letters, blog posts, and interviews and on social media forums. The word "optimistic" shows up frequently in the annual letters he pens for the foundation. The foundation's weekly newsletter, in which it shares updates about its work, is called "The Optimist." When Gates assesses the foundation's work, acknowledging that there is still far to go, he insists on hope. Every uptick on a curve showing improved crop yields, every breakthrough in the mechanism for vaccine delivery, every data point about a death averted, is a victory. It is proof that the foundation's work has value, and that there is reason to keep going. After all, to de-emphasize optimism is to give up, shut down, and go home.

Gates came to philanthropy with a fix-it approach, starting out with the ambition and naïveté of a newbie and the arrogance of a software king confident that by directing his fortune toward technological innovation in global health and development, his foundation could solve—or at least come close to solving—specific but seemingly intractable problems within decades. He has shared many aspects of his philanthropic journey, including his learnings and experiences, and the challenges and wins. But perhaps the one overarching lesson that Gates has learned is that progress is finicky and nonlinear, and its pace is sometimes so slow that a watched pot will boil over, and a snail will have reached its destination. Complicated as it is by underfunding, changing political affiliations, conflict, droughts, floods, cultural mores, conspiracy theories, and chaos, the story of global public health and development is a story of missed targets and abandoned strategies, of real-time adjustments and wasted opportunities. Is it better to direct efforts to prevent a disease or focus on its treatment? What good is a vaccine if it remains out of reach for the poorest communities? The ideal is constantly accommodating the real. For a man inclined to see the world as a series of solvable challenges, it has been a long and humbling test of patience, an unending game of Whac-A-Mole.

The Gates Foundation's work has had enormous impact in many regions of the world, particularly in sub-Saharan Africa and South Asia. Trends in global morbidity and mortality rates provide one way to gauge the foundation's success given the broad and deep nature of its involvement in global health. For the two-decade period ending in 2020, the maternal mortality rate—the number of women who die at childbirth—fell by 34 percent. For children under five years old, who are most susceptible to death from disease and undernutrition, the rate fell by 60 percent.[1] In its annual report for 2022, the WHO credits "major investments and improvements in communicable disease programs, such as those dedicated to human immunodeficiency virus (HIV), tuberculosis (TB) and malaria" for declines in the prevalence of those diseases and the number of deaths caused by them, although challenges stemming from the pandemic have caused recent setbacks.

Still, despite the decades of efforts and billions of dollars spent by multilateral organizations, nonprofits, and governments, diseases like malaria and polio are yet to be eradicated. The WHO began trying to eradicate malaria—a key focus of the Gates Foundation—in 1955. There are victories: The total number of estimated deaths has fallen in recent decades, and the incidence of new malaria cases fell between 2000 and 2019. But they rose again in 2020 and 2021, largely in African countries, as pandemic-related disruptions prevented treatments from reaching those regions.[2] At the same time, malaria-carrying mosquitoes are developing resistance to the pesticides sprayed on bed nets that the foundation and other health agencies distribute, creating new challenges even as the existing ones evade conquest.

Polio, another big priority for the Gates Foundation, too has proved impossible to uproot. The highly infectious and crippling disease cannot be cured, but multiple vaccinations can prevent it. In 1988, the nonprofit Rotary International started the Global Polio Eradication Initiative (GPEI). The foundation, which has made $5 billion in total grants to end polio, is a primary partner to Rotary, supporting its efforts to administer vaccines. The vaccine alliance GAVI, also backed by the foundation, is another big supporter of the Rotary initiative. In 2011, Gates proclaimed that polio can be eradicated with enough financial support. Three years later, the WHO declared polio a global health emergency, and the health community promised to eradicate it by 2018. India, which once accounted for the largest number of polio cases, was declared free of the wild poliovirus in 2014—a victory of immense significance made possible by the work of multiple organizations including the Gates Foundation, as well as the Indian government. Emboldened by that success, Gates predicted in 2017 that the end of polio worldwide was near.[3] The global health community came close to fulfilling that prediction, but the 2019 coronavirus was a huge setback, and polio still exists in countries such as Afghanistan and Pakistan.[4] At the same time, a strain of virus mutated from the oral polio vaccine itself has led to new cases. In the spring of 2023, a New York man was found to have polio. The polio eradication initiative has now set 2026 as a new target. "To be blunt, we are also closer than ever to losing the gains we have fought so hard for [if] GPEI doesn't identify substantial new resources soon," Gates said at the launch of the new strategic plan, calling for more resources.[5]

The world has missed other global health and development targets. In 2000, the same year that the Gates Foundation got going, the United Nations announced its Millennium Development Goals, a series of eight targets that its member states agreed to try to meet by 2015. The foundation used those goals as a roadmap to set its own priorities, focusing on improvements in public health and vaccinations. Then 2015 came and went. Progress was uneven, and the world fell short of many of the millennium goals. The United Nations next formulated the set of targets called the Sustainable Development Goals that it hoped to meet by 2030. In addition to the traditional goals of achieving gender equality, ending poverty and hunger, and improving access to education, the revised document established new and pressing targets: reducing economic disparity, combating climate change, and promoting sustainable growth. The goals have also shaped the recent priorities of the Gates Foundation, but it's already clear that the world is unlikely to fulfill them by 2030. The pandemic had created massive roadblocks, choking off access to vaccines because supply chains broke down and healthcare systems were too overwhelmed to administer routine immunizations. In April 2023, as the pandemic ebbed, the Gates Foundation, along with global agencies like the WHO and UNICEF, announced an urgent vaccination campaign called "The Big Catch-Up." With more than 25 million children not fully vaccinated during the pandemic, preventable diseases such as measles and yellow fever were on the rise, according to the foundation. Two devastating wars have taken a fresh toll on humanity. Since Russia invaded Ukraine in February 2022, tens of thousands of Ukrainians have died or been injured; amputees await prosthetic limbs, war widows grieve as they await aid. In October 2023, Hamas attacked Israel, triggering a destructive counterattack that bombarded hospitals, schools, and shelters, and killed more than 30,000 people within months, leaving survivors desperate for help and humanitarian organizations racing to provide relief. In 2022, Gates said that the pandemic and the war in Ukraine had created enough new challenges for the world that there was even more of a need for philanthropy. He said he would transfer $20 billion of his fortune to the foundation's endowment, including $15 billion that he had pledged in 2021, adding to the nearly $70 billion in assets it currently holds.[6]

In recent years, Gates has picked climate change as his next big focus, directing his energy and resources toward fighting the effects of warming weather in the same determined way that he sought to eradicate certain diseases and solve specific problems in areas such as nutrition and vaccination. In his 2021 book *How to Avoid a Climate Disaster*, Gates explains the breakthroughs the world needs to avert calamity and lays out the steps needed to get there. In a video advertising the book, he draws a line from his earliest days at Microsoft, referring to the "wild idea" that made him rich and famous: "What could we do if there was a computer on every desk?" His latest wild idea, he says in the video, is to get emissions down to zero by 2050 while meeting the planet's basic needs. Averting a climate disaster will be even greater than landing on the moon, eradicating smallpox, or putting a computer on every desk, he says. Innovation, he insists with an almost childlike optimism, will get us all out of this mess. "It's our power to invent that makes me hopeful." He told *Wired* magazine that his optimism about beating climate change reflected his success in general. "It's a characteristic of someone who drops out of school thinking they can create a software company and hires a lot of people and then it actually works." Furthermore, he told the magazine, it's the huge successes of the foundation "that pushes you into the wow-what-can-I-do category."[7]

In the book, however, he sidesteps the most important, and most obvious, point about climate change: With competing national agendas, fractured domestic politics, apathetic corporations, and investors who settle for dutiful gestures, even the wisest strategies and smartest innovations will make little difference. Without buy-in from the rest of the world, the arsenal of a single man—even if it contains the smartest minds, billions of dollars, a bottomless reservoir of determination, relentless hope, and the shrillest of alarms—can only go so far in defeating the foul gathering clouds of wildfires, hurricanes, melting ice caps, and raging temperatures. Gates is hardly blind to that criticism, but he argues that investing in the right technologies now will prepare the world for when there is no time for innovation or politicking left.

With the additional funds from Gates, the foundation will have to give out $9 billion annually by 2026 to keep its tax-deductible status as a nonprofit. "I will move down and eventually off of the list of the world's richest people," the billionaire wrote in a blog post.[8] His giving has already pushed him down the list of billionaires, although the nature of wealth invested in the markets is such that it can rise and fall. In 2018, *Forbes* estimated his net worth at $90 billion. By 2022, it had risen to $129 billion, even after the separation of assets with French Gates, making him the world's fifth richest individual. At the same time, the Gates Foundation is structured as a spend-down entity, which means that it intends to deplete its resources steadily and fold when it has bequeathed its last dollar. Unlike the Rockefeller Foundation, which has a perpetual endowment that allows it to continue its philanthropy more than nearly 90 years after its founder's passing, the Gates Foundation is expected to wind down within the next 25 years. The governing documents can be modified, but unless they are, the foundation is likely to disappear sometime within the twenty-first century.

One goal of a spend-down foundation is to ensure that the intention of the founders remains intact, and that it doesn't become a source of employment for future generations or executives who run the entity. In this case, though, it is driven more by the foundation's urgency. "The decision to use all of the foundation's resources in this century underscores our optimism for progress and determination to do as much as possible, as soon as possible, to address the comparatively narrow set of issues we've chosen to focus on," according to a statement on the foundation's website.

What, then, is the long-term impact of a spend-down foundation through which a hubristic billionaire technologist pursued his dream of fighting some of humanity's most stubborn problems—problems that predated him and will outlast him, even as new ones arise? Any optimist will tell you that history is not a reason to give up on the future. But money, ambition, and optimism are modest beacons that can guide us only so far through the unmapped caverns of a troublesome world. What Gates will leave behind, in the end, is a palimpsest, a document of ambition upon which future generations of billionaires and philanthropists can scribble their own dreams and goals, effacing, rebuilding, and reimagining the Sisyphean task of improving our lot.

In *The Great Gatsby*, the narrator, Nick Carraway, reflects on the nature of Gatsby's love for Daisy Buchanan, and the desperate lengths to which he went to rekindle their romance. "He had come a long way to this blue lawn, and his dream must have seemed so close that he could hardly fail to grasp it," Carraway writes—the line that Gates and French Gates loved so much they had it painted on the ceiling of the library in the home they formerly shared. But in Fitzgerald's slim Jazz Age novel, Carraway's last words are hauntingly sad, evoking not only that which was gone but that which had never been attainable in the first place: "He did not know that it was already behind him, somewhere back in that vast obscurity beyond the city, where the dark fields of the republic rolled on under the night."

Acknowledgments

This book came about because Ben Loehnen of Avid Reader Press, the only person I knew in publishing, listened to my poorly formed pitch and immediately spotted its potential. As a first-time author, I'm deeply grateful to Ben for giving me a chance. Thanks to the team at Avid Reader and Simon & Schuster, including Carolyn Kelly, Janet McDonald, and Amy Medeiros, who polished my work and gave physical and digital form to my words. Thanks also to my agent Dan Mandel, who translated the mysteries of the book business.

Special thanks to Carolyn Ryan, Ellen Pollock, and Rich Barbieri at *The New York Times*, who graciously gave me the time and space to report and write. I am indebted to my *Times* colleagues, in particular Matthew Goldstein, Steve Eder, and Emily Flitter, without whose reporting and generosity this would have been a poorer work. Thanks also to my team for their patience as I periodically disappeared to work on this book, and to those who picked up the slack.

I owe a big debt of gratitude to the people who spoke to me for this book, including many whose names I have withheld upon their request, and the dozens of authors, journalists, and academics who documented so much of the history that I have relied upon to build the narrative.

Thanks to my author friends and colleagues, and to those in the broader media industry, for sharing their knowledge about the book publishing process and offering me valuable advice.

Thanks to Craig Karmin, without whose partnership at *The Wall Street Journal* the first stories about Bill Gates would never have been written, and for the discussions—over negronis—about ideas that became this book.

Thanks to Dennis K. Berman, who provided thoughtful feedback on my unpolished manuscript and pushed me to refine my arguments.

I am grateful for Jui Chakravorty, my confidante and counsel, and for my dear friends Lilla Zuill, Karen Cheung, and Taryn Luciani—strong, accomplished women whose unstinting support and cheerleading helped me recover from multiple bouts of self-doubt. Special thanks to Rachel Slade, my brilliant author friend, whose insights into the premise of this book made it clearer and richer, and whose hand-holding throughout the writing process was invaluable.

Thanks to the family I hold close: Mom and Dad, for the roots to ground me and the wings to fly; and my brother Dev, sister-in-law Rachel, and my nephews Daniel and Declan for warmth, safety, and unconditional love.

And finally, thanks to Alex Orozco, for being there from the beginning, for knowing when to push and when to listen, for leavening the tough moments with humor, and for always making the opposite case.

Author's Note

This is a work of reportage that relies on hundreds of interviews with sources, including many who spoke with me on the condition that their names be withheld. Some of the sources sought anonymity to speak freely without fear of repercussions; others would have declined to be interviewed at all. Where possible, I have added attributions in the text and tried to be specific about the nature of the anonymous source, so that the reader may better assess the information presented. If specific attribution is not provided, the reader should assume that the information is synthesized from multiple accounts of an event or experience. Bill Gates, his representatives at Gates Ventures, and representatives of the Gates Foundation did not participate. Once presented with the information in this book, they stonewalled for months. Following multiple entreaties, both organizations initially said they would not comment on "hearsay." Just days before the book went to print, a representative of Gates Ventures offered some comments, which are reflected in the text.

Notes

Introduction

1. Emily Flitter and James B. Stewart, "Bill Gates Met with Jeffrey Epstein Many Times, Despite His Past," October 12, 2019, *The New York Times*.
2. Bill Gates, "The Day I Knew What I Wanted to Do for the Rest of My Life," *GatesNotes*, September 20, 2019.
3. The Federal Reserve, "Distribution of Household Wealth in the U.S. Since 1989."
4. Will Wilkinson, "Don't Abolish Billionaires," *The New York Times*, February 21, 2019.

Chapter 1: Why We Love Billionaires

1. *Express* staff, "Take Me to Your Leaders," *Idaho Mountain Express*, July 8, 2021.
2. Nathan J. Robinson, "Why Is the Pursuit of Money Such an American Obsession?" *Current Affairs*, December 11, 2021.
3. Chase Peterson-Withorn, "From Rockefeller to Ford, See Forbes' 1918 Ranking of the Richest People in America," *Forbes*, September 19, 2017.
4. "The Only Four Hundred," *The New York Times*, February 16, 1892.
5. Steve Forbes, "Our First 100 Years," *Forbes*, September 19, 2017.
6. Lydia Kiesling, "Rags-to-Riches Stories Are Actually Kind of Disturbing," *The New York Times Magazine*, April 5, 2022.
7. Carl M. Cannon, "Billionaires: Have Americans' Views Changed?" *RealClear Opinion Research*, July 29, 2022.
8. Jeffrey P. Bezos, "Statement by Jeffrey P. Bezos Founder & Chief Executive

Officer, Amazon before the U.S. House of Representatives Committee on the Judiciary Subcommittee on Antitrust, Commercial, and Administrative Law," July 29, 2020.

9. Mark Zuckerberg, "Hearing Before the United States House of Representatives Committee on the Judiciary Subcommittee on Antitrust, Commercial, and Administrative Law, Testimony of Mark Zuckerberg, Facebook Inc.," July 29, 2020.

10. "The Gilded Age: Gilded Is Not Golden," *PBS*, February 6, 2018.

11. "Giving USA: Total U.S. Charitable Giving Declined in 2022 to $499.33 Billion Following Two Years of Record Generosity," Lilly Family School of Philanthropy, Indiana University, June 20, 2023.

12. Amanda B. Moniz, "Giving in America: A History of Philanthropy," *AASLH History News* 72, no. 4 (2017): 28–32.

13. Alexis de Tocqueville [translated by Henry Reeve], "Of the Use Which the Americans Make of Public Associations in Civil Life," *Democracy in America*, vol. II, book 2, sect. 2, chap. V.

14. National Park Service, *Statue of Liberty*, "Joseph Pulitzer."

15. Warren E. Buffett, "Comments by Warren E. Buffett in Conjunction with His Annual Contribution of Berkshire Hathaway Shares to Five Foundations," June 23, 2021.

16. Warren E. Buffett, "My Philanthropic Pledge," 2010.

17. *Giving USA 2023: The Annual Report on Philanthropy for the Year 2022*, a publication of Giving USA Foundation, 2023, researched and written by the Indiana University Lilly Family School of Philanthropy.

18. Forbes Wealth Team, "America's Top Givers 2022: The 25 Most Philanthropic Billionaires," *Forbes*, January 19, 2022.

19. Colin Moynihan, "To Honor Gift, Public Library Will Add Donor's Name a 6th Time," *The New York Times*, February 28, 2019.

20. David M. Rubenstein, "The Magna Carta Returns to the Archives," *Prologue Magazine*, 42 (2010): 4.

21. Chuck Collins and Helen Flannery, "Gilded Giving 2022: How Wealth Inequality Distorts Philanthropy and Imperils Democracy," Institute for Policy Studies, July 2022.

22. Board of Governors of the Federal Reserve System, "Total Financial Assets Held by Private Foundations," Federal Reserve Bank of St. Louis, June 30, 2023.

23. National Philanthropic Trust, "Charitable Giving Statistics," National Philanthropic Trust.

24. Philip Rojc, "Major Philanthropy Sector Groups Are Dragging Their Feet or Outright Opposing DAF Reform. Why Is That?" *Inside Philanthropy*, May 23, 2023.

25. Chuck Collins and Helen Flannery, "New Data Tells Us Where Donor-Advised Fund Dollars Go—And Don't Go," *Nonprofit Quarterly*, April 27, 2022.

26. Patrick Radden Keefe, "The Family that Built an Empire of Pain," *The New Yorker*, October 23, 2017.

27. Robin Pogrebin, "Met Museum Removes Sackler Name from Wing Over Opioid Ties," *The New York Times*, December 9, 2021.
28. Indiana University Lilly Family School of Philanthropy, "What America Thinks of Philanthropy and Nonprofits," April 2023.
29. Patrick M. Rooney, "The Growth in Total Household Giving Is Camouflaging a Decline in Giving by Small and Medium Donors: What Can We Do About It?" *Nonprofit Quarterly*, August 27, 2019.

Chapter 2: The Ur Nerd of Capitalism

1. Paul Allen, *Idea Man* (New York: Portfolio/Penguin, 2012), 61, 69–91.
2. Nathan Ensmenger, "Beards, Sandals, and Other Signs of Rugged Individualism: Masculine Culture within the Computing Professions," *Osiris* 30 (2015): 38–65.
3. Bill Gates, "The Day I Knew What I Wanted to Do for the Rest of My Life," *GatesNotes*, September 20, 2019.
4. Ken Auletta, *World War 3.0* (New York: Random House, 2001), 155.
5. Allen, *Idea Man*, 9. Also see: Bill Gates, "Remarks of Bill Gates, Harvard Commencement, 2007," *The Harvard Gazette*, June 7, 2007.
6. Bill Gates, "An Open Letter to Hobbyists," February 3, 1976.
7. Associated Press, "Mary Gates, 64; Helped Her Son Start Microsoft," *The New York Times*, June 11, 1994.
8. Cathy Booth, "Steve's Job: Restart Apple," *Time*, August 18, 1997.
9. Walter Isaacson, *Steve Jobs* (New York: Simon & Schuster, 2021), 171–79.
10. IBM Archives, "The Birth of the IBM PC."
11. Nathan Ensmenger, *The Computer Boys Take Over* (Cambridge, MA: MIT Press, 2012), 52–53, 62, 79.
12. Stewart Brand, "Spacewar," *Rolling Stone*, December 7, 1972.
13. Thomas Streeter, "Romanticism in Business Culture: The Internet, the 1990s, and the Origins of Irrational Exuberance," in *Toward a Political Economy of Culture: Capitalism and Communication in the Twenty-First Century*," ed. Andrew Calabrese and Colin Sparks (Lanham, MD: Rowman & Littlefield, 2004), 286–306. Also see: Interview with Thomas Streeter, "Romancing the Internet," *Journal of Communication Inquiry*, May 22, 2012.
14. Andy Reinhardt, "What Matters Is How Smart You Are," *Businessweek*, August 25, 1997.
15. Laurence Zuckerman, "With Internet Cachet, Not Profit, A New Stock Is Wall St.'s Darling," *The New York Times*, August 10, 1995.
16. Paul Andrews and Michele Matassa Flores, "Internet Wars—Microsoft Vs. Netscape: Goliath Takes On David—Navigator Still Ahead—But Losing Ground," *The Seattle Times*, March 11, 1997.
17. Andrews and Flores, "Internet Wars."

18. Interview with Marc Andreessen, "Find the Smartest Technologist in the Company and Make them CEO," *McKinsey Quarterly*, June 22, 2022.

19. Survey of Current Business, "U.S. Digital Economy: New and Revised Estimates, 2017–2022," *The Journal of the U.S. Bureau of Economic Analysis*, December 6, 2023.

20. Occupational Outlook Handbook, U.S. Bureau of Labor Statistics.

21. Author calculations, based on data from PitchBook.

22. David Rensin, "A Candid Conversation with the Sultan of Software about Outsmarting His Rivals," *Playboy*, July 1994.

23. Streeter, "Romanticism in Business Culture."

24. Pierre Azoulay, et al., "Age and High-Growth Entrepreneurship," *NBER Working Paper No. 24489*, April 2018.

25. Roger Parloff, "This CEO Is Out for Blood," *Fortune*, June 12, 2014.

26. David Yaffe-Bellany, "A Crypto Emperor's Vision: No Pants, His Rules," *The New York Times*, May 14, 2022. Also see: David Yaffe-Bellany, "The Man Who Was Supposed to Save Crypto," *The Daily*, November 18, 2022.

27. Thomas D. Snyder, ed. "120 Years of American Education: A Statistical Portrait," *National Center for Education Statistics*, January 1993, 85–86.

28. Robert X. Cringely [pen name], *Triumph of the Nerds: The Rise of Accidental Empires*, PBS documentary, June 1996.

29. Bill Gates, "If You Want to Understand Silicon Valley, Watch *Silicon Valley*," *GatesNotes*, November 19, 2018.

30. Jordynn Jack, "'The Extreme Male Brain?' Incrementum and the Rhetorical Gendering of Autism," *Disability Studies Quarterly*, 31 (2011): 3. Also see: "Q&A with Autism and Gender Author Jordynn Jack," *University of Illinois Press Blog*, May 19, 2014.

31. Allison Master, Sapna Cheryan, and Andrew N. Meltzoff, "Computing Whether She Belongs: Stereotypes Undermine Girls' Interest and Sense of Belonging in Computer Science," *Journal of Educational Psychology* 108, no. 3 (2016): 424–37.

32. Sapna Cheryan, et al., "The Stereotypical Computer Scientist: Gendered Media Representations as a Barrier to Inclusion for Women," *Sex Roles* 69 (2013): 58–71.

33. Richard Waters, "Reid Hoffman, Mr. LinkedIn," *Financial Times*, March 16, 2012.

34. "Women in the Workplace 2021," LeanIn.org.

35. Ellen Huet, "Kleiner Perkins Trial Details Firm's All-Male Ski Trip and Dinner Party," *Forbes*, February 25, 2015.

36. Joseph Bernstein, "Elon Musk Has the World's Strangest Social Calendar," *The New York Times*, October 11, 2022.

37. Emily Chang, "Oh My God, This Is So F---ed Up: Inside Silicon Valley's Secretive, Orgiastic Dark Side," *Vanity Fair*, January 2, 2018.

38. Alex Williams, "As the Nerds Turn by Marc Andreessen," *The New Stack*, June 24, 2014.

Chapter 3: Rockstar to Robber Baron

1. Jack Beatty, "A Capital Life," *The New York Times*, May 17, 1998.
2. David E. Sanger, "High-Tech Rebel," *The New York Times Magazine*, September 11, 1988.
3. James Gleick, "Making Microsoft Safe for Capitalism," *The New York Times Magazine*, November 5, 1995.
4. John Seabrook, "E-mail from Bill," *The New Yorker*, December 26, 1993.
5. John Heilemann, "The Truth, the Whole Truth, Nothing But the Truth," *Wired*, November 1, 2000.
6. Ron Chernow, *Titan: The Life of John D. Rockefeller, Sr.* (New York: Random House, 1998), 136.
7. Stuart Elliott, "Haven't Heard of Windows 95? Where Have You Been Hiding?" *The New York Times*, July 31, 1995.
8. Kristi Gates, interview in *Inside Bill's Brain: Decoding Bill Gates*, Netflix, 2019.
9. David Rensin, "A Candid Conversation with the Sultan of Software About Outsmarting His Rivals," *Playboy*, July 1994.
10. Paul Allen, *Idea Man* (New York: Portfolio/Penguin, 2012), 32, 91.
11. Jane Pauley interview with Bill Gates, *Today*, NBC, 1989.
12. Timothy Egan, "Microsoft's Unlikely Millionaires," *The New York Times*, June 28, 1992.
13. Blaine Harden, "Microsoft Millionaires Still Pondering Wealth," *The Washington Post*, August 3, 2003.
14. "Racial Wealth Divide in Seattle," Prosperity Now.
15. Todd Bishop, "No Bull Bill: Bill Gates' Blunt Legacy," *Seattle Post-Intelligencer*, June 23, 2008.
16. Rensin, "A Candid Conversation."
17. Ken Auletta, *World War 3.0* (New York: Random House, 2001), 152.
18. Suzanne Taylor and Kathy Schroeder, *Inside Intuit: How the Makers of Quicken Beat Microsoft and Revolutionized an Entire Industry* (Cambridge: Harvard Business Review Press, 2003).
19. Lawrence M. Fisher, "Microsoft in $1.5 Billion Deal to Acquire Intuit," *The New York Times*, October 14, 1994.
20. David Einstein, "The Lawyer Who Took on Microsoft," *SFGate*, March 20, 1995.
21. Elizabeth Corcoran, "Microsoft Halts Merger with Intuit," *The Washington Post*, May 21, 1995
22. Kathy Rebello, "Inside Microsoft," *Bloomberg*, July 14, 1996.
23. Gleick, "Making Microsoft Safe for Capitalism."
24. Joseph Nocera, "The Microsoft Word," *The New York Times*, December 24, 1995, https://archive.nytimes.com/www.nytimes.com/books/99/01/03/specials/gates-road.html.
25. Jim Clark with Owen Edwards, *Netscape Time: The Making of the Billion-Dollar Start-Up That Took on Microsoft* (New York: St. Martin's Griffin, 1999), 15.

26. Lawrence M. Fisher, "A Legal High-Wire Artist Takes On Silicon Valley Giants," *The New York Times*, April 5, 1995.

27. Andrew I. Gavil and Harry First, *The Microsoft Antitrust Cases: Competition Policy for the Twenty-First Century* (Cambridge, MA: MIT Press, 2014), 3.

28. Nick Wingfield, "To Rebuild Trust, Facebook's Zuckerberg Looked to Microsoft," *The Information*, December 10, 2018.

29. Daisuke Wakabayashi, "Google Employees Are Free to Speak Up. Except on Antitrust," *The New York Times*, October 13, 2020.

30. Om Malik, "In Silicon Valley Now, It's Almost Always Winner Takes All," *The New Yorker*, December 30, 2015.

31. Jason Calacanis, "10 Things We Learned from Mitch Kapor," LinkedIn, August 13, 2013.

32. "Client Profile: Microsoft Corp," summary, OpenSecrets, 2023.

33. "Client Profile: Amazon.com," summary, OpenSecrets, 2021.

34. Tim Wu, "How Google and Amazon Got Away with Not Being Regulated," *Wired*, November 13, 2018.

35. Lina M. Khan, "We Must Regulate A.I. Here's How," *The New York Times*, May 3, 2023.

36. John Jurgensen, "In Bill Gates's Mind, A Life of Processing," *The Wall Street Journal*, September 10, 2019.

Chapter 4: The Pivot

1. Jared Cohon, "College Tour, Carnegie Mellon University," *Carnegie Mellon Today*, February 21, 2008.

2. Nick Wingfield, "Pamela Edstrom, Who Helped Shape Microsoft's Public Image, Dies at 71," *The New York Times*, March 31, 2017.

3. Steve Hamm, "Bill Gates: 'I'm Humble. I'm Respectful.'" *Bloomberg*, February 9, 1998.

4. Steve Lohr, "The Chairman's Vision," *The New York Times*, June 16, 2000.

5. Frank Rich, "Love That Bill," *The New York Times*, March 7, 1998.

6. Ken Auletta, *World War 3.0* (New York: Random House, 2001): 131.

7. Steven Levy, "Behind the Gates Myth," *Newsweek*, August 29, 1999.

8. John Jurgensen, "In Bill Gates's Mind, A Life of Processing," *The Wall Street Journal*, September 10, 2019. Also see: Gates, "The Day I Knew What I Wanted to Do for the Rest of My life," *GatesNotes*, September 20, 2019.

9. "When in Seattle, Bono Bunks with Bill Gates," *Reuters*, May 2005.

10. Robert A. Guth, "Stock Analysts Note Microsoft 'Bye' Sign: No Gates at Meeting," *Wall Street Journal*, July 31, 2006.

11. Guth, "Wealth of Ideas: Bill Gates Issues Call for a Benevolent Capitalism," *The Wall Street Journal*, January 24, 2008.

12. Cohon, "College Tour, Carnegie Mellon University."

13. Robert A. Guth, "In Secret Hideaway, Bill Gates Ponders Microsoft's Future," *The Wall Street Journal*, March 28, 2015.

14. David Pogue, "Reconsidering Bill Gates," *The New York Times*, June 22, 2005.

15. Tore Gjerstad and Gard Oterholm, "Bill Gates and Jeffrey Epstein Met with Nobel Committee Chair," *DNMagasinet*, October 2, 2020. Also see: Khadeeja Safdar and Emily Glazer, "Jeffrey Epstein Appeared to Threaten Bill Gates Over Microsoft Co-founder's Affair with Russian Bridge Player," *The Wall Street Journal*, May 21, 2023. Also see: Kate Briquelet, "Bill Gates Thought Jeffrey Epstein Was His Ticket to a Nobel Prize," *The Daily Beast*, May 18, 2021. Also: Emails of Jeffrey Epstein obtained under Freedom of Information Request by *The New York Times* regarding the lawsuit by the U.S. Virgin Islands against Epstein's estate.

16. Philip Galanes, "The Mind Meld of Bill Gates and Steven Pinker," *The New York Times*, January 27, 2018.

17. Jurgensen, "In Bill Gates's Mind, a Life of Processing."

18. Katherine Rosman, "Bill Gates: The Billionaire Book Critic," *The New York Times*, January 2, 2016.

19. Bill Gates, "The Future Our Grandchildren Deserve," *GatesNotes*, December 20, 2022.

20. Theodore Schleifer, "Bill Gates Will Never Be the Same," *Vox*, May 18, 2021.

Chapter 5: Besties with Buffett

1. David Von Drehle, "Meg Greenfield, Editor Extraordinaire," *The Washington Post*, May 14, 1999.

2. Remarks of Warren E. Buffett, "Afternoon Session—2000 Meeting," Warren Buffett Archive, April 29, 2000.

3. Bill Gates, "Testing Mattresses with Warren Buffett," *GatesNotes*, June 6, 2017.

4. Warren Buffett, email to the author, October 22, 2015.

5. Warren E. Buffett, "Remarks at University of Nebraska, Lincoln," *Buffett Online*, September 30, 2005.

6. Andrew Carnegie, *The Gospel of Wealth* (New York: Carnegie Corporation of New York, 2017).

7. *Changes in U.S. Family Finances from 2019 to 2022*, "Table 2. Family Median and Mean Net Worth, Selected Characteristics of Families, 2019 and 2022 Surveys," Board of Governors of the Federal Reserve, November 8, 2023.

8. Bill Gates, "By 2026, the Gates Foundation Aims to Spend $9 Billion a Year," *GatesNotes*, July 13, 2022.

9. Gates, "Gates Foundation Aims to Spend."

10. John M. Goshko, "Ted Turner to Give U.N. $1 Billion," *Washington Post*, September 19, 1997.

11. Maureen Dowd, "Ted's Excellent Idea," *The New York Times*, August 22, 1996.
12. Warren Buffett, Bill Gates, and Melinda French Gates discussed the initiative on *Charlie Rose*, June 16, 2010.
13. Judith Miller, "He Gave $600 Million, and No One Knew," *The New York Times*, January 23, 1997.
14. "Going Big," *The Atlantic Philanthropies*.
15. Stephanie Strom, "Pledge to Give Away Fortunes Stirs Debate," *The New York Times*, November 10, 2010.
16. Hans Peter Schmitz and Elena M. McCollim, "Billionaires in Global Philanthropy: A Decade of the Giving Pledge," *Society* 58, no. 2 (2021): 120–30.
17. Calculations by the author.
18. Warren E. Buffett, "Comments by Warren E. Buffett in Conjunction with His Annual Contribution of Berkshire Hathaway Shares to Five Foundations," Berkshire Hathaway, June 23, 2021.
19. Chuck Collins and Helen Flannery, "Gilded Giving 2022: How Wealth Inequality Distorts Giving and Imperils Democracy," *Inequality.org*, July 28, 2022.
20. Kerry A. Dolan, *Forbes*, June 5, 2022.

Chapter 6: Melinda without Bill

1. Bill Gates, "Melinda Has a Terrific Book Coming Out," *GatesNotes*, April 9, 2019.
2. Emily Glazer and Khadeeja Safdar, "Melinda Gates Was Meeting with Divorce Lawyers Since 2019 to End Marriage with Bill Gates," *The Wall Street Journal*, May 9, 2021.
3. O. Casey Corr, "Melinda French Gates: A Microsoft Mystery—She Married High-Profile Bill Gates, But Wants Her Life Kept Private," *Seattle Times*, June 4, 1995.
4. Patricia Sellers, "Melinda Gates Goes Public," *Fortune*, January 21, 2008.
5. Julia Reed, "Melinda Gates Focuses the World's Largest Foundation on Gender," *The Wall Street Journal*, November 2, 2016.
6. OECD, "Philanthropy and Gender Equality: Insights on Philanthropy for Gender Equality," *OECD Development Centre*, 2019.
7. David Marchese, "Melinda Gates on Tech Innovation, Global Health and Her Own Privilege," *The New York Times Magazine*, April 15, 2019.
8. Abby Schultz, "20 Minutes With: Haven Ley of Pivotal Ventures," *Barron's*, November 16, 2020.
9. Melinda Gates, "Here's Why I'm Committing $1 Billion to Promote Gender Equality," *Time*, October 5, 2019.
10. Melinda Gates, "How to Start the Conversation About Gender Equality," *The New York Times*, March 7, 2020.
11. Melinda Gates, *The Moment of Lift* (New York: Flatiron Books, 2019), 208–9.

10. Jan-Willem van Prooijen and Karen M. Douglas, "Conspiracy Theories as Part of History: The Role of Societal Crisis Situations," *Memory Studies* 10, no. 3 (2017): 323–33.

11. Bill Gates, "The Next Outbreak? We're Not Ready," March 18, 2015.

12. Ike Sriskandarajah, "Where Did the Microchip Vaccine Conspiracy Theory Come from Anyway?" *Reveal*, June 5, 2021.

13. Jay Greene, "The Billionaire Who Cried Pandemic," *The Washington Post*, May 2, 2020.

14. Matthew Smith, "World's Most Admired," *YouGov*, September 22, 2020.

15. KK Ottesen, "Bill Gates on Climate Change, Covid and Whether He Has Too Much Influence," *The Washington Post*, February 26, 2021.

Chapter 10: Why We Hate Billionaires

1. Kathryn Kvas and Vignesh Seshadri, "How to Become a Billionaire in 2021," *The New Yorker*, March 18, 2021.

2. Carl M. Cannon, "Billionaires: Have Americans' Views Changed?" RealClear Opinion Research, July 29, 2022.

3. Jesse Walker, Stephane J. Tepper, and Thomas Gilovich, "People Are More Tolerant of Inequality When Expressed in Groups," *Proceedings of the National Academy of Sciences* 118, no. 43 (2021).

4. Jeff Grabmeier, "People Love the Billionaire, but Hate the Billionaires' Club," *Ohio State News*, October 18, 2021.

5. U.S. Census Bureau, "Real Median Household Income in the United States," *FRED*, Federal Reserve Bank of St. Louis, August 16, 2022.

6. Martin-Brehm Christensen, et al., "Survival of the Richest: How We Must Tax the Super-Rich Now to Fight Inequality," Oxfam International, January 2023.

7. John Weinberg, "The Great Recession and Its Aftermath," *Federal Reserve History*, November 22, 2013.

8. U.S. Census Bureau, "Real Median Household Income in the United States."

9. Justin Wolfers, "Piketty's Book on Wealth and Inequality Is More Popular in Richer States," *The New York Times*, April 23, 2014.

10. Idrees Kahloon, "Thomas Piketty Goes Global," *The New Yorker*, March 2, 2020.

11. Emmanuel Saez and Gabriel Zucman, "Exploding Wealth Inequality in the United States," Washington Center for Equitable Growth, October 20, 2014.

12. Emanuel Saez and Gabriel Zucman, "The Rise of Income and Wealth Inequality in America: Evidence from Distributional Macroeconomic Accounts," *Journal of Economic Perspectives* 34, no. 4 (2020): 3–26.

13. Ben White, "Soak the Rich? Americans Say Go for It," *Politico*, February 4, 2019.

14. Richard A. Epstein, "A Plague of Billionaires?" *Hoover*, April 18, 2022.

15. Warren E. Buffett, "Stop Coddling the Super-Rich," *The New York Times*, August 14, 2011.

16. Marc Benioff, "We Need a New Capitalism," *The New York Times*, October 10, 2019.

17. Kaya Yurieff, "Mark Zuckerberg on Billionaires: 'No One Deserves to Have That Much Money," *CNN Business*, October 4, 2019.

18. Ben White, "Corporate America Freaks Out Over Elizabeth Warren," *Politico*, October 23, 2019.

19. Eli Saslow, "The Moral Calculations of a Billionaire," *The Washington Post*, January 30, 2022.

20. William H. Gates and Chuck Collins, *Wealth and Our Commonwealth: Why America Should Tax Accumulated Fortune* (Boston: Beacon Press, 2003; repr. 2004).

21. Federal Reserve, Survey of Consumer Finances.

22. Kerry A. Dolan, "America's Self-Made Women List 2023," *Forbes*, June 1, 2023.

23. Sara McLanahan and Gary Sandefur, *Growing Up with a Single Parent: What Hurts, What Helps* (Cambridge: Harvard University Press, 1994).

24. Alan B. Krueger, "The Rise and Consequences of Inequality in the United States," Remarks as Prepared for Delivery, January 12, 2012.

25. Raj Chetty et al., "The Fading American Dream: Trends in Absolute Income Mobility Since 1940," *Science* 356, no. 6336 (2017): 398–406.

26. Raj Chetty, David J. Deming, and John N. Friedman, "Diversifying Society's Leaders? The Determinants and Causal Effects of Admission to Highly Selective Private Colleges," *Opportunity Insights*, October 2023.

27. Michael Dell, *Direct from Dell: Strategies that Revolutionized an Industry* (New York: HarperBusiness, 1999), 3–11.

28. Catherine Clifford, "How a College Dropout Grew Whole Foods into the Company Amazon Just Bought for $13.7 billion," CNBC, August 28, 2017. Also see: Nick Paumgarten, "Food Fighter," *The New Yorker*, December 27, 2009.

29. Henry S. Farber, et al., "Unions and Inequality over the Twentieth Century: New Evidence from Survey Data," NBER Working Paper No. 24587, May 2018.

30. Travis Baker, "New Highway Tunnel Means Bill Gates Gets What He Wants," *Kitsap Sun*, December 22, 2006.

31. *Seattle Post-Intelligencer* staff, "Gates' Money Wasn't Enough," *Seattle Post-Intelligencer*, July 4, 2004.

32. Richard Wilk and Beatriz Barros, "Private Planes, Mansions and Superyachts: What Gives Billionaires Like Abramovich and Musk Such a Massive Carbon Footprint," *The Conversation*, February 16, 2021.

33. Michael Waldman, "Billionaires Provided 15 Percent of Funding for the Midterms," Brennan Center for Justice, November 22, 2022.

34. Maggie Haberman, Jonathan Swan, and Shane Goldmacher, "Koch Network Raises Over $70 Million for Push to Sink Trump," *The New York Times*, June 29, 2023.

35. Joshua Kaplan, Justin Elliott, and Alex Mierjeski, "Clarence Thomas and the Billionaire," *ProPublica*, April 6, 2023.

36. Justin Birnbaum, "America's Richest Sports Team Owners 2022," *Forbes*, September 27, 2022.

37. Michael Kavate, "A Half-Billion from Detroit's 'Shadow Mayor' Latest Sign of Donors' Power in Cities," *Inside Philanthropy*, March 30, 2021.

38. Jeff Ernsthausen and Justin Elliott, "How a Tax Break to Help the Poor Went to NBA Owner Dan Gilbert," *ProPublica*, October 24, 2019.

Conclusion

1. World Health Statistics 2022: Monitoring Health for the SDGs, Sustainable Development Goals," May 19, 2022.

2. World Malaria Report 2022, December 8, 2022.

3. Ray Sipherd, "Bill Gates: For Polio the Endgame Is Near," CNBC, December 14, 2017.

4. Apoorva Mandavilli, "A Multibillion-Dollar Plan to End Polio, and Soon," *The New York Times*, June 9, 2021.

5. Robert Fortner, "Has the Billion Dollar Crusade to Eradicate Polio Come to an End?" *BMJ* 374, no. 1818 (2021).

6. Maria Di Mento, "Bill Gates Made 2022's Biggest Charitable Donation: $5 Billion," Associated Press, December 30, 2022.

7. Steven Levy, "Bill Gates Is Upbeat on Climate, Capitalism and Even Politics," *Wired*, March 18, 2021.

8. Bill Gates, "By 2026, the Gates Foundation Aims to Spend $9 Billion a Year," *GatesNotes*, July 13, 2022.

Further Reading

Alger, Horatio, Jr. *Ragged Dick and Struggling Upward.* New York: Penguin Books, 1985.

Allen, Paul. *Idea Man.* New York: Portfolio/Penguin, 2012.

Aschoff, Nicole. *The New Prophets of Capital.* London, New York: Verso, 2015.

Auletta, Ken. *World War 3.0: Microsoft and Its Enemies.* New York: Random House, 2001.

Bank, David. *Breaking Windows: How Bill Gates Fumbled the Future of Microsoft.* New York: Free Press, 2001.

Bishop, Matthew, and Michael Green. *Philanthrocapitalism: How Giving Can Save the World.* New York: Bloomsbury, 2008.

Carnegie, Andrew. *The Gospel of Wealth.* New York: Carnegie Corporation of New York, 2017.

Chang, Emily. *Brotopia: Breaking Up the Boys' Club of Silicon Valley.* New York: Portfolio/Penguin, 2019.

Chernow, Ron. *Titan: The Life of John D. Rockefeller, Sr.* New York: Vintage Books, 2004.

Clark, Jim, with Owen Edwards. *Netscape Time: The Making of the Billion-Dollar Start-Up that Took On Microsoft.* New York: St. Martin's Griffin, 1999.

Dell, Michael. *Direct from Dell: Strategies that Revolutionized an Industry.* New York: HarperBusiness, 1999.

Easterly, William. *The Tyranny of Experts: Economists, Dictators, and the Forgotten Rights of the Poor.* New York: Basic Books, 2015.

Ensmenger, Nathan. *The Computer Boys Take Over: Computers, Programmers, and the Politics of Technical Expertise.* Cambridge: MIT Press, 2012.

Fitzgerald, F. Scott. *The Great Gatsby.* New York: Scribner Classics, 2018.

Frank, Robert. *Richistan: A Journey Through the American Wealth Boom and the Lives of the New Rich.* New York: Three Rivers Press, 2007.

Freeland, Chrystia. *Plutocrats: The Rise of the New Global Super Rich.* London: Allen Lane, 2012.

Gates, Melinda. *The Moment of Lift: How Empowering Women Changes the World.* New York: Flatiron Books, 2019.

Gavil, Andrew I., and Harry First. *The Microsoft Antitrust Cases: Competition Policy for the Twenty-First Century.* Cambridge, MA: MIT Press, 2014.

Giridharadas, Anand. *Winners Take All: The Elite Charade of Changing the World.* New York: Vintage Books, 2019.

Isaacson, Walter. *Steve Jobs.* New York: Simon & Schuster Paperbacks, 2021.

Kidder, Tracy. *The Soul of a New Machine.* Boston: Back Bay Books, 2000.

Kohlenberger, Judith. *The New Formula for Cool: Science, Technology, and the Popular in the American Imagination.* Transcript Publishing, 2016.

Lewis, Michael. *The New New Thing: A Silicon Valley Story.* New York: W.W. Norton, 2000.

Loomis, Carol, ed. *Tap Dancing to Work: Warren Buffett on Practically Everything, 1966–2012.* New York: Portfolio/Penguin, 2012.

Lowe, Janet. *Bill Gates Speaks: Insights from the World's Greatest Entrepreneur.* New York: John Wiley and Sons, 1998.

Lowenstein, Roger. *Buffett: The Making of an American Capitalist.* New York: Random House Trade Paperback Edition, 2008.

Manes, Stephen, and Paul Andrews. *Gates: How Microsoft's Mogul Reinvented an Industry—and Made Himself the Richest Man in America.* New York: Touchstone, 1994.

Mayer, Jane. *Dark Money: The Hidden History of the Billionaires Behind the Rise of the Radical Right.* New York: Doubleday, 2016.

McGoey, Lindsey. *No Such Thing As a Free Gift: The Gates Foundation and the Price of Philanthropy.* London: Verso, 2015.

O'Mara, Margaret. *The Code: Silicon Valley and the Remaking of America.* New York: Penguin Press, 2019.

Phillips, Kevin. *Wealth and Democracy.* New York: Broadway Books, 2002.

Piketty, Thomas. *Capital in the Twenty-First Century.* Cambridge: The Belknap Press of Harvard University Press, 2017.

Putnam, Robert D. *Our Kids: The American Dream in Crisis.* New York: Simon & Schuster, 2015.

Reich, Rob. *Just Giving: Why Philanthropy Is Failing Democracy and How It Can Do Better.* Princeton: Princeton University Press, 2019.

Rohm, Wendy Goldman. *The Microsoft File: The Secret Case Against Bill Gates.* New York: Random House, 1998.

Saez, Emmanuel, and Gabriel Zucman. *The Triumph of Injustice: How the Rich Dodge Taxes and How to Make Them Pay.* New York: W.W. Norton, 2019.

Samuel, Lawrence R. *The American Dream: A Cultural History.* New York: Syracuse University Press, 2012.

Schultz, Howard, and Dori Jones Yang. *Pour Your Heart into It: How Starbucks Built a Company One Cup at a Time.* New York: Hachette Books, 1997.

Sherman, Rachel. *Uneasy Street: The Anxieties of Affluence.* Princeton: Princeton University Press, 2017.

Stone, Brad. *The Everything Store: Jeff Bezos and the Age of Amazon.* New York: Back Bay Books, 2014.

———. *Amazon Unbound.* New York: Simon & Schuster, 2021.

Streeter, Thomas. *The Net Effect: Romanticism, Capitalism, and the Internet.* New York: NYU Press, 2011.

Tocqueville, Alexis de. *Democracy in America.*

Wallace, James, and Jim Erickson. *Hard Drive: Bill Gates and the Making of the Microsoft Empire.* New York: HarperBusiness, 1993.

Zinn, Howard. *A People's History of the United States.* New York: Harper Perennial Modern Classics, 2015.

Index

About the Author

Anupreeta Das is the finance editor of *The New York Times*, overseeing coverage of Wall Street, including banking, investing, markets, insurance, and consumer finance. Previously, Das spent nearly a decade at *The Wall Street Journal*, where she helped run the paper's coverage of business and technology, focusing on corporations and the issues affecting them. Das was also a reporter at the *Journal*. She holds degrees from Boston University, the London School of Economics, and the University of Delhi.